Praise for *Remix Judaism*

"Roberta Kwall provides a new way to be Jewish in America! The book's 'remixed' approach to contemporary Judaism means developing practical paths based in historical traditions. For anyone interested in the vibrancy of the Jewish community and religion, this book provides critical grounds for thought—and action."
—Naomi Cahn, Harold H. Green Professor, George Washington University Law School

"Professor Kwall, one of the prominent scholars of modern American Jewry, wrote *Remix Judaism* as a follow-up to *The Myth of the Cultural Jew*. Her new book touches the lives of so many of us who live in a non-Orthodox world yet strive to maintain a strong connection to our Judaism. With more than thirty-four years in a pulpit, I have dealt with congregants of all ages and backgrounds who have been dealing with the issues identified by Kwall. Her diverse sources are masterfully woven into the fabric of her narrative. There is no question in my mind that this work will be a guiding light to so many of us. If I could, I would make *Remix Judaism* required reading for all non-Orthodox Jews."
—Rabbi Chuck Diamond, former rabbi of the Tree of Life–Or L'Simcha, Pittsburgh

"In *Remix Judaism*, Roberta Kwall draws nimbly and intelligently from the wellsprings of Jewish tradition and practice so as to allow American Jews to forge a Judaism that is both meaningful and authentic. Kwall is a keen observer of the contemporary Jewish scene, and she offers a clear program for modern Jewish life that has the capacity to address and motivate individuals and community. Her creative and rooted vision of Judaism is both exciting and inspiring. *Remix Judaism* will deservedly garner a wide readership!"
—Rabbi David Ellenson, chancellor emeritus, Hebrew Union College–Jewish Institute of Religion and professor emeritus of Near Eastern and Judaic studies, Brandeis University

"*Remix Judaism* is a sourcebook of great Jewish ideas and a guidebook for living Jewishly in the twenty-first century. Roberta Kwall manages to be both descriptive and prescriptive, charting a path for how Jewish living can thrive in contemporary society. This is not a book for the future; this is a vital book for right now."

—Rabbi Avi Finegold, founder, The Jewish Learning Lab, Montreal

"In *Remix Judaism* Roberta Kwall puts forward a convincing case for liberal Jews holding tight to certain Jewish rituals and traditions even as they seek a Judaism flexible and meaningful enough to transmit to their children. It's what every synagogue tries to do, but her book aims to reach those Jews who don't hear the message because they're not in the pews. It's an important message for our community at this critical time."

—Sue Fishkoff, editor of *J. The Jewish News of Northern California* and author of *The Rebbe's Army: Inside the World of Chabad-Lubavitch* and *Kosher Nation: Why More and More of America's Food Answers to a Higher Authority*

"*Remix Judaism* is a thought-provoking book filled with justification, stories, and ways to lead an assimilated lifestyle while being intentional about your Judaism. It encourages an individualistic approach to what Judaism means to you as an individual, couple, or family at any stage in your life and how to pass on your tradition and culture to those around you. As a millennial Jewish summer camp professional who works with the next generation of the Jewish people, I believe Kwall's remix Judaism is the direction my campers should embody as they begin their own journeys to discovering their Jewish identities."

—Gabrielle Gordon, assistant director, Camp Young Judaea Midwest

"Lucidly and engagingly written, Roberta Rosenthal Kwall's *Remix Judaism* is a must-read for Jews and other 'willing listeners' seeking to deepen their connection to Judaism in ways other than through traditional Jewish legal observance. Emphasizing 'tradition' rather than 'law,' Kwall advocates a 'remix' strategy of personal choice of rituals and traditions rooted in the normative Jewish legal tradition that are infused with personal meaning and practiced consistently. Blending personal narratives and a scholar's perspective, Kwall illustrates 'remixes' of Shabbat, Jewish food traditions, marriage, children's education and b'nai mitzvah, grandparenting, mourning, and *tikkun olam*. Kwall's emphasis on the importance of Jewish education; the joyful, thoughtful, and consistent appropriation of Jewish traditions; and the contemporary need to balance the normative Jewish legal tradition with a search for personal meaning makes *Remix Judaism* an indispensable starting point for all those seeking a rich, meaningful Jewish life outside the scope of traditional Jewish legal observance."

—Alyssa M. Gray, Emily S. and Rabbi Bernard H. Mehlman Chair in Rabbinics, Hebrew Union College–Jewish Institute of Religion

"*Remix Judaism* is a critically important work. In a world where young people face unprecedented alienation and breakdown of meaning, Jewish living has so much to offer. But with so many young Jews distanced from their heritage, it must be presented in ways that resonate and meet them where they are. Professor Kwall understands these opportunities and challenges, and her book serves as a guide on how to access and make meaningful our sacred resources of wisdom, culture, and spirituality."

—Rabbi Ari Hart, Skokie Valley Agudath Jacob Synagogue, Skokie, IL

"In *Remix Judaism*, Roberta Kwall presents a lovingly constructed portrait of postmodern, postdenominational Judaism in North America. Her extensive research is studded with touching, insightful anecdotes that will delight and inspire, inviting the reader into self-reflection and into dialogue with the tradition. Kwall's thoughtful examination of the foundational pillars of Jewish life, and the diverse ways in which they are 'remixed' by Jews today, brings her audience into a new appreciation for the multifaceted, multivalent nature of modern Jewish life. This marvelous book will provide Kwall's diverse audience with a joyful affirmation of the way in which today's diverse 'remix Judaism' provides for heightened meaning in one's life."

—Rabbi Oren J. Hayon, Congregation Emanu El, Houston

"Kwall lovingly interweaves her personal Jewish journey with the unique stories of fellow travelers. The result: a more expansive and inclusive understanding of Jewish culture. Whether you agree or disagree with *Remix Judaism*'s premise, you'll be inspired by Kwall's use of Jewish culture as a springboard for intergenerational discussion."

—Hayim Herring, author of *Connecting Generations: Bridging the Boomer, Gen X, and Millennial Divide*

"*Remix Judaism* does a fantastic job of drawing on Jewish text and real-life anecdotes to help people who really want to build Jewish community see multiple ways to do it. Kwall's love of Jewish tradition, of creativity, and of Jewish peoplehood shines through the chapters of this book. Whether one considers oneself observant or secular, atheist or believer, *Remix Judaism* ultimately helps the reader envision a colorful and diverse Jewish future that transcends denominations and mines the gold at the heart of Jewish tradition."

—Rabbi Lizzi Heydemann, Mishkan Chicago

"One of the most beautiful and compelling truths about Judaism is that it evolves and keeps pace with modernity. Roberta Rosenthal Kwall's book is a timely contribution to this generation's search. This book captures the wonder of Jewish traditions and makes them accessible to all who are searching."

—Rabbi Karyn D. Kedar, Congregation BJBE, Deerfield, IL; author of *The Bridge to Forgiveness: Stories and Prayers for Finding God and Restoring Wholeness* and *Amen: Seeking Presence with Prayer, Poetry, and Mindfulness Practice*

"In her insightful book Professor Roberta Kwall offers a challenge to the worldwide Jewish community and especially the liberal community in North America. Citing example after example, she offers a path for all those who want to make their Judaism meaningful. Steeped in modern Jewish sociology, survey studies, personal interviews, and stories from the field, Kwall demonstrates that a Jewish tradition that is open to personal meaning, flexibility, and innovation can make a difference even in the lives of those who may not feel impelled by its legal structure. Kwall has produced a book that will challenge Jewish clergy, educators, and thought leaders, as well as those who want to find their path in Judaism through their own practice. It is a book worth reading and thinking about, and for that we should be thankful for the insights of the author and the passion with which they are expressed."

—Rabbi Vernon Kurtz, rabbi emeritus North Suburban Synagogue Beth El, past president American Zionist Movement, past president international Rabbinical Assembly

"Roberta Rosenthal Kwall's work reveals a deep examination of the unfolding nature of Jewish tradition in modernity, especially here in

America. Kwall's analysis proves relevant for people in all stages of life. Her unique background allows her the ability to craft explanations that make this a great resource for those who are new to the Jewish tradition as well as those for whom the Jewish tradition is familiar territory."

—Rabbi Nolan Lebovitz, Adat Shalom, Los Angeles

"*Remix Judaism* sets out to enable the reader to find meaning in and create an authentic Jewish life. Responding to recent research on trends in the American Jewish community, Kwall recognizes the realities of twenty-first-century life and offers ways in which Judaism may provide guidance, relevance, and insight for living in these times. Kwall believes in the preservation of the religious and cultural traditions of Judaism and at the same time strives to make Judaism accessible, opening doorways into Jewish practice and exploration in an empowering way."

—Rabbi Dr. Laura Novak Winer, Hebrew Union College–Jewish Institute of Religion

"In *Remix Judaism*, Kwall makes the case that Judaism is an aspirational tradition where diversity and disagreement can be simultaneously a tremendous challenge and our greatest strength. Kwall's writings always challenge my thinking through her combination of meticulous research, well-crafted arguments, copious references to traditional and modern Jewish sources, and fidelity to Jewish tradition. For a person who cares about the future of Judaism, this book presents a tremendous opportunity to take a journey with Kwall and think deeply about what it means to care about Judaism in this generation and generations to come."

—Rabbi Joshua Rabin, senior director of synagogue leadership, United Synagogue of Conservative Judaism (USCJ)

"When I chose a Jewish life, I was hungry for anything that could tell me exactly what I was signing up for. Judaism is ancient and traditional, but it is also dynamic and ever-adaptable. Roberta Kwall has written the book I needed then, and what a joy to read it now and remind myself of the breadth of Jewish life and ingenuity."

—Al Rosenberg, director of strategy and communication, OneTable

"Everyone knows that Jewish life in America is changing, but can American Jews take control of that change? In *Remix Judaism*, Roberta

Kwall lays out a way to think about Jewish identity and practice that embraces all Jews and encourages American Jews to 'remix' their tradition with care, thought, and an eye toward sustainable transmission for future generations. Packed with religious insights, recent studies, and concrete suggestions, Kwall has produced a book for anybody interested in the future of Judaism in America."

—Shira Telushkin, author of "Thou Shalt" Jewish advice column,
Tablet Magazine

"Roberta Kwall's informative and passionate new book melds some of the most meaningful Jewish customs and traditions with modern societal values and sensitivities. Her book provides enjoyable ways to preserve Jewish culture, in such areas as Shabbat and holidays, life events, the roles of parents and grandparents, *tikkun olam*, and much more. So many of the things we do on a day-to-day basis present opportunities to infuse them with Judaism, thus making them more meaningful and enjoyable. This book is a great guide to accomplishing that."

—Mark Trencher, president, Nishma Research

"Roberta Kwall grapples with the challenges and opportunities of an open and diverse society to offer pathways for engagement and deepened connection to Judaism for cultural and secular Jews."

—Rabbi Deborah Waxman, president, Reconstructing Judaism

"Writing with much sympathy and in an accessible, nondoctrinaire style about the complexities of living as an active Jew in contemporary America, Roberta Kwall has set herself the task of encouraging the broad spectrum of non-Orthodox Jews to give Judaism a second look because she is convinced their lives will be enriched immeasurably through the teachings and practices of their ancestors. *Remix Judaism* extends an invitation to all Jews to engage with the ever-evolving, millennia-old Jewish tradition."

—Jack Wertheimer, professor of American Jewish history,
Jewish Theological Seminary

REMIX JUDAISM

Preserving Tradition in a Diverse World

Roberta Rosenthal Kwall

ROWMAN & LITTLEFIELD
Lanham • Boulder • New York • London

Published by Rowman & Littlefield
An imprint of The Rowman & Littlefield Publishing Group, Inc.
4501 Forbes Boulevard, Suite 200, Lanham, Maryland 20706
https://rowman.com

6 Tinworth Street, London SE11 5AL, United Kingdom

British Library Cataloguing in Publication Information Available

Library of Congress Cataloging-in-Publication Data
Names: Kwall, Roberta Rosenthal, 1955– author.
Title: Remix Judaism : preserving tradition in a diverse world / Roberta Rosenthal Kwall.
Description: Lanham : Rowman & Littlefield, [2020] | Includes bibliographical references and index.
Identifiers: LCCN 2019046964 (print) | LCCN 2019046965 (ebook) | ISBN 9781538129555 (cloth) | ISBN 9781538129562 (epub)
Subjects: LCSH: Judaism—Customs and practices. | Jewish way of life. | Orthodox Judaism—Relations—Non-traditional Jews.
Classification: LCC BM700 .K89 2020 (print) | LCC BM700 (ebook) | DDC 296.7—dc23
LC record available at https://lccn.loc.gov/2019046964
LC ebook record available at https://lccn.loc.gov/2019046965

♾ ™ The paper used in this publication meets the minimum requirements of American National Standard for Information Sciences Permanence of Paper for Printed Library Materials, ANSI/NISO Z39.48-1992.

To Sander and those who will follow him.
My first grandchild—a sense of continuity.

CONTENTS

FOREWORD

Being Jewish, as Roberta Kwall knows all too well, is vexingly hard to define. Perhaps with the exception of sharing a history and not believing in the divinity of Jesus, there is no single aspect of Jewish identity that all Jews can agree upon. No single race or ethnicity defines us, nor, as Kwall observes at the very beginning of her book, can all Jews agree on religious practice. It's not just the wide spectrum of religious observance and beliefs, but it's that, outside Orthodoxy, many of us are agnostic, if not atheist, and few of us find religious law to be as binding as civil law.

Instead, Jewish identity is a kind of amalgamation of Jewish components—with each of us drawing from a different mix of history, ritual, texts, language, culture, food, nostalgia and more, to form our own version of being Jewish. Sometimes it seems like a soup or stew that has so many variations that people have difficulty agreeing on any one essential ingredient.

Many Orthodox Jews look at this reality and conclude, sometimes a bit smugly, that non-Orthodox Judaism is doomed to extinction. Similarly, many Israeli Jews—whether religious or not—conclude that Judaism outside the Jewish State cannot survive. But where they see a group of lost souls assimilating themselves out of existence, Roberta Kwall sees possibility. And I think she is right.

And Kwall is right on target when she observes, "For a Jew to appreciate and want to perpetuate the tradition, I do not believe it is necessary that he or she see the law as 'binding' or representing the direct word of God. It is enough that one appreciates the beauty of Jewish tradition and desires to benefit from its content and wisdom."

I know this because, while I was raised with no formal Jewish education and by parents who often seemed to desire to run away from Jewishness, my adult life has embodied what Kwall coins "Remix Judaism."

Just weeks before I wrote this foreword, my younger daughter had what was essentially a "remix" bat mitzvah. As her older sister had three years earlier, she had an alternative ceremony held not at a synagogue, but at the Marlene Meyerson Jewish Community Center in Manhattan. Called "Off the Bimah B Mitzvah," it differed from traditional bar/bat mitzvah ceremonies in several ways: It was a group ceremony, rather than an individual one. And instead of chanting from their Torah portion and Haftarah, each child spent a year working on a project related to the Torah portion associated with their Hebrew birth date and gave a speech about it.

The most moving part of the bat mitzvah was when, after each child gave their presentation, all the guests—from a wide range of Jewish and other backgrounds—spread out around the room (in this case, a well-decorated gymnasium) to form a large circle and then, together, carefully held a fully unrolled Torah scroll. With the scroll spread out and its entire contents visible, each child and their immediate family stood in front of the spot on the parchment where the Torah portion corresponding to their Hebrew birthday was located and then read one line from it.

I love the way this ritual made the Torah tangible and made it easy for people to see how all its different pieces fit together. And even though we weren't studying each portion on the traditional date it is read in the annual Torah-reading cycle, the children were learning that the portions are related to a place in the calendar, and each one got a sense of ownership over the part that coincides with their birth date.

As Kwall writes in the introduction, "remix Judaism" is a way of connecting Jews "who are not, and likely never will be, observant by conventional measures" to Jewish teachings and practices. As she observes, "The power and beauty of Jewish tradition can speak to everyone because the tradition's rituals offer so much potential for deriving attributions of personal meaning. Second, all Jews can access this power and beauty through meaningful Jewish education."

Of course the bat mitzvah is one of the easiest Jewish customs to tinker with, since much of what we think is tradition nowadays is relatively new—not just the bat mitzvah, which only became a thing in the mid-twentieth century but also the bar mitzvah, which isn't all that much older. Once marked quite modestly, with a boy called to the Torah for a weekday Torah reading and a few toasts in his honor at the kiddush afterward, the bar mitzvah only became a big communal affair in the twentieth century.

For our family, it was particularly easy to tinker with the bat mitzvah because we were working from a relatively clean slate. While my father was forced to have a bar mitzvah at a Conservative synagogue in the 1950s—and resented it—neither my sister nor I had (or even attended many) bat mitzvah celebrations growing up. My husband isn't Jewish. So on neither side of the family was there any pressure for our daughters to have bat mitzvah celebrations, much less ones that followed specific protocols.

Given my upbringing, and because I intermarried, my adult Jewish life has been one of picking, choosing, and remixing. My Jewish practices are quite idiosyncratic and often inconsistent: I do a partial fast on Yom Kippur, in which I eat just enough to curb intense hunger and lightheadedness (and enough caffeine to stave off headaches) but avoid eating anything pleasurable or flavorful. At Passover, I don't purge my house of *chametz*, but I do abstain from leavened foods. For *Shabbat* (the Sabbath), we light the candles and say the blessings—though we usually do a shortened *kiddush* [blessing over wine], and sometimes the *motzi* [blessing over bread] is over pizza or a regular loaf of bread, rather than challah. While our rituals are quite abridged and our *Shabbat* observance rarely includes any time in a synagogue, we did, early in our marriage, designate *Shabbat* as a quasi-sacred family day. During the school year, Saturday is the one day my husband, a high school teacher, does no work at all. While his Sundays are filled with grading papers and exams, and mine are usually consumed with errands and household chores, Saturday is the day we reserve for family excursions. Similarly, an annual family vacation to Maine serves as a sort of yearly *Sabbath*, one in which we stay in a cottage with no Internet access or TV and do *Shabbat*-like activities together: jigsaw puzzles, reading and board games, along with lots of swimming and kayaking.

More important than Jewish observance to me is Jewish knowledge. And thankfully, a Jewish education is much easier to obtain today—and at all stages of life—than it once was, thanks to innovative educational programs (like the one at the JCC that my children benefited from) and accessible websites like My Jewish Learning (which I edited for several years) and Sefaria. I am grateful that, through a college semester in Israel, my decades working in Jewish journalism, and my several years at My Jewish Learning, I have compensated for my lack of formal childhood education to become a reasonably literate Jew. I am hardly an expert, but I feel culturally competent, as if I have a feel for the breadth of Jewish history and tradition and I know how to find out what I don't know.

It can be overwhelming to have everything up for grabs—and often I second-guess myself, worry that I am not Jewish enough or that I'm not doing enough to raise my children as Jews (although I alternate between thinking this is important and thinking that, in the vast scheme of things, Jewish identity is a rather abstract and even first world problem-like thing to worry about). But "remix Judaism" actually provides far more structure and ritual than simply living a secular, modern American life in which so many people are lonely and overwhelmed by infinite choices. It is a good compromise between these two extremes, one in which one's life is completely defined by religion and one in which life is defined by individualism and materialism. It's nice to be able to take what works for me and reject those pieces of the tradition that do not. It is nice to have a life—and give a life to my children—that is not exclusively secular, in which certain things aren't up to us, that we have a tradition and community from which to draw guidance.

As my experience illustrates, Kwall definitely gets it right when she writes, "The sacred texts of the tradition reveal multiple meanings on their face. For example, even the Bible incorporates numerous, and sometimes competing, views of God. The history of the Jewish people is complicated, as is the Jewish tradition itself. Judaism has never been a one-size-fits-all religion."

Julie Wiener
June 16, 2019

ACKNOWLEDGMENTS

We often hear the phrase "when one door closes another opens." As I was completing my last book, *The Myth of the Cultural Jew: Culture and Law in Jewish Tradition*, I began to experience an urgent desire to apply my theoretical observations to a more practical setting. Living and writing as a Jew who straddles the traditional and liberal communities, I have a keen sense that many people want to embrace Jewish tradition in ways that will work for them but are not quite sure how to go about this process. My primary mentor for my last book, Rabbi Vernon Kurtz, wisely advised me not to take on this issue in connection with a book that was primarily directed to an audience of Jewish professionals and legal scholars. But even as I wrote my concluding chapter, I knew that this would be the goal of my next project.

When I began writing *Remix Judaism* three years ago, a Jewish studies colleague advised me to "write this book for my daughters." I have kept this sage observation continually in mind as I crafted the content for this book. I am so grateful to my three daughters, Shanna, Rachel, and Nisa, and their respective partners, Andrew, Jeremy, and Jordan, for providing me with the best possible inspiration for this book.

My husband, Jeffrey Kwall, also has played a crucial role in the development of this book, and I am so grateful to him not only for his perceptive comments on chapters but also for his willingness to discuss the content of this book on what must have seemed like a never-ending basis.

I also want to express my gratitude to my parents, Millie and Abe Rosenthal, *z"l*. Without their endless love and support, none of my personal or professional accomplishments would have been possible. I miss them both dearly.

I believe in the power of *beshert* (something that is meant to be) and my relationship with my agent Amaryah Orenstein of GO Literary exemplifies this concept. Even when she agreed to represent me, I had no idea of the tremendous role she would play in the successful completion of this project, which included careful reading, brainstorming, sage advice on the publication process, and overall just being there whenever I needed her. When Amaryah came into my life, I gained not only an incomparable agent, but also a dear friend.

My editor, Rolf Janke at Rowman & Littlefield, is everything one could want in an editor. I am so grateful to him for understanding the importance of this project and facilitating its publication in such a gracious and seamless way. Also, I want to thank Jon Sisk, senior executive editor, for his many efforts; his assistant Dina Guilak; Courtney Packard for her capable assistance with production and design; Chloe Batch for the cover design; my production editor Janice Braunstein; and copy editor Naomi Mindlin, all at Rowman & Littlefield.

I also owe a large debt of gratitude to Julie Wiener for her willingness to write the foreword and the substantial thought she put into framing such an appropriate prelude to my book.

My law school dean, Jennifer Rosato, also supported me by advocating for my spring 2019 research leave. My three exceptional student research assistants at DePaul University College of Law were also integral: Shprintza Block, Marisa Pogofsky, and Hannah Sullivan. In addition, I am grateful to DePaul colleagues Lawrence Arendt and David Bell for the administrative assistance they provided in connection with this project.

I also want to thank Dean Amnon Lehavi of the Radzyner Law School, Interdisciplinary Center (IDC) in Israel for inviting me to teach "Jewish Law and the American Jewish Movements" for the past couple years. This book benefited greatly from the many conversations I had with the faculty and Israeli law students during my visits.

A special thank you to my friend and colleague Deborah Tuerkheimer who provided encouragement and support during our weekly pre-*Shabbat* telephone calls. Another special thank you to Vernon Kurtz, who read every chapter and provided helpful insights throughout this process.

I benefited in many different ways from the following friends and colleagues who played significant roles throughout this process. These individuals provided a diverse range of support that included reading and commenting on discrete chapters, engaging in conversations that helped to shape my thinking, sharing research, providing inspiration through their personal narratives, forging invaluable connections, furnishing books and other useful materials, facilitating presentations where I could discuss my work, and offering friendship and support: Liz Alpern, Susan Bandes, Adina Bankier-Karp, Ali Begoun, David Begoun, Adena Berkowitz, JoAnne Blumberg, Naomi Cahn, Barry Chazan, Steven Cohen, Daniella Greenbaum Davis, Elliot Dorff, Molly Dugan, Avi Finegold, Naomi Firestone-Teeter, Stacey Flint, Betsy Forester, Laura Frankel, Judy Franks, Steven Franks, Alex Freedman, Marissa Freeman, Wendi Geffen, Alicia Gejman, Jessica Grose, Amy Guth, Ellen Gutiontov, Stanley Gutiontov, Diane Halivni, Shai Halivni, Wendy Helton, Leslie Hill Hirschfeld, Jill Jacobs, Jonathan Jacobson, Mindy Jacobson, Shosh Korrub, Liel Leibovitz, Arielle Levitan, Phil Lieberman, Kathryn Liss, Anna Marx, Linda McClain, Barbara Miller, Patricia Keer Munro, Althea Pestine-Stevens, Sonja Pilz, David Raphael, Al Rosenberg, Lisa Rosenkranz, Shmuel Rosner, Carol Schneider, Michael Schwab, Katherine Schwartz, Maureen Sechan, Michelle Shain, Joel Shalowitz, Madeleine Shalowitz, Steven Shapiro, Cindy Sher, Marc Sherman, Adam Shinar, Gila Silverman, Alex Sinclair, Peri Sinclair, Donna Kwall Smith, Stephen Sniderman, Sandy Starkman, Kim Treiger, Mark Trencher, Barbara Tuerkheimer, Frank Tuerkheimer, David Wechsler, Susan Wechsler, Gary Weintraub, Jack Wertheimer, Laura Novak Winer, Joshua Yuter, and Lior Zemer.

This book is dedicated to my first grandchild, Sander, who was born exactly two years into this project, and to my grandchildren whom we pray will follow in the years to come. Many years ago I read the book *Revelation Restored* by David Weiss Halivni, who dedicated his book to his first grandchild with the same beautiful language I use in my dedication. I always hoped that one day I might be able to use this language in a book of my own and I thank him for his inspiration.

Sander quickly changed our lives in a fundamental way. My passion for transmitting Jewish tradition suddenly took on an even greater intensity as we experienced the beginning of the second generation of our offspring. As I write these words, my greatest hope is that one day Sander, and the grandchildren who join him, will read these pages and want to pass along a love of Jewish tradition.

Tam v'nishlam shevah le-El borei olam (This book is complete, praise be to God, Creator of the universe).

Roberta Rosenthal Kwall
July 2019/*Tammuz* 5779

INTRODUCTION
Why Remix Matters

How many times have you heard someone say that he or she is a cultural Jew? Perhaps you have even used this phrase to describe yourself. Cultural Jews generally see Jewish culture, and Jewish identity, as positive values. Cultural Jews often enjoy Jewish-themed literature and entertainment, foods associated with the Jewish people, and playing the well-known game of "Jewish geography" with new acquaintances. They also take great pride in the notable achievements of other Jews. In general, though, many cultural Jews are relatively disinterested in the religious side of Judaism.

Jewish culture still is fairly robust in the United States. If the entertainment industry is a reliable barometer, Jewish culture seems to be thriving now more than ever as Jewish themes and topics are continually showcased in television and movies. Some treatments even feature Jewish ritual in seemingly authentic formats such as Hebrew prayers during a Bar Mitzvah or funeral service.

Paradoxically, many cultural Jews feel it is important for their children, grandchildren, and even great-grandchildren to share their Jewish identity and cultural affiliation. This feeling aligns with the reality that today's American Jews are proud to be Jewish. They see *being Jewish* as an important part of their lives and they have a strong sense of belonging to the Jewish people. Many Jewish baby boomers still prefer their children to marry Jewish mates, and hope that their grandchildren, even those who are the product of intermarriage, will be raised at least partially Jewish. These desires exist even among some baby boomers who themselves have intermarried.

Of course, not all cultural Jews share this desire for cultural transmission. In October 2013, Gabriel Roth, the senior editor at *Slate* magazine, wrote an opinion piece entitled "American Jews Are Secular, Intermarried, and Assimilated: Great News!" Here is his argument in a nutshell: "As an intermarried Jewish nonbeliever, I think it's time we anxious Jews stopped worrying and learned to love our assimilated condition—even if it means that our children call themselves half-Jewish and our grandchildren don't consider themselves Jews at all."[1]

Roth directs his comments to "cultural Jews" such as himself "who host Seders with progressive Haggadahs and read contemporary novels with Jewish themes and never go to synagogue." He argues that in the context of a lifestyle that is otherwise devoid of Jewishness, "these activities have no intrinsic meaning—they are just tactics to placate our own parents and encourage the next generation to identify as Jews." Roth asks: "How much value can 'Jewish heritage' have if it signifies nothing beyond its own perpetuation?"[2]

When I initially read Roth's piece, I confess I was deeply disturbed. Still, Roth is not entirely wrong when he rails against the performance of meaningless tradition. Although his concern is to assuage the guilt his cohorts feel for not being better Jews, I see the relevance of his critique differently. In twenty-first-century America, meaningful Jewish identity must be actively cultivated if it is to continue. Jews who want their offspring to identify as proud Jews, and feel a strong sense of peoplehood and connection to Judaism generally, must work at achieving this result. Roth is absolutely on target to the extent that he argues that what some cultural Jews do will not be enough to perpetuate Judaism.

When seen in this light, Roth's article reveals the core problem of the American Jewish condition. Many, if not most, American Jews want their grandchildren to be Jewish in theory, but in practice they are not so sure what that means, either for themselves or their progeny. They would have difficulty giving a precise answer to the question of why they identify as Jewish, and why they hope their children and grandchildren will continue this identification.

The evidence is pretty clear that most American Jews do not believe strict religious observance is fundamental to their Jewish identity. The

2013 Pew Report, the most recent comprehensive study of the American Jewish community, found that "observing Jewish law" was "essential to Jewish identity" for only 19 percent of the respondents.[3] But if observing the laws of the Jewish religion is not important to the vast majority of American Jews, how would they define their Jewish identity? The answer to this question is far from clear in the Pew Report and other sources. At best, we know that American Jewish identity is multifaceted and fluid, particularly among millennials.[4]

We live in a very diverse Jewish world regarding a variety of areas such as politics, geography, and even race.[5] In this book, I use the term "diverse" to mean that people's practices and beliefs occupy what seems like an ever-expanding spectrum largely characterized by a movement away from traditional religious observance. The majority of identified Jews in the United States fall somewhere along a spectrum ranging from still fairly traditional (although not Orthodox) to purely cultural. This spectrum includes a wide range of Jewish involvement.

Here are some benchmarks that can be used to define distinct places along this spectrum. The most engaged of these Jews may consider themselves religious, attend synagogue quite regularly, and are deeply enmeshed in a vibrant Jewish community. Moving along the spectrum, there are many Jews who do not consider themselves conventionally religious but still are affiliated with a synagogue and deeply engaged in Jewish causes and certain traditional observances. There are also Jews who are actively engaged in Jewish causes but not affiliated with a synagogue and vice versa.

The least engaged Jews on this spectrum may have warm feelings for their Jewish heritage, perhaps due to fond memories of *bubbe*'s matzo ball soup or their upbringing in a more traditional Jewish environment. Even so, they are not actively involved in Jewish organizations, causes, or observances on a regular basis. In other words, aside from upbringing, Judaism essentially does not factor into their lives. Significantly, many Jews occupy different places along this spectrum at various points. Perhaps one unifying factor is that nearly all of these Jews value Jewish ancestry and culture enough to identify as Jewish, and are proud of this identification. Throughout these pages, I refer to the diverse group of Jews on this spectrum collectively as either non-Orthodox or liberal Jews.

Often people ask me where faith in God fits into the picture of Jewish identity and transmission. This topic is complicated. It seems to be the case that among many Jews, including a sector of some religious Jews, faith and observance do not necessarily go hand in hand. I have known many Jews with a deep faith in God but who are not ritualistically observant. I also know seemingly observant Jews who are not entirely certain about the strength of their faith. The firm where I worked as a young lawyer in Chicago had a Torah study group that met regularly, and I still vividly recall the discussion that ensued after I commented on the relative silence about faith among Jews I knew. Our Modern Orthodox group leader asked the only other Orthodox member of the group whether he believed in God. The other group member, seemingly shocked by our leader's question, replied "of course I do!" And our leader replied—very plainly and clearly—that one could not necessarily assume this even among those who identify as Orthodox.

Although in theory Judaism demands loyalty to a monotheistic perspective, in practice the Jewish religion tends to focus on actions rather than belief. Actions are believed to influence emotions, and therefore Judaism emphasizes what people do, even more than what they believe. As a religion major in college, I have long been keenly aware that the types of conversations common among my religious Christian friends are generally very different from those that take place in Jewish circles. In my experience, most Jews typically do not discuss their faith in God publicly.

Israel represents another complicated aspect of Jewish identity and transmission in today's world. Although there is reason to believe that for many Jews caring about Israel is still a marker of American Jewish identity,[6] the positive nature of Israel's influence on this identity is diminishing, particularly among younger Jews. The current political situation plays a role in this decline, but so does decreasing Jewish engagement in general among the non-Orthodox. This reality is problematic from the standpoint of transmitting Jewish tradition. As I develop more fully below, the flavor and rhythm of Jewish tradition in Israel is unique, even among Israelis who consider themselves secular. Exposure to this environment can have a significant positive impact on those Jews willing and able to spend time in Israel.

With this book, I hope to open a dialogue with all Jews, and other willing listeners, about how to strengthen their connection to the teachings and practices of the Jewish tradition in a way that comports with the sensibilities of Jews who are not, and likely never will be, observant by conventional measures. I develop the concept of "remix" Judaism as the means of strengthening this connection. This project is driven by two deeply held personal convictions. First, the power and beauty of Jewish tradition can speak to everyone because the tradition's rituals offer so much potential for deriving attributions of personal meaning. Second, all Jews can access this power and beauty through meaningful Jewish education, and especially through the narrative sources of Jewish tradition known as *aggadah*. The remainder of this chapter lays the groundwork for how a remixed approach to Jewish tradition has the potential to enhance appreciation for Jewish tradition, and preserve its existence, among a wide spectrum of non-Orthodox Jews.

UNBUNDLING JEWISH IDENTITY, CULTURE, LAW, AND TRADITION

Judaism is not just a religion; it is also a way of life. This way of life has shaped the Jewish people throughout the centuries and even today it has much to do with why even assimilated Jews still identify as Jewish.

Unfortunately, when it comes to unbundling Jewish identity, it seems to be the case that everyone is speaking a different language. Sometimes these language differences feel more like dialects that still allow for a degree of communication. Often, though, the differences are so fundamental that people simply cannot hear one another, and in truth, may not wish to.

A good starting point for this discussion is the concept of Jewish law. I co-directed a center for Jewish Law and Judaic Studies at my law school for six years and the most common question I received from people was "What exactly is Jewish law?" Even Jews who consider themselves traditional would ask me this question. I came to understand that most people think Jewish law is relevant only to religious ritual, which explained why many people simply could not understand how and why a center for Jewish law would have a place in secular legal studies.

Typically, I responded to these questions by explaining that Jewish law, known as *halakhah* in Hebrew, is an organic legal system that covers virtually all aspects of human behavior. It is not confined to what we do on the Jewish holidays and in synagogue. The scope of Jewish law extends to just about every area of human existence—such as personal relationships, property, inheritance, sex, clothing, ethics, health concerns, and business. People typically found this explanation of Jewish law interesting, but, of course, it always led to the next question: "Why do we have to follow Jewish law today?" After all, when a person does not obey secular law, there will likely be tangible consequences. But who is in charge of prosecution and punishment if someone eats pork or disregards *Shabbat*, the Jewish Sabbath?

To many Jews who are steeped in the theology of Torah most closely associated today with Orthodoxy, the answer is obvious and needs little explanation. Torah comes from God and it is our binding obligation as Jews to follow the law. Also, the consequences of violating Jewish law may never be experienced in this world.

Personally, I appreciate the Jewish tradition's perspective that Jewish law is binding upon the Jews as the word of God. But I suspect the concept of faithfully following Jewish law in its entirety, because God commanded that we do so, does not resonate with most non-Orthodox Jews—even those who profess a strong faith in God.

I recall my own reaction the first time I saw one of my friends wearing a wig to comply with the *halakhic* norm that married women should cover their hair. I asked her what made her decide to do this, and her response was unqualified: "I knew this is what God wanted of me." I remember thinking that I must have missed this memo! To me, the requirement of a head covering seems much more culturally imposed rather than a requirement issued from the Divine.

We live in an age in which many people do not respect the authority of contemporary religious figures, let alone the rabbis who shaped Jewish law hundreds of years ago. Our society prizes autonomy and customization. People tend to observe ritual when they find it to be personally meaningful. We pick and choose that which we feel is meaningful and have no second thoughts about discarding everything else.

This is exactly the problem Gabriel Roth identifies. But I disagree completely with his proposed solution that cultural Jews should embrace their assimilated selves. In my conversations with Jews from a wide variety of backgrounds and levels of education, I began to notice an important shift in the understanding of my message when I replaced the largely unfamiliar language of "Jewish law" with the more comfortable and familiar language of "Jewish tradition." The language of Jewish "law" suggests hard and fast rules and consequences for disobedience that are foreign to most non-Orthodox Jews. On the other hand, Jewish "tradition" connotes positive associations and the desire for transmission.

So what exactly is Jewish tradition and how does it differ from Jewish law? Jewish tradition can be analogized to an umbrella that covers both the concrete legal components formulated by the rabbis as well as the more amorphous cultural aspects of the religion practiced by the people over the centuries. In other words, Jewish tradition includes both Jewish law and Jewish culture.

Most people do not recognize this interconnection between Jewish law and culture. In truth, however, throughout history the rabbis shaped *halakhah* in response to surrounding cultures. These cultures included both the cultures of the Jews specifically as well as the host nations in which Jews have lived for centuries. The reality of foreign influence is especially apparent in the Jewish laws regarding life cycle events, such as birth and death, which are realities for everyone.

The line between the legal precepts and the practices of the people has always been a fuzzy one. There are many examples of practices that began with the people and became codified into law by the rabbis. For example, much of what we now think of as basic practices for keeping a kosher kitchen, such as permanent separation of meat and dairy dishes, began as stringencies adopted by the people in the Middle Ages that were eventually elevated into legal requirements by the rabbis.

Similarly, what we think of as Jewish culture has been greatly influenced by the existence of the law the rabbis formulated. Here are just a couple of examples. When self-denominated cultural Jews light Chanukah candles or celebrate a Passover Seder, the roots of these behaviors come from Jewish law even if many Jews do not recognize this origin. Also, the liberal causes and social action models so many American Jews find attractive derive from language in the Torah about leaving the edges of fields untouched so that the poor and socially disadvantaged can benefit. In reality, other than the popularity of bagels and lox, there are very few cultural Jewish practices that do not have some basis in *halakhah*.

In short, Jewish law and culture are completely intertwined, and this relationship lies at the heart of the Jewish tradition. For most of its history, the core of Judaism was understood to be a binding law that was infused with cultural elements. Today, the majority of Jews see Judaism as more cultural in nature, and many do not appreciate the law's impact upon this culture.

Despite this paradigm shift, Jewish tradition can serve as the foundation for inspiring and educating Jewish adults and children to appreciate the beauty of the religion. For a Jew to appreciate and want to perpetuate the tradition, I do not believe it is necessary to see the law as "binding" or representing the direct word of God. It is enough that one appreciates the beauty of Jewish tradition and desires to benefit from its content and wisdom.

JEWISH TRADITION MORE ORGANIC IN ISRAEL

A culturally sensitive approach to Judaism for non-Orthodox Jews entails using the language of "Jewish tradition" rather than "Jewish law." Still, the operative word here is "Jewish." Not surprisingly, we see evidence of this organic affinity for Jewish tradition most strongly in Israel, despite the well-publicized struggles there between religious and secular Jews.

A 2016 report by the Pew Research Center, its first major study of the entire Israeli population, concluded that despite some decline in observance in recent years, Israeli Jews still are more likely than Jews in the United States to adhere to Jewish traditions. For example, the survey found that 80 percent of non-Orthodox Israeli Jews do not eat pork, and 43 percent claimed they always or usually light *Shabbat* candles. The comparative data on these markers for non-Orthodox Jews in the United States reveals much lower percentages.[7]

Although the Israel Pew Report still provides plenty of evidence that secular Jews are thriving in Israel, the concept of "secular" has a very different meaning in Israel than in the United States.[8] There are logical explanations for the differences between Israeli and American secularism: Jewish culture is the majority culture in Israel, the country operates according to Jewish time, and the nation's primary language is

Hebrew. All Jews in Israel cannot help basking in the history and practice of Jewish tradition, regardless of their personal level of observance.

When Israelis contemplate the dangers of assimilation, they think of intermarriage—something that realistically happens mostly to Jews living outside of Israel.[9] Also, although Jews in both Israel and the United States display a strong sense of Jewish peoplehood, this concept has a flavor in Israel unlike anywhere else. For example, consider the national sirens that are sounded on both *Yom Hazikaron* (Israel's Day of Remembrance honoring fallen soldiers) and *Yom Hasho'ah* (Holocaust Remembrance Day). During these two-minute siren blasts, the entire country comes to a complete stop. This remarkable manifestation of Jewish peoplehood is completely unthinkable outside of Israel. The Israel Pew Report reveals that the vast majority of Israeli Jews believe "being connected with Jewish history, culture and community" is "central to their Jewish identity." The Pew Report on the American Jewish community does not demonstrate this same type of connection.[10]

In short, Israel's surrounding culture is steeped in Jewish tradition, including the *halakhic* elements. As a result, the secular Jewish environment enables many Israelis to lead very Jewish lives, even if they do not feel bound by the commandments. Many secular Israelis probably do not realize or contemplate the extent to which Jewish tradition, both the culture and the *halakhah*, surrounds them and shapes their existence. Their overall absorption of the religious elements of the tradition is taken for granted. Therefore, non-Orthodox Israeli Jews, including those who claim to be secular, manifest a greater and more organic connection to Jewish tradition compared to non-Orthodox American Jews.

But on my last trip to Israel I realized that non-Orthodox Jews living in Israel also can benefit from an explicit remixed approach to Jewish tradition. For the past couple of years, I have been teaching Israeli law students at Radzyner Law School a course called "Jewish Law and the American Jewish Movements." Although the vast majority of my students are secular Israelis, their personal practices actually embody a remixed version of Jewish tradition that is consistent with the approach developed here. Still, despite being surrounded by much more Jewish tradition than non-Orthodox Jews in the Diaspora, they have to grapple with their resentment toward Judaism stemming from their perceived coercion of the country's Chief Rabbinate.

Alex Sinclair, an expert on Israeli education who lives in Israel, has written that Israelis "can learn a lot from American Jews about meaning-oriented Judaism," a statement that confirms my instinct about the relevance of a remixed approach to Judaism in Israel.[11] Through my teaching and visits to Israel, and the many conversations I have had with Jewish professionals there, I have come to see that much of the content of this book also is relevant for secular Israelis who find themselves practicing more tradition than most Americans but who have conflicting feelings toward the benefits of Jewish tradition given the impact of the Rabbinate. For secular Israelis, as well as Diaspora Jews, it is important to develop personal meaning in their observed traditions, as this proactive engagement will optimize the chances for ongoing transmission.

CONNECTION TO TRADITION THROUGH REMIX JUDAISM

Diaspora Jews clearly face a completely different cultural landscape than their Israeli brethren. They live in majority cultures that are not based on Jewish or Hebrew roots or on Jewish time. They live on land that is not the historic Jewish homeland. For the most part, they do not speak, read, or write the Hebrew language.

Author Gal Beckerman's parents recognized this distinction immediately upon their immigration to the United States from Israel. He wrote that one of their "biggest adjustments" was "figuring out how to pass on their Jewishness," something they had never thought about while in Israel. Their solution was to celebrate the onset of *Shabbat* on Friday night. The traditional Friday night rituals signified to him "home and something deeply rooted." Eventually, he and his wife wanted to provide their children with this same feeling toward Jewish tradition. Beckerman describes the importance of the regularity of this special family time on Friday night as "the few minutes in our lives when we enter a special zone that's different from the rest of the week."[12] The selection of aspects of the religious tradition, and regular performance, provides the foundation for how Judaism can be transmitted by non-Orthodox Jews through a remixed approach.

The United States has the largest concentration of Jews living outside of Israel. Sadly, the Jewish content of American-Jewish culture is becoming less apparent and important to those American Jews who do not recognize or appreciate the *halakhic* roots of Jewish culture. This reality complicates the way in which American Jews contemplate and define their Jewish identities.

Despite these problems, the Pew Report on the American Jewish community clearly demonstrates that American Jews are identified Jews. This finding is critical because if identified Jews have access to Jewish tradition through education and other tools, they can learn to appreciate its beauty and relevance. They can be persuaded to incorporate some, if not many, elements of the tradition into their lives even if they are not willing to follow Jewish law in its entirety. The ritualistic aspects of the tradition can be used effectively to communicate a wealth of content for living meaningful lives.

It is vital for all Jews to be taught why and how Jewish tradition can provide the basis for the particulars of the cultural tradition about which they do care. This tradition has played a pivotal role in shaping the Jewish people over the millennia. It has allowed Jews to connect the past with the present, and it can furnish a path to the future. Elements of the Jewish tradition can touch the heart, soul, and mind of every willing Jew, and add meaning to life.

Jews who do not feel bound to observe Jewish law in the most conventional way still must be persuaded to deepen their connection to Jewish tradition. I understand that an approach lacking a focus on an obligation to observe Divine commandments will be cause for concern in many strictly observant Jewish communities. I also appreciate the success that many Orthodox groups such as Chabad, through their outreach programs, have achieved with non-Orthodox Jews. But Jewish outreach, known as *kiruv*, is not a one-size-fits all proposition. Although I applaud those non-Orthodox Jews who have grown in their faith and practice through the type of *kiruv* commonly practiced in the Orthodox world, large numbers of Jews will never set foot anywhere near an Orthodox community or rabbi. These Jews need to be encouraged with a different model, both conceptually and practically.

The idea of developing a deeper connection to Jewish tradition can appeal to Jews who believe in the Divine origins of Jewish law, as well as to those who question the concept of God but have positive feelings toward their Jewish roots. Many Jews, regardless of their personal beliefs about God, can appreciate that Jewish tradition is a part of our collective past and is something worthy of continuity.

So how would this concept work in practice? An important starting point is that the past has relevance and cannot be discarded. But sometimes the present calls for a "remix" of past tradition. The idea of "remix" appropriately suggests starting with something familiar as a base, and then adding to it or somehow personalizing its relevance. [13]

Jewish educators have described much of the current relationship many Jews, especially millennials, have with Jewish tradition as a process of remix that entails selection, rejection, and modification. Doctors Erica Brown and Misha Galperin have argued that the current popularity of customized products and experiences can be used advantageously by Jews seeking to embrace "the beauty of remix identities." This is particularly true for younger Jews "who still respect the 'original' enough to take hold of it and make it their own." [14] College student Amanda Gordon implicitly affirmed the concept of remix in an article in the *New York Jewish Week* when she wrote that she feels "a personal sense of urgency to adapt and reinterpret" Jewish rituals "to keep them relevant." [15]

A remixed approach to Judaism must be invoked with care, however, to ensure that remixed practices retain authenticity by maintaining "a legitimate link to the community." [16] A study of moderately affiliated American Jews at the turn of the twenty-first century revealed a growing trend of selecting among new and inherited practices and texts "to find the combination they as individuals can authentically affirm." [17] The problem, however, is that authenticity cannot be determined exclusively according to individual practice and opinion. From the standpoint of a particular cultural or religious tradition, authenticity must also be judged with reference to the norms of tradition in question.

It is possible for individuals to find an authentic yet personal meaning in tradition when three conditions exist: (1) people exercise individuality as to what rituals and traditions they elect to incorporate in their lives; (2) people infuse the elements they choose with their own personal meaning; and (3) people *consistently* perform the elements they practice in a way that embraces, at least to *some degree*, the authenticity of historical tradition. If these conditions are met, it is highly likely that both the individuals and the communities of which they are a part will be successful in transmitting meaningful, specific elements of Jewish tradition as well as a more global appreciation for its beauty and relevance. The key is selecting practices that retain an authentic link to Jewish history and community, infusing them with a sense of personal meaning, and consistent performance.

These ideas can be illustrated with three examples. The first example centers on one of the most beautiful and renowned Jewish traditions—the lighting of candles to mark the beginning of *Shabbat*. According to the Torah, it is forbidden to create a fire on *Shabbat*.[18] Because the Jewish day begins and ends at sundown, Jews who observe Jewish law are required to light *Shabbat* candles about eighteen minutes before sundown on Friday night. This prescribed timing dates back to the Talmudic period[19] and represents a fence around the law created by the rabbis to prevent inadvertent violations.

For Jews who believe Jewish law is the binding word of God, it is forbidden to light *Shabbat* candles after the prescribed time. Still, many Jews who do not adhere to the letter of Jewish law find meaning in lighting *Shabbat* candles and want to participate in this tradition. They also want to pass this tradition down to their children. As a result, they may choose to light *Shabbat* candles later than the prescribed time, after *Shabbat* has actually begun. These Jews want to inaugurate the celebration of *Shabbat* with an authentic ritual, even if they choose to perform this ritual in a way that actually violates Jewish law. Often those who light candles find enhanced meaning in this tradition, such as time for personal reflection and thanksgiving and a feeling of being connected to the Jewish people over space and time. These personal attributions can be more significant to many people than the legal regulations concerning timing.

The second example involves the *ketubah*, the Jewish marriage contract given by a Jewish groom to his bride. At one time, the *ketubah* was a legal necessity devised by the Talmudic sages to protect women in the event of unwanted divorce or their spouse's death.[20] Today, the legal protections furnished in the *ketubah* are largely irrelevant in the United States given that civil law governs the economic aspects of marriage and divorce. Even from the standpoint of Jewish law, the *ketubah*'s function has been minimized. Still, its use throughout the centuries has established the *ketubah*'s place as an important symbol of Jewish marriage.

I believe the *ketubah*'s popularity has endured largely because this tradition is easily amenable to personal attribution. Today, the *ketubah* can be equated to the attestation of Jewish marriage in cultural terms. The reality of this modern interpretation of the *ketubah* is supported by its frequent use in wedding ceremonies involving both intermarried and same-sex couples, neither of which would qualify as a valid Jewish marriage based on traditional *halakhah*.

The third example involves a young mom, Leslie, who lives in the Chicago area and who, by her own admission, is not traditionally observant. Yet, each night, all three of her sons sing the first line of the *Shema*, Judaism's declaration of faith and its most foundational prayer, in Hebrew. Leslie began this practice when her oldest was having difficulty settling down at night due to fear of having bad dreams. Given that he was in a Jewish preschool at the time, Leslie suggested that they sing the *Shema* in the hopes that it would bring him comfort. Now, all three of her boys recite this prayer by themselves before they go to bed, a practice she hopes they will remember and cherish into their adult years.

The bedtime ritual Leslie has established for her sons embodies all of the elements of a remixed approach to Judaism. Religious Jews recite the first paragraph of the *Shema* before going to sleep every night. She has adopted a version of this traditional practice that works for her family and she makes sure that it is performed every night. She did not begin this family ritual out of a desire to observe Jewish law, but rather to provide her boys with a sense of routine and comfort at the end of their very chaotic days. Still she loves the idea that everyone in her family is "mindful of God in those last moments before sleep" and that her boys "end their day with a bit of Torah on their lips."[21] Such remixed Jewish rituals, when performed with consistency and in sufficient number, can go a long way toward instilling a positive Jewish identity and love for Jewish tradition in children who are not growing up in Orthodox or traditionally observant homes.

THE EDUCATIONAL POTENTIAL OF
JEWISH NARRATIVE (*AGGADAH*)

Jews are known as the "People of the Book" because education always has been the backbone of Jewish tradition. Many people do not realize that from the outset of the Jewish religion, *aggadah* has played a central role in shaping Jewish identity and the Jewish worldview. *Aggadah* includes narratives found in the Jewish Bible as well as in rabbinic sources, and it incorporates wisdom, speculation, and even folklore. Many of the biblical narratives, especially those involving Moses, as well as the patriarchs Abraham, Isaac, and Jacob, still are somewhat familiar to those Jews who have had a rudimentary Jewish education. *The aggadah* contained in the Talmud, which is understood as the central book of Jewish law and tradition,[22] is far less known to the majority of today's Jews.

In 2013, Dr. Ruth Calderon, a secular Israeli, was elected to the Knesset. She used her introductory speech to teach Talmud and to express her love for Jewish learning. The passage she chose to teach focuses on the story of a rabbi who became so engrossed with his studies that he failed to come home for his annual one-day visit to his wife on the eve of Yom Kippur. At the same moment the wife shed a tear of disappointment, the floor on which the rabbi was sitting collapsed and he fell to his death.[23] Calderon explained to the Knesset that this tragedy teaches that one who adheres to the Torah at the expense of being sensitive to human beings is not religious. During her talk, Chairman Yitzhak Vaknin, an ultra-Orthodox Jew from the *Shas* party, observed: "I think the idea she is saying is wonderful." At that moment, two Knesset members with diametrically opposed worldviews found a mutual language from the tradition they both cherish.[24]

Cultures are shaped by their stories. In the case of the Jewish people, both biblical and Talmudic *aggadah* have had a profound impact throughout history in shaping the Jewish psyche and in contributing to the richness and wisdom of the tradition. Today, *aggadah* can be especially helpful in educating all Jews, but especially the non-Orthodox, about the beauty and particularity of the Jewish tradition. *Aggadah* is accessible to people who lack rigorous Talmudic training since the stories often contain a universal message with broad appeal. They resonate with people who are disinterested in the legal technicalities of Jewish learning and practice. *Aggadah* also is particularly useful for teaching children who might be especially receptive to the moral lessons these narratives contain.

When I speak at Reform and Conservative synagogues, I sometimes open my talk with a remixed version of this Talmudic story featuring a non-Jewish scientist who becomes so absorbed in his research that he forgets to come home to celebrate his wedding anniversary with his wife. The wife is all dressed up and waits for him for a long time, and eventually sheds a tear. At that moment, there is an explosion in his laboratory and he dies. I ask my audience to think about the emotions this story engenders. Usually I sense they become sad and contemplative. I then ask my audience if this story sounds familiar to anyone and usually the answer is no. Later, I share with them the original text and tell them it is from the Talmud. This often elicits a surprised, but positive, reaction. Sometimes people approach me afterward and tell me how much they enjoyed this particular aspect of my talk. During these moments, I sense that even this small exposure to *aggadah* has opened the door for some more Jewish learning.

As is the case with the narrative Dr. Calderon chose to teach, *aggadah* often involves stories that are universally relevant but, given their biblical or Talmudic origin, they are packaged in a way that represents a uniquely Jewish perspective and historical context. For these reasons, *aggadah* is a very effective mechanism for transmitting particular Jewish content that can serve as the basis for remix and appropriation by future generations. *Aggadah* serves as a means of connecting with Jewish tradition in an authentic manner. Throughout this book, I draw from the wealth of Jewish narrative in order to give readers a flavor for *aggadah* so they can develop an appreciation for its importance and potential in Jewish education.

ALL JEWS HAVE A STAKE IN THIS ENTERPRISE

The *ketubah* example discussed earlier, as it relates to intermarriage and gay marriage, raises another important question. If the norms of the historical tradition play an important part in determining whether an individual's choices can be considered authentic, how, and by whom, should the determination of authenticity be made? Practices that are considered authentic in a less traditional community can be viewed as completely unacceptable in a more traditional community. So it is fair to ask: *Who gets to decide?*

There is no easy answer to this question. The following chapters illustrate how an approach focusing on connection to tradition, in conjunction with authentic remix, might play out in the bread and butter of daily Jewish life. The focus of this book is on the day-to-day choices we make in connection with ordinary matters such as family, food, holidays, and life cycle events. Some chapters focus on core concepts of Jewish tradition such as *Shabbat*, holidays, and *tikkun olam* (repairing the world). Other chapters explore remix in the context of life cycle events such as Bar or Bat Mitzvah, marriage, and death. I also examine the promise of remix in connection with topics such as food and grandparents that, although not unique to the Jewish religion, have a particular relevance for transmission of Jewish tradition.

This book is intended for the growing number of Jews in the United States and elsewhere who want a more meaningful Jewish existence for themselves and their progeny outside of the parameters of a strictly observant lifestyle. It is also intended for the leaders of Jewish communities that are aligned with this mission, and for the increasing number of non-Jews involved with Jewish families. I seek to foster a discussion about how a vital, meaningful, contemporary Judaism can benefit people by touching their hearts and minds.

As discussed earlier, Jewish tradition has been shaped by the bottom-up choices of the people in combination with the top-down legal rulings of the rabbis. My focus in this book is largely about what can be done from the bottom up. I intend this book as a guidebook to jumpstart thinking about Jewish tradition for individuals and families rather than as a template for institutions and their affiliated movements. Still, many of the themes I discuss have relevance for those groups and movements that serve non-Orthodox Jews.

I am also hopeful that at least some Jews who do live according to *halakhah* will see value in this project even if it advocates a model of observance for non-Orthodox Jews that would not be appropriate for themselves or for their own community's *kiruv* efforts. The literal translation of *kiruv* is to bring someone close. I see this project as *kiruv* because it is intended to bring Jews outside of the Orthodox model closer to Jewish tradition.

All identified Jews have a stake in this enterprise because its success will result in the preservation of a rich and vibrant Jewish tradition for a greater number of Jews. Many conventionally religious Jews understand that a stronger appreciation for Jewish tradition across the board will strengthen the Jewish community on a global level, despite inevitable differences in degrees and manners of observance. Several years ago, one of my students—an Orthodox Jew—told me that his grandfather used to say that the Jewish people are like a symphony, and therefore, all parts are needed for the whole to function well. I cherish that sentiment and strongly believe in its truth.

My approach to Judaism does not merely tolerate differences, but instead embraces them as vital to the continuity and health of the Jewish people. Differences of opinion are the backbone of Talmudic discourse. Today, the left end of the spectrum attempts to push the boundaries by incorporating what it sees as needed change; the right end counters this tendency by pushing back against innovation to ensure what it sees as continued authenticity; and the middle seeks to navigate between these approaches. Multiple perspectives strengthen, rather than diminish, the whole. When all sectors accept the inevitability of differences and appreciate the good-faith function of each place on the spectrum, the Jewish people are at their strongest and are most able to maintain a sense of unity despite a lack of uniformity.

I

A CELEBRATION OF *SHABBAT* AND HOLIDAY TRADITION

Writer Ahad Ha'am once said that "more than Jews have kept the Sabbath, the Sabbath has kept the Jews."[1] Ahad Ha'am, the founder of the Cultural Zionist movement who was by no means fastidious concerning ritual observance, wrote these words in 1898 in a magazine column lauding a group of liberal, nonreligious Berlin Jews who were protesting the growing trend by Reform synagogues to move the Sabbath from Saturday to Sunday.

The historical context of the Reform movement provides an interesting backdrop to Ahad Ha'am's sentiments. The initial leaders of Reform Judaism in the early nineteenth century acted within a framework that was steeped in Jewish knowledge and tradition. They relied on the Talmud and other classical Jewish sources as support for their changes and believed they were upholding the continuity of the Jewish tradition. By the middle of the century, however, Reform leaders rejected elements of long-standing Jewish tradition. They began to advocate new practices such as changing the Jewish Sabbath to Sunday. Ahad Ha'am wrote with approval that the protesters "have banded together to defend the Sabbath with all the means at their disposal as a historic institution belonging to our entire people."[2]

The Jewish Sabbath, *Shabbat*, is the cornerstone of Jewish life and culture. The centrality of *Shabbat* to the Jewish people has a strong history dating back to the Torah, and *Shabbat* observance is the only ritual included in the Ten Commandments. One of the Torah's most clear pronouncements is the prohibition against creating fire on *Shabbat*.[3] But the Torah itself contains relatively little information about how to observe *Shabbat*.

It was the rabbis in the early centuries of the Common Era who fleshed out the details of *Shabbat* observances. They expanded on the Torah's prohibitions by codifying thirty-nine specific types of activities that are absolutely prohibited on *Shabbat*. This list includes baking, planting, sewing, carrying, writing, and extinguishing fire.[4]

The Talmudic sages then added to these prohibitions a long list of other tasks they believed were derivations of these primary categories. For example, since planting is one of the original prohibitions, they also prohibited watering a plant as a derivative type of labor. The sages also came up with an additional list of prohibitions that were designed to prevent people from accidentally violating or subverting the spirit of *Shabbat*. For example, since the primary use of a pen is to write, and writing is prohibited, they also prohibited moving a pen on *Shabbat*.[5]

Observant Jews today refrain from driving, using electricity, conducting business, using and handling money, as well as a host of other activities. Using electricity and starting a car engine are prohibited because they are believed to be analogous to creating a fire. Very observant women avoid wearing makeup on *Shabbat* since the application of cosmetics is considered an act of creation. A New Jersey woman named Sharon Langert runs the Fashion-isha website for observant Jewish women that provides fashion and other advice, including how to keep makeup in place for the twenty-five-hour duration of *Shabbat*. She claims that some women use a permanent Sharpie pen for eyeliner while others set their facial foundation with hairspray.[6]

I realize how these restrictions may sound to the vast majority of Jews who do not observe the laws of *Shabbat*. It must be understood, however, that for Jews who operate according to the assumption that all of Jewish law, *halakhah*, represents Divine command, there is no other choice. Still, *Shabbat* is the property of all Jews, not just those who believe in a particular view of the Divine or a particular view of Jewish law. Therefore, Jews who believe in the value of Jewish tradition and its staying power need to think more carefully about how to reclaim *Shabbat* in a way that comports with their individual lifestyles and levels of observance.

Given the centrality of *Shabbat*, it is not surprising that it furnishes a paradigmatic illustration of how the richness of Jewish tradition can be celebrated and transmitted even absent adherence to many of the technical aspects of the *halakhah* surrounding *Shabbat*. Writer Daniella Greenbaum Davis observed in a *Wall Street Journal* editorial that although most American Jews are not Orthodox, "even without strict observance, the experience of Sabbath can keep them too."[7] When I read her editorial, which referenced Ahad Ha'am's remark quoted earlier, it reminded me that a friend once told me that he celebrates, rather than observes, *Shabbat*. I think he meant that rather than adhering to all of the *Shabbat* laws and customs meticulously, he preferred to make the day special by focusing on its celebratory components. I believe this approach is consistent with the very distinction Davis, a millennial Modern Orthodox Jew, is suggesting.

Even if *Shabbat* is not observed to the letter of the law, its celebration on a weekly basis has tremendous potential to safeguard Jewish tradition in a world of increasing secularization. It allows for a much-needed break from our fast-paced existence by carving out sacred time and space on a consistent basis uninterrupted by electronics and other background noise. *Shabbat* facilitates time with loved ones and spiritual contemplation.

Beyond *Shabbat*, the concept of celebrating, as opposed to observing, Jewish tradition has powerful implications for how non-Orthodox Jews can establish a deeper connection with Judaism. In general, I believe we can unbundle the celebration of nearly all Jewish holidays with four key elements: *differentiation, disconnection, joy, and the selection of tradition, performed consistently.*

With several Jewish holidays, notably *Shabbat*, the High Holidays, and other holy days of the year during which times most forms of work are prohibited, Jewish tradition requires a spiritual *differentiation* through *disconnection* with our usual routines. The idea here is that we strive to create a space for a type of spiritual elevation that is difficult to achieve with our normal existence. Through this differentiation and disconnection, we are also able to focus on experiencing *joy*, a luxury that we do not normally have given all of our competing daily demands. On these special days, a focus on joy is not only appropriate but actively encouraged.

Of course many people want to experience periodic disconnection and afford a greater space for joy. But the Jewish tradition prescribes a *particular way* of accomplishing these goals with respect to each holiday. For those seeking a path for sustaining a transmissible tradition outside of strict observance of Jewish law, attention must be paid to *selecting specific aspects from the Jewish tradition as consistent markers* of one's holiday celebrations.

The following discussion concentrates mainly on *Shabbat* but it also illustrates how these elements can apply to other Jewish holidays. *Shabbat* provides an ideal example for how the remix philosophy discussed in the Introduction can guide liberal Jews in their selection, and adaptation, of authentic Jewish tradition. Recall that remix allows, and even encourages, Jews to tap into the pool of tradition and yet maintain considerable latitude in their execution of this tradition. This latitude affords liberal Jews the space to infuse their selections of Jewish tradition with personalized meaning. The goal is not to dot the *i*'s and cross the *t*'s of the legal prescriptions for observance, but rather to embrace a celebration of Jewish tradition while navigating the line between authenticity and innovation.

I know that for those who are part of Jewish communities living within the *halakhic* system, my framing of *Shabbat* and other holiday celebrations may be largely unacceptable. In traditional communities, people observe the law and then may, or may not, seek to find personal meaning in its observance. But the reality is just the opposite in liberal Jewish communities where most people need to find a personal meaning *in order to* celebrate tradition.

At this point, I would like to share some of my personal narrative in the hope that it will provide readers with a sense of where I am coming from with respect to *Shabbat* specifically and Jewish tradition generally. Regardless of my personal level of observance, my Jewish journey has fostered a deep appreciation for a pluralistic perspective. My desire to help non-Orthodox Jews strengthen their connection to Jewish tradition is an outgrowth of this perspective.

I grew up in a working-class New Jersey town. Although I do not have siblings, I was so lucky to have had two wonderful parents whom I now dearly miss. My parents discussed the fact that we were Jewish all the time but when I was very young, I do not recall our family regularly celebrating *Shabbat*. My father was raised in a strictly Orthodox home but his job as a salesman for Florsheim shoes meant that he had to work nearly every Friday night and Saturday. Still, it was very important to him that I receive what he called a "good Jewish education." My parents joined a Conservative synagogue when I was in third grade and enrolled me in its after-school Jewish education program. Even though I was a year behind students of the same age, I soon learned that I loved everything about being Jewish and quickly caught up. I was strangely drawn to the rules and the history, even if I found the Hebrew language tough going.

By the time I turned twelve, I decided I wanted to keep kosher as well as observe *Shabbat*. Because our synagogue was not in walking distance to our home, I rode in a car and did not think too much about this one way or the other. I had a vague idea that among our Conservative community, driving to synagogue was fine. Still, I did not go out with friends on *Shabbat* afternoons after services and did not watch television. As a teenager, I spent a lot of time at my synagogue between choir rehearsal, youth group, and *Shabbat* services on Friday nights and Saturday mornings. My mother always went with me. I also *davened* (prayed) three times a day during that time, satisfying the *halakhah* for men (women's obligations regarding prayer are more flexible). It was a rather unusual life for a teenager who was not raised in an Orthodox environment, but I was happy.

I continued, more or less, this version of observance throughout high school, college, and law school, although I usually did not go to services on *Shabbat* once I entered college. The truth is that I was not overly fond of the Hillel crowd at my university, and so I taught young children at a Jewish cultural school located in the Hillel building on Friday afternoons, but went back to my dorm room before services began.

When I met my husband during law school, Friday nights were our logical date night because I did not do any schoolwork on *Shabbat*. My husband was raised in a traditional Jewish home and was comfortable with my pattern of observance. At that time, I gave little thought to whether going out on Friday nights to activities around the campus was "kosher." I was committed to not working on *Shabbat* and I defined work according to my personal understanding and inclinations.

After we graduated and married, we moved to Chicago and immediately joined a synagogue. We occasionally attended *Shabbat* services, and always went to synagogue for the major Jewish holidays. Following the birth of our first daughter, I began to feel the immense pressure of being a parent and working full time. Despite this pressure, I decided that attending weekly *Shabbat* services was a must because I wanted to pass this tradition on to our children. But I consciously relinquished my earlier practice of refraining from work and even routine daily activities on *Shabbat* afternoons. I felt I needed the time to run errands, chauffeur our three daughters to birthday parties and activities, and even do some occasional work. For about fifteen years, our family pattern was pretty constant: traditional *Shabbat* dinners and mandatory *Shabbat* morning services for the whole family. On Saturday afternoons, I did what I felt needed to be done with the demands of children, managing a home and my career.

When I was in my midforties, I started to seriously reevaluate what had become my new normal regarding overall observance, but especially *Shabbat*. I had begun some more serious study of the tradition and realized that, for myself, I could no longer justify some of the things I was doing. This began a slow journey that has resulted in my becoming even more observant in some ways than when I was a teenager. For example, I no longer drive on *Shabbat*, even to enjoy a *Shabbat* dinner at the home of friends who live too far for us to walk.

To be sure, my current level of observance sometimes presents challenges for my family. I stopped driving when our girls were still living at home, which meant my husband had to handle these duties solo on Saturdays. And it is still hard to get all of my Friday evening meal prepared by four o'clock in the winter so that I do not have to cook on *Shabbat*. Even now I sometimes wish I could accept more social invitations and work opportunities that require travel on Friday nights or Saturdays. There is definitely a sense of limitation presented by this level of observance, particularly when one is part of a family that, in general, is not observing in the same way.

On the other hand, there are many benefits that come with this consistent type of *Shabbat* observance, not the least of which is the ability to take a much-needed *Shabbat* nap (known as the *Shabbos schluf* in Yiddish) on Saturday afternoons in the winter, and long nature walks with my husband in the summer. *Shabbat* is a time I can consciously dedicate to a more mindful perspective. If it were not for my consistent commitment to observe *Shabbat*, it would be easy to fill my time on Saturdays with other activities, be they leisure or work. In fact, I remember all too well just how easy it would be!

And to be clear, I still very much draw my own lines with respect to *Shabbat* observance. I am very strict about travel, fire, cooking, using a computer, playing music, and nearly all household tasks, but more liberal in terms of flipping on a light switch or using a landline telephone to speak with a family member or close friend. I understand and respect the nature of balancing my needs against those of my family and needing to compromise on occasion.

My own Jewish journey has taught me how to appreciate the benefits of *Shabbat* for me personally, and has also given me perspective on how to discuss observance generally with our daughters and others who are not as interested in traditional observance. If I had to do it over again, perhaps I would have done some things differently but then again, the time I spent "on the other side" enables me to identify with a more liberal Jewish mind-set. The elements I develop and apply in this chapter concerning *Shabbat* and other holidays are still helpful to me when I am faced with situational challenges, and my hope is that they can be helpful to other Jews who are seeking to find some place—no matter how small—for *Shabbat* and holiday tradition in their lives.

DIFFERENTIATION

> On the seventh day God finished the work that He had been doing, and He ceased on the seventh day from all the work that he had done. And God blessed the seventh day and declared it holy, because on it God ceased from all the work of creation that He had done.
> —Genesis 2:2–3

Those who think about *Shabbat* from a faith-based perspective will readily appreciate the sentiments of Orthodox Rabbi Lord Jonathan Sacks, the former Chief Rabbi of Britain and the Commonwealth, who observed: "On *Shabbat*, the world belongs to God, not us." Sacks amplified this idea when he added that on *Shabbat*, man renounces his mastery over "nature and animals" and "we become God's guests . . . recognizing the limits of human striving."[8] Many people may not know that the Biblical text commanding rest even extends to one's animals.[9] Conservative Rabbi David Wolpe has articulated a similar philosophy:

"The predominant rule of the Sabbath is to live in harmony with what is, not to seek change; this day is for renewal, not transformation. The Sabbath asks us not to be creative but restorative; not to give out but to take in; to sanctify time and recall our souls to their Source."[10]

The more universal message inherent in these religiously based perspectives is that on *Shabbat*, we dedicate ourselves to intake rather than output. We give up control in order to raise ourselves to a more mindful and spiritual place where we have the freedom to concentrate on those things that truly matter. In other words, ceding control actually enhances rather than limits our freedom. As Reform Rabbi Daniel Judson has written: "If you can't rush off to the shopping mall or work just a little bit more, you can create sacred space in your life to linger over conversation or to be intimate with your partner."[11] In a similar vein, Rabbi Sacks reminds us that time management skills teach that urgent things must be attended to before matters that are important but not urgent. *Shabbat* is "time dedicated to the things that are important but not urgent":[12] family, friends, community, expressing gratitude, reflecting on our past, present and future.

This universalistic appeal of *Shabbat* was the focus of an article by Ariel Okin, appearing in the online version of *Vogue* magazine, that stated: "it doesn't matter if you're Jewish, Hindu, Muslim, Buddhist, Catholic, Christian, agnostic, atheist. *Shabbat*—the concept of spending quality time with friends and family while taking a break from scrolling on Instagram—is for everyone. It is an ancient antidote to our modern ailments." Okin, who mentions she is Jewish "but not Orthodox or extremely observant," explains to her readers that *Shabbat* is a time for mindfulness, expressing gratitude, and engaging in meaningful conversation.[13]

Although *Shabbat* has a universalistic appeal, the Jewish tradition provides a clear path for how to differentiate this day according to a religiously observant perspective. As any Orthodox person involved in *kiruv* (outreach) knows, there are more than a few Jews who start down the road of *Shabbat* and other Jewish observances with baby steps and end up a *baal teshuva*, the term used for newly observant Orthodox Jews. Still, the majority of Jews will not be persuaded to observe *Shabbat* in such a rigorous manner no matter how many benefits they are told will result from this behavior. For these Jews, a plausible goal would be to achieve a state of mindfulness about *Shabbat* that will facilitate engaging in activities that are not otherwise readily possible given the demands of work, family, and life in general.

In his book *Being Jewish*, journalist and professor Ari Goldman discusses his interviews illustrating how Jews who are mindful of *Shabbat* exhibit a rich diversity of behavior as to how they differentiate the day. Most of his examples entail some form of remix Judaism since they involve patterns of observance that do not wholly comport with Jewish law. For example, Goldman discusses the Jewish Federation executive who drives his car on *Shabbat* but not on the freeways since that reminds him of work, and the Orthodox college student who sleeps with his girlfriend on Friday nights but tears open his package of condoms early in the day (so as to avoid the prohibition on tearing).[14] Goldman's examples serve as a useful reminder that there is indeed a distinction between the law and the spirit of the tradition.

This idea of differentiating *Shabbat* even through activities that may violate the law is at the heart of remix Judaism. For Jews who are not otherwise driven to observe Jewish law based on Divine command, the details of observance will never be the goal. Instead, the focus must be achieving a state of mindfulness about *Shabbat* and developing an appreciation for the benefits of this special element of Jewish tradition. Rabbi Sacks reminds us that the idea of a seven-day week "was born in the Torah and spread throughout the world via Christianity and Islam, both of which borrowed it from Judaism." It is sobering to realize that "we have years because of the sun, months because of the moon, and weeks because of the Jews."[15] The Jewish religion continues to demonstrate to the world just how therapeutic it can be to spend one day a week (or even part of a day) not as creators but rather as mindful contemplators.

The concept of differentiation applies to virtually all Jewish holidays since, by their very nature, holidays are in some way different from regular days. The Jewish festival of Passover is differentiated by the nature of the foods that are consumed according to the tradition. The Ninth of *Av*, the saddest day in the Jewish calendar, is differentiated by its somber mood and the virtual absence of joy.[16] At the other end of the spectrum, the holidays of Purim and Simchat Torah are differentiated by an almost party-like atmosphere even in places of worship. Rosh Hashanah and Yom Kippur are differentiated by the concepts of forgiveness and fresh starts. The festival of Sukkot is differentiated by

eating, and sometimes even sleeping, in a *sukkah*, the temporary outdoor structure symbolizing this holiday. Shavuot, another major Jewish
festival, is differentiated by opportunities for Jewish-related study that
traditionally last all night. Chanukah is differentiated by the importance
of light and special foods containing oil, an ancient source for light.

Although nearly every Jewish holiday is characterized by a thick
cultural, religious tradition that enables a differentiation of the day,
Shabbat is unique. Its regularity has always provided a consistent opportunity for the Jewish people to remember their past and celebrate
their present and future. For these reasons, I believe *Shabbat* offers the
most compelling invitation to Jewish tradition.

DISCONNECTION

> In the tempestuous ocean of time and toil there are islands of still-
> ness where man may enter a harbor and reclaim his dignity. The
> island is the seventh day, the Sabbath, a day of detachment from
> things, instruments and practical affairs, as well as of attachment to
> the spirit.[17]
> —Rabbi Abraham Joshua Heschel

It is difficult to achieve the state of mindfulness important for *Shabbat*
just by adopting ways of differentiating the day. Although it is vital for
some people to mark part of their celebration of *Shabbat* by engaging in
activities for which they do not otherwise have time, *Shabbat* must also
include an element of affirmative release from the day-to-day. From a
religious perspective, *Shabbat* should not entail any form of active creativity, and Jewish law is very clear on what constitutes creativity. This
level of observance is not realistic for most Jews but the more fundamental point is that *Shabbat* provides us with a ready-made opportunity
for something everyone needs—a consistent measure of disconnection.

Rabbi Jonathan Sacks has observed that there is something so funda-
mentally creative about resting. He writes that "without rest for the
body, peace for the mind, silence for the soul, and a renewal of our
bonds of identity and love, the creative process eventually withers and
dies." He calls *Shabbat* "humanity's greatest source of renewable energy, the day that gives us the strength to keep on creating."[18]

Jewish law authorities widely believe that "the seventh day has long functioned as an incubator for the most spiritually creative and productive hours of the week."[19] The Torah itself provides the blueprint for this idea by its numerous references to being "refreshed" during *Shabbat*.[20] This point is further underscored by the Talmudic sage Rabbi Shimon ben Lakish, who taught that the cessation of physical labor on *Shabbat* leads to the gift of an "additional soul,"[21] and in the Jewish tradition, the concept of "soul" has been linked to artistic creativity. In the twentieth century, Rabbi Mordecai Kaplan, the founder of the Reconstructionist movement, specifically acknowledged how *Shabbat* facilitates human creativity in the coming week just as an artisan must retract from his painting to contemplate his next creative steps.[22]

The "eureka" moment during which a flash of creative genius suddenly strikes and enables the resolution of an artistic or other type of struggle is familiar to many people. The origin of this phenomenon is traced back to Archimedes, the renowned Greek mathematician, who was asked to determine whether a particular crown given to the king as a gift was made of pure gold. Archimedes knew that he could provide an answer if he was able to determine the volume of the crown since he could then measure that against an equal volume of pure gold. Unfortunately, however, the crown was of an irregular shape and did not lend itself to being measured in volume. Frustrated, the mathematician put the problem aside and took a bath: "As he lowered himself into the tub, Archimedes noticed the bath water rise, and it suddenly occurred to him that the displacement of bath water must be exactly the same as the volume of his body." He realized that to solve his dilemma, he only needed to drop the crown into a tank of water and measure the water's displacement. According to legend, he was so elated by his discovery "that he leapt out of the bath and ran naked through the streets shouting Eureka! (I have found it!)."[23]

The Archimedes narrative illustrates the relationship between a break period and enhanced creativity. Disconnection facilitates percolation time, an essential factor in human creativity according to the testimony of artists and other creators from a wide range of disciplines. Their narratives attest to the "gestational period" underscoring creativity—that timeframe in which the creative juices flow internally, almost imperceptibly. This inner labor—termed "the unconscious machine" by mathematician Henri Poincaré—is what creators underscore as the pivotal component of creativity.[24]

For nearly a century, scientific research has focused on the impact of percolation time, and the connection between a break period and increased creative output. These studies highlight the importance of disconnection and examine its precise function and operation in spurring human creativity. In the early twentieth century, Graham Wallas laid the groundwork for future psychological studies of the relationship between an incubation period and active creativity by highlighting the experience of an academic psychologist who was also a preacher. Wallas discussed how the preacher believed his weekly sermons were much better if he posed the problem to be discussed the prior Monday rather than later in the week, even if he ultimately devoted the same number of hours to his task. According to Wallas, the preacher's practice of beginning a project and setting it aside for periods of unconscious, or partially conscious, reflection was a significant element in his creative success.[25] He believed that this practice was particularly crucial to more difficult forms of creative thought involving subjects such as science and literature.

Wallas' focus on the incubation period and its unconscious component of creativity has received significant attention in psychological research, particularly in the late twentieth and early twenty-first centuries.[26] Of course it is no surprise that providing a break from fatigue can be beneficial in renewing creative energy. Significantly, though, the current research goes further by showing how incubation with unconscious thought may contribute to creative problem solving in a proactive way.

Unconscious thought is characterized by either thought without attention, or with attention directed elsewhere.[27] Studies suggest that such unconscious thought, "reminiscent of lay people's idea of 'sleeping on it,'" spurs creativity by prompting ideas that "are less obvious, less accessible, and more creative."[28] Evidence exists that unconscious processing is "an active, generative, and creative mode of thought" that is superior to conscious thought in many respects, particularly for complex problems. One study used interesting language stating that unconscious thought promotes greater creativity because it "ventures out to the dark and dusty nooks and crannies of the mind."[29]

Another recent focus of the research on unconscious thought concerns the significance of mind wandering that occurs during the incubation process. Several researchers believe that mind wandering "could be linked to enhanced creativity, particularly for problems that have been previously encountered."[30]

It seems as though modern science is now catching up to Judaism's ancient insight about *Shabbat*. The traditional mode of marking *Shabbat* requires disconnection and includes long periods of prayer and worship. Scientists are now telling us that these circumstances are tailor-made to facilitate human creativity by providing opportunities for unconscious thought, percolation, and mind wandering.

Technically, there is nothing wrong with thinking, but not speaking with others, about work on *Shabbat*. A popular *Shabbat* song affirms this idea with the explanation that the Torah was given to man and not to perfect angels.[31] It is almost as if, by allowing internal contemplation of our work but barring physical creativity, the Jewish tradition understood the psychological principles of human creativity even before modern science affirmed them.

Moreover, the duration of *Shabbat* may well provide the optimal period of unconscious processing that will spur the resumption of highly creative activity. One study concerned with consumer psychology found that creative output is maximized with a moderate unconscious phase that is neither too short nor too long.[32] A related theme in the psychological literature concerns the sequencing of unconscious thought with respect to conscious thought. The literature demonstrates that the superiority of unconscious thought is fostered by a prior period of conscious thought, perhaps followed by another period of conscious thought after the incubation period.[33] This cyclical dimension of creativity, rest, and resumed creativity is familiar to anyone who observes *Shabbat*.

Based on this science, researchers are now recommending increased opportunities for people to unconsciously process problems and incubate solutions. These findings support the need for digital detox, a concept that is gaining a foothold in our culture and consciousness largely through the efforts of Reboot's National Day of Unplugging. Reboot is a nonprofit organization that is dedicated to rekindling Jewish connections among young Jews and the greater community through programs dedicated to both upholding and reimagining Jewish traditions. The annual Day of Unplugging, launched in 2010, takes place over the course of a *Shabbat* (sundown Friday to sundown Saturday), and has drawn participants from every state, more than two hundred countries, and participating organizations representing Catholicism, Islam, Hinduism, and Buddhism.[34]

As discussed earlier, Jewish tradition prescribes a particular way to accomplish disconnection on *Shabbat* by refraining from specific types of work that violate the tradition. There are other holidays that also mandate a very similar type of disconnection. Yom Kippur, the holiest day of the Jewish calendar, is the epitome of disconnection given that Jews are supposed to refrain from everything that is prohibited on *Shabbat*, as well as other activities such as eating, drinking, and having sexual relations. Yom Kippur is a day reserved for a complete spiritual renewal through seeking forgiveness for our sins—both those committed against God *and* those we commit against our fellow human beings.

There are also several days in the Jewish calendar that have rules similar to *Shabbat* except for some minor adjustments that allow a bit more latitude. These days are designated in the Torah and known today generally as *Yom Tov*, which translates from Hebrew to English as "good day."

So what are the *Yom Tov* days that require this special form of disconnection that is similar to *Shabbat*? Some of these days, most especially Rosh Hashanah and Passover, are still very familiar to American Jews. The term *Yom Tov* applies to both days of Rosh Hashanah, the Jewish New Year, but only to the first two and last two days of Passover, the spring holiday commemorating the Israelites' exodus from Egypt and slavery. Passover is an eight-day holiday in the Diaspora, but the intervening days are not considered as holy as the others. In Israel, where *Yom Tov* days in general track the shorter times prescribed in the Torah, Passover lasts for just seven days with only the first and last ones being *Yom Tov* (the reason for the difference between Israel and everywhere else relates to the difficulties in ancient days of alerting distant communities to the actual start of holidays given that the Jewish calendar is a lunar one).[35]

Other days of *Yom Tov* include the first two days of Sukkot, a seven-day festival that falls five days after Yom Kippur (in Israel just the first day is *Yom Tov*), and two more days immediately following Sukkot respectively called Shemini Atzeret and Simchat Torah (in Israel, these two days are combined into one day). Finally, Shavuot, another major *Yom Tov* festival, occurs seven weeks after Passover. In the Diaspora, Shavuot is two days but in Israel it is also just a one-day holiday. The Reform movement consciously abandoned the second day of most *Yom Tov* holidays and, instead, advocates the same length of celebration as in Israel.

On any day of *Yom Tov*, the rules concerning disconnection are a bit looser so that one is permitted to carry objects, light fire from a preexisting flame, and cook or bake food that will be consumed just on that same day (remember that a day in the Jewish calendar runs from sundown to sundown). But these rules are of little practical importance to most liberal Jews, for whom *Yom Tov* days are much like any other with the exceptions of Rosh Hashanah and the first night or two of Passover.

Still, all *Yom Tov* days, even those that are not more widely known or observed today, offer a special space for celebration and connection to Jewish tradition. In fact, the whole point of the rules of disconnection for both *Shabbat* and *Yom Tov* is to help people focus on the various spiritual meanings of the holidays, on quality time with family and friends, and on experiencing joy.

JOY

> R. Chizkiyah said in the name of Rav: You will one day give reckoning for everything your eyes saw which, although permissible, you did not enjoy.
> —Qiddushin 4:12, Jerusalem Talmud

As this Talmudic source suggests, in general Judaism is not a religion that encourages deprivation. On the contrary, the element of joy—known in Hebrew as *simcha*—is one of the cornerstones of the religion. Rabbi Jonathan Sacks explains the fundamental importance of joy, claiming that it provides a major theme in the last book of the Torah, Deuteronomy. Sacks observes that "joy lives in the moment," and "has to do with a sense of connection to other people or to God." Joy is "a social emotion" and "is the exhilaration we feel when we merge with others."[36]

God would like us to be joyful
Even when our hearts lie panting on the floor. [37]

There are different ways to understand the concept of "joy" as it relates
to the celebration of *Shabbat*. The prophet Isaiah referred to *Shabbat*
as *oneg*, or a delight. [38] Joy, as interpreted by Rabbi Sacks, is a state of
mind that facilitates relationship building. But joy can also embrace an
emphasis on physical pleasure. Even in ancient times the rabbis understood the importance of physical pleasure in affirming how *Shabbat*
should be celebrated to ensure its staying power in Jewish history:
"Sanctify Shabbat with food and drink, with splendid clothes. Delight
yourself with pleasure and God will reward you for this very pleasure"
(Deuteronomy Rabbah 3:1).

As this *aggadah*, or passage of narrative, from the post-Talmudic
rabbinic literature reveals, the joy one experiences on *Shabbat* should
include a sense of physical pleasure derived from material experiences.
Even though the laws of *Shabbat* entail a substantial list of "do not's"—
such as spending money, writing, using computers and cell phones—
there is a compelling list of "do's" that include spending time with
family, friends, and community, enjoying good food, wearing nice clothing, reflecting, and relaxing.

For the majority of Jews, *Shabbat* becomes a more attractive concept when the focus is on the perceived personal benefits of celebration
rather than on the restrictions. An emphasis on the theology of *Shabbat*
observance is not going to serve as a compelling way of capturing most
Jews today. Although some traditional Jews might take issue with this
view, I believe it represents reality. After all, who would not want to
experience a weekly time dedicated to pleasure in the form of physical
benefits?

Judaism is a religion that is attentive to the importance of physical
beauty, particularly with regard to performing religious ritual. The Talmud encourages beautiful objects to be used in various ritual observances. There is even a name for this concern with physical beautifica-
tion of the commandments—*hiddur mitzvah*. One example of this concept is the custom of setting a beautiful dinner table for *Shabbat*, complete with a white tablecloth, and adorning the home with flowers.

In addition to deriving joy from physical beauty, people are encouraged to participate in other types of pleasurable physical experiences on
Shabbat. What better ways to experience physical joy than through sex

and delicious food—two of the hallmarks of *Shabbat* observance? According to rabbinic tradition, having sex with one's spouse is a particularly important *Shabbat* activity: "How often are scholars to perform their marital duties? Rav Judah in the name of Samuel replied: 'Every Friday night.' . . . Judah the son of R. Hiyya and son-in-law of R. Jannai would spend all his time in the schoolhouse but every Sabbath eve he came home" (Ketubbot 62b, Babylonian Talmud).

As the chapter on marriage discusses in more detail, sex is seen as an important part of life, provided it is channeled appropriately through the bonds of matrimony. Judaism recognizes and embraces the joy that sex brings to a relationship, and therefore it is not surprising that the Jewish tradition singles out this activity as one that should be encouraged on *Shabbat* for the joy it brings.

And then there is the food! As will be discussed in more detail in the next chapter, Jews have had a long history of getting joy out of food. And good food is an especially important part of the *Shabbat* celebration. Even the great sage Shammai understood that the joy of food was an essential part of the *Shabbat* celebration, and he was mindful of preparing for *Shabbat* throughout the rest of the week:

> They said about Shammai the Elder that every day he ate in honor of Shabbat: If he found a good quality animal he would say: "This is for Shabbat." If he found an even better one, he would save the second one [for Shabbat] and eat the first one. (Betzah 16a, Babylonian Talmud)

In today's food-obsessed culture, the linkage of special food with *Shabbat* can be a particularly compelling draw.

Esti, an Orthodox woman I know who does *kiruv* (outreach), takes a yearly trip to Israel with some of her students, mostly non-Orthodox women. She has told me that baking challah for *Shabbat* is the tradition that her students are "drawn to most profoundly" when they return to the States. She believes the reason for this connection is simple. In her words, challah "fills the home with a delicious smell that connects the whole family to the warmth and pleasure of being Jewish." But for observant Jews like Esti, challah represents more than just a special food we associate with *Shabbat*. The real importance of challah relates to the *mitzvah* (commandment) of "separating the challah" (*hafrashat* challah)—a particular action required by Jewish law—in which the owner of a certain amount of dough must separate, set aside, and burn a part of this dough as a symbol of the Biblical priestly offering. This *mitzvah* traditionally has been associated with women because, according to Jewish tradition, they are responsible for those commandments that sanctify everyday activities and nourish the family physically and spiritually.[39]

Esti sees the authentic significance of this *mitzvah* as a reminder "that the things that we claim ownership of really belong to God, who in turn blesses us that we should enjoy the wonderful things in this world." This is a beautiful sentiment, of course. Realistically, though, outside of the most traditionally observant communities, most people do not know, or even care, about the *halakhah* associated with challah, or that it originated in the Torah in the context of setting aside part of the bread as a gift to God.[40]

Today, the personal significance of challah for most people is as an authentic marker of *Shabbat*. When seen in this way, challah on *Shabbat* also captures the essence of the concept of remix. Although the *mitzvah* of separating challah originated in one context, its main significance today for most Jews is distinct from this origin because the focus is on challah as a food that symbolizes *Shabbat*. This symbolism is enhanced by the recitation of the *motzi*, a general blessing over bread said before eating challah on *Shabbat*, a custom that also differentiates *Shabbat* for non-Orthodox Jews who do not routinely say this blessing before consuming any type of bread throughout the week.

Remix can entail not only personalizing the relevance of the tradition, but also its downright subversion. A 2017 article titled "Gumbo Shabbat in New Orleans—Treif but True?" illustrates this phenomenon. Sophia Marie Unterman, a young writer and teacher who grew up in Kansas as a Reform Jew, was living in New Orleans when she wrote this piece. She writes with gusto of hosting weekly *Shabbat* dinners that arguably are "the least kosher either side of the Mason-Dixon line." Still, for her, Jewish identity is "a means of adapting in non-Jewish spaces" and "embracing the contradictions" she encounters in those spaces:[41]

> To me, mine is not a less Jewish Shabbat because there is shellfish and bread-breaking long after sundown, but a just-as-meaningful one; it's a time to take a break from an insane workweek, relax with

> loved ones over a well-earned meal, give thanks for those elements,
> and keep my favorite family tradition alive.[42]

It may be difficult for people who maintain a practice of traditional observance to read these words. Some people simply will dismiss the author's efforts as completely misguided and even sinful. But I believe her desire to mark *Shabbat* by hosting weekly *Shabbat* dinners, even though the food is blatantly *treif* (not kosher), should be seen as something positive. She is saying that Jewish tradition matters to her and that she wants to keep it alive. Maybe not all of the tradition and maybe not in the way more religious people would condone. But when reading her article, one cannot escape feeling her passion for Judaism. In today's day and age this is not something to be taken lightly.

Joy is an inherent part of most Jewish holiday celebrations. Even Yom Kippur, a solemn day in which it is not permitted to eat or drink, is known as the White Fast because the mood is joyful given the themes of forgiveness and spiritual renewal. The Torah actually commands us to be joyful on the harvest festival of Sukkot,[43] which presents endless possibilities for creating wonderful, fun-filled family memories. In fact, there seems to be more awareness of this holiday in some liberal Jewish communities due to an increased interest in building a *sukkah*. After all, who doesn't love a weeklong party dining al fresco and even sleeping under the stars?

Most other Jewish holidays are also marked by large doses of joy.[44] Given its proximity in the calendar to Christmas, Chanukah, for example, is an eight-day holiday that is generally familiar to Americans. Although Chanukah is a relatively minor Jewish holiday, its celebration entails special foods, games, songs, the lighting of the menorah (traditional candles), and of course, small presents.

Less known highly joyous holidays include Simchat Torah and Purim. On Simchat Torah, the cycle of Torah reading for the year is finished and begun anew. It is a time for dancing with the Torah scrolls, eating yummy treats such as candy apples, and yes, even indulging in a bit of liquid spirits! Purim marks the triumph of the Jews' survival in ancient Persia in the face of threatened destruction, as recounted in the Book of Esther, known as the *Megillah*. This holiday is characterized by a carnival-like atmosphere during the prayer service and the donning of costumes for both children and adults.

Celebrating these special days can go a long way toward accomplishing the goal of transmissibility of Jewish tradition, even without complete adherence to the requirements of Jewish law. These holidays have tremendous potential for creating unique childhood memories that can be used as the basis for adults seeking to transmit Jewish tradition to their own children. My earliest Jewish memory is going to synagogue with my mother, along with my dearest childhood friend Sue and her mother, to hear the *Megillah*. I was probably around four at the time and although the details of this outing are a bit fuzzy, I recall the synagogue itself and eating strawberry ice cream.

But for non-Orthodox Jews who are not living within the system of Jewish law, transmission of a thick Jewish tradition cannot be accomplished without consistent practice. The Jewish tradition has shaped the Jewish people on a collective basis over the years, and despite the myriad differences in belief and practice that exist, a core degree of Jewish particularity can be found. This core particularity derives from its recognizable consistency.

SELECTION AND CONSISTENT CELEBRATION OF TRADITION

There are holiday practices particular to Jewish tradition that still have staying power among a wide cross-section of Jews. For example, the comprehensive 2013 Pew study of the American Jewish community found that 78 percent of people who identified Judaism as their religion participated in a Passover Seder in the prior year, and 62 percent fasted for all or part of Yom Kippur.[45] Although the percentages were significantly lower for other ritual markers, including some related to *Shabbat*, it is fair to say religious, cultural traditions still are embedded in the lives of the Jewish people collectively and kept alive among individuals even if to varying degrees.

The essence of tradition, however, is that it must be passed down from one generation to the next. Unterman, the host of the Gumbo *Shabbat* meals in New Orleans, was inspired by how her mother cooked a huge dinner every Friday night and her family's consistent recitation of *Shabbat* prayers and candle lighting. Despite the fact that this young woman could now be spending her Friday nights according to a bacchanalian New Orleans tradition, she chooses instead to find meaning in Jewish tradition by hosting her own *Shabbat* experience for her friends, both Jews and non-Jews. Her narrative shows that she values Jewish tradition enough to embrace it and make it her own, even if she is remixing some of its elements. She is neither negative nor apathetic toward her roots. Children who grow up with a positive take on *Shabbat* are more likely to want to re-create this experience for themselves and their families, even if that experience entails some remix of the tradition.

While writing this book I attended a Bat Mitzvah and heard a wonderful story involving a remixed approach to *Shabbat*. During the young woman's speech, she mentioned that her mother, who is an emergency-room physician at a hospital in Chicago, is rarely able to join the rest of the family for *Shabbat* dinner. So it has become their family practice to drive forty-five minutes each way to her mother's hospital every Friday night after they have dinner and bring her a home-cooked *Shabbat* meal to eat during her shift. This family is fairly traditional in their level of observance so they likely know that driving on *Shabbat* is not permitted according to Jewish law. But this particular application of a remixed *Shabbat* celebration clearly resonates in a very positive way with this young woman. In listening to her speak about their special family *Shabbat* tradition, it is clear that it will provide the basis for a unique childhood memory she will hold dear.

Of course, a celebration of *Shabbat*, or any other ritual for that matter, must embrace enough of the particulars of the tradition to imbue the practice with a sense of authentic Jewish content. If transmission of Jewish tradition is a goal, *Shabbat* cannot be marked only by universalistic components absent any incorporation of the tradition's particularities. The Reboot Sabbath Manifesto provides a wonderful illustration of the operation of remix with respect to observing *Shabbat* that balances the universal and the particular. Recall that Reboot is a group concerned with "rebooting" Judaism's rituals, culture, and traditions. Its Sabbath Manifesto, a creative project designed to slow down lives in an increasingly hectic world, revolves around ten core principles. In addition to avoiding technology, Reboot aims to encourage participants to "connect with loved ones; nurture your health; get outside; avoid commerce; light candles; drink wine; eat bread; find silence; give back."[46]

The principles of avoiding technology, avoiding commerce, lighting candles, drinking wine, and eating bread are derived from the laws of *Shabbat* and therefore represent an authentic link with the tradition, even though they can be embraced by everyone. The other five principles also perfectly capture the spirit of *Shabbat*, and even if they do not have as clear a link to the *halakhah*, they too can be embraced universally.

The Reboot Sabbath Manifesto underscores the importance of focusing on some aspects of the tradition. It downplays the rules of law in favor of an approach characterized by adaptation and remix. This process of selecting authentic elements of *Shabbat* observance, and infusing these choices with personal attribution, facilitates the creation of meaningful staples of Jewish tradition for individuals and families. The beauty of *Shabbat* is that it allows for so many possibilities of choice—so many "do's"—that can form the basis of crafting a personalized and very much cherished and transmissible *Shabbat* tradition.

Inaugurating *Shabbat* with candle lighting and a festive meal are two of the most renowned highlights of a traditional *Shabbat* celebration. Both of these traditions are capable of being performed in a traditional manner, as well as being "remixed" so that they retain a degree of authenticity despite being tweaked in a way to afford a sense of personalized meaning. For example, many choose to light *Shabbat* candles after sunset on Friday night, despite the prohibition of creating fire on *Shabbat*. For those who make this choice, the tradition of lighting candles on Friday night is what matters as opposed to the legal technicalities of *Shabbat* observance.

Journalist Alina Dizik began lighting *Shabbat* candles after visiting a concentration camp while in college. Since that time, she has lit candles every Friday night, no matter where in the world she happens to be. Even now, she does not light them "by the book" but in her own way that works for her and her life. Although she does not observe all that Jewish law requires for *Shabbat*, she tries not to work on Friday nights and for now, this is enough. Still, she muses that when her daughter gets older, she will "perhaps light candles earlier with her" and "maybe even learn to cook a Shabbat dinner."[47]

Similarly, Amy Guth, a journalist and radio show host based in Chicago, is committed to weekly candle lighting but since *Shabbat* in Chicago begins very early in the winter months, there are inevitably some nights when "the logistics trump everything else and that makes for a murky *Shabbat* start time." When that happens, Amy admits to a "sense of fret when she is late to the dance," but it is never a question of whether or not to observe *Shabbat*. For her, *Shabbat* generally is "less about the *halachot* [laws] . . . more about prioritizing the natural world's definitions of day and night, seasons and years, and of being in rhythm with the rest of my people." She feels an acute separation from her people when she cannot light her candles on time because, for her, "each one of us who takes the time to light *Shabbat* candles and observe *Shabbat* adds to the collective light of our people."[48]

Amy's personal attribution for candle lighting emphasizes global Jewish peoplehood, but there are so many other ways those who light candles can ascribe meaning to this tradition. This capacity for creating a personal attribution is a critical element of a remixed approach to Jewish tradition. Lighting *Shabbat* candles is a means of connecting not just with Jews living today in all parts of the world, but also with those who came before—our ancestors. I always think of my mother, father, and grandparents when I light candles. My mother-in law used to tell me that she would always speak to her deceased husband after she lit her *Shabbat* candles.

Candle lighting also is a particularly special way of forging multigenerational bonds between grandparents, parents, and children when they have the opportunity to light *Shabbat* candles together. My daughters readily embrace the opportunity to light the candles with me when they join us for a *Shabbat* dinner. Although we only have one grandchild at this point and he is still very young, he does spend some Friday nights sleeping over at our home. I look forward to the time when he can light the candles with me and I can teach him the appropriate blessing.

Lighting *Shabbat* candles also is a wonderful way to mark physically the separation between the grind of the everyday workweek and the onset of something different and special. It is an extra bonus that *Shabbat* also coincides with the beginning of the secular weekend, when many people are off from work and school. This timing also allows for creating some distinct types of personal attributions, such as taking a few moments to express gratitude for the highlights of the past week and to reflect on hopes for the coming week.

Journalist and former *Meet the Press* moderator David Gregory has observed that *Shabbat* dinner is his favorite Jewish ritual: "I'm always trying to go deeper into the ritual, to really feel the transcendence, through prayer, through the martini I have on Friday nights, through studying Torah, through the conversations we have around the table, and to just lose myself in the light of Shabbat."[49]

Of course, Friday night can be special family time whether or not *Shabbat* is part of the equation. But inviting *Shabbat* into your home on Friday nights, even for part of the evening, is low-hanging fruit for those who care—even to some degree—about perpetuating Jewish tradition. My friend Sarah is not a particularly religious person; she probably would call herself a cultural Jew. Recently, however, she told me that although her family always sat down together to Friday night dinner, she did not make this dinner a celebration of *Shabbat*. She now laments this decision and wishes she had lit candles and had a more traditional Friday night. She hopes that one day, she will get to celebrate *Shabbat* with her grandchildren.

Sarah's sentiments are not uncommon. Philanthropist Edgar Bronfman wrote in his book, *Why Be Jewish*, that he regretted not giving his children any Jewish tradition as they were growing up, including a Friday night meal to welcome *Shabbat*.[50] This failure still haunted him in his eighties, and it was one of the reasons he spearheaded several of his Jewish charitable ventures later in life.

When people are raising young families, life is complicated and unless religious traditions are important to one or both parents, it is easy to get overwhelmed in the day-to-day. People may care about Judaism in theory, but practicing the tradition can get pushed aside when there is no countervailing, perceived religious obligation to observe. Because family and home are such critical sources of identity, it is especially important for young families to carve out at least some space for creating a thicker cultural, religious tradition.

Although some millennials are less likely to embrace traditional modes of observance than their parents, many do still enjoy connecting with Judaism around holidays.[51] Such connections are being encouraged on a more formal basis through organizations such as Moishe House and OneTable. Marissa, a friend of one of my daughters, works for OneTable in Chicago, an organization that provides the infrastructure for twenty- and thirty-something postcollege Jews, who do not yet have children, to host or attend a *Shabbat* dinner with their peers. OneTable's message is about the importance of ending the week with *intention* by celebrating a *Shabbat* dinner together with friends. Note how this organization seeks to encourage the attribution of fostering intentionality for *Shabbat* on the part of its target audience, which includes both Jews who have experienced *Shabbat* dinner previously as well as those for whom it is new territory. Marissa tells me there is a high degree of continuing participation, especially among those who volunteer to host these dinners.

Although the *Shabbat* dinner often gets top billing in the overall *Shabbat* celebration, particularly among individuals who do not strictly keep the Sabbath according to Jewish law, it must be remembered that *Shabbat* presents a variety of opportunities for food and fellowship. I spent the *Shabbat* after the contentious 2016 presidential election on New York's Upper West Side with my dear friend Rena, whose family is Modern Orthodox. Following *Shabbat* services on Saturday morning, she hosted a wonderful luncheon that included two families with two very different sets of political views. Anyone familiar with New York culture knows that folks from this part of the country do not mince words. Having lived in the more tempered Midwest for more than thirty years, I grew a bit uncomfortable with the direction the conversation took, especially when one of the guests called another "immoral." That said, at the end of the meal, we joined together for the traditional blessing after the meal, known as *birkat ha'mazon*. If a few feathers were ruffled before this time, it was clear how much everyone at the table cherished their common heritage, notwithstanding the strongest of political differences. Leaving the table without reciting this prayer together was just not an option. We joined together in singing and afterward, nerves were just a bit less raw and the anger was diminished enough for apologies to be made. This experience is an important reminder that Jewish space and ritual, particularly as embodied in the traditional formulas that accompany *Shabbat* meals, can be a wonderful antidote to the very challenging discourse that sometimes infiltrates even our *Shabbat* experience.

Today, most of us see both religion and politics as subjects that create divisiveness rather than unity and, of course, there is good reason for this perception. Even so, as I was reminded during this *Shabbat* luncheon in New York, the importance of a religious tradition, even one that is observed in diverse ways, can provide a path for healing when people allow themselves access to the tradition. We all need healing on

a regular basis—healing from a hard week at work, from difficult encounters with loved ones, and from more global crises that occur in our
country and the world at large. At its core, the *Shabbat* experience is
about healing as much as disconnection and joy.[52]

> Two ministering angels accompany man on the eve of the Sabbath
> from the synagogue to his home, one good and one evil. And when
> he arrives home and finds the lamp burning, the table laid, and the
> couch [bed] covered with a spread, the good angel exclaims, "May it
> be this way on the next Sabbath," and the evil angel unwillingly
> responds, "Amen." But if not, the evil angel exclaims, "May it be this
> way on the next Sabbath," and the good angel unwillingly responds,
> "Amen." (Shabbat 119b, Babylonian Talmud)

This passage from the Talmud made a strong impression on me as a
child. I recall being touched by the vivid imagery of the good and evil
angel, and each one being forced to agree to a future of the home that
neither one wanted. I cannot recall exactly when or how I learned this
narrative but I have carried it with me through the years. As an adult, I
appreciate the timeless truth this narrative teaches. It is a poignant
expression of the importance of consistent behavior in transmitting tradition and serves as a reminder of how difficult it is to change patterns
once they become set.

Particularly in this day and age, consistency in observance of tradition must be tied to positive experiences that will build strong memories. Clearly, a strong family tradition of joyful *Shabbat* celebration will
go a long way toward accomplishing the goal of instilling a desire among
children to duplicate this experience in their own homes. As a society,
we have been taught to value and appreciate the benefits of "multicul-
turalism." But living as a minority in the Diaspora, the truth is that Jews
must work harder to ensure that Jewish tradition continues to be part of
the "multi." A key component of this work means carving out the time
and space to celebrate *Shabbat*, as well as the other Jewish holidays.

2

FOOD

A Recipe for Remix

Given the historically prominent position of the dietary laws, there is no doubt that food occupies an important place in Jewish religious tradition. But food also represents an important aspect of a more general Jewish cultural identity that has been shaped by both Jewish law, as well as social practices.

> The Lord appeared to [Abraham]. . . . Looking up, he saw three men standing near him. As soon as he saw them, he ran from the entrance of the tent to greet them and, bowing to the ground, he said, "My lords, if it please you, do not go on past your servant. Let a little water be brought; bathe your feet and recline under the tree. And let me fetch a morsel of bread that you may refresh yourselves. (Genesis 18:1–5)

> Rav Yehudah said in the name of Rav: Welcoming guests is greater than receiving the presence of God. (Shabbat 127a, Babylonian Talmud)

The first narrative featuring the patriarch Abraham reveals that he left God to greet and feed his guests (who turn out to be angels sent by God). The story continues with the preparation of a substantial meal for the guests. Both opening narratives illustrate the prominent place that welcoming guests, and food, have long occupied in Jewish culture. Judaism also embraces the enjoyment of food as a gift from the Divine. Despite the numerous fasting days that occur throughout the annual Jewish calendar, it is clear that food is seen as a blessing and its enjoyment encouraged, subject to the constraints provided by Jewish law.

> Wine gladdens the heart of man . . . and bread fills man's heart.
> —Psalms 104:15

When I began writing this chapter, my agent suggested I spend some time browsing through Jewish cookbooks to learn more about how the stories of renowned chefs and authors reveal their unique perspectives on the intersection between Jewish food and Jewish tradition generally. One thing that struck me almost immediately was the difficulty of defining "Jewish food." Jewish culture is similar to most other cultural traditions to the extent that it contains unique types of cuisines that have, over the course of the centuries, become associated with the Jewish people. Foods such as chicken soup, chopped liver, corned beef, brisket, and bagels and lox take center stage in the list of well-known Jewish staples. But the locales in which the Jews have lived across the globe have produced many different foods and types of cuisines that are less familiar to American Jews, as well as non-Jews. At our first synagogue in Chicago, we met a young couple from Iran. I distinctly remember the husband telling us that he could not understand all the fuss Jews make about bagels. In his view, pita was infinitely superior!

Author Anita Hirsch observed in her book *Our Food: The Kosher Kitchen Updated* that there are only three traditional Jewish foods: matzo, cholent, and gefilte fish.[1] She designates these foods because of their explicit connection to *halakhah*, Jewish law. Matzo is mentioned in the Torah primarily in the context of the Passover story. Although neither cholent, a meat-based stew, nor gefilte fish has a biblical pedigree, they are both products of a onetime more widespread compliance with *halakhah*. Cholent is a slow-cooked dish that can be fully cooked prior to the Sabbath (*Shabbat*), but can simmer for hours after the onset of *Shabbat* without violating *halakhah*. Gefilte fish's popularity was also the result of *Shabbat*'s legal restrictions. Hirsch writes: "Because Jews cannot separate flesh from the bone on *Shabbat*, clever cooks decided to separate the fish from the bone prior to Friday evening, and stuffed the fish skin with the chopped, boned fish. Eventually the stuffing of the skin was forgotten."[2] I would perhaps add to this list *charoset*—the sweet mixture consisting of apples, nuts and other fruit we eat during the Passover seder representing the mortar our ancestors used to make bricks during their slavery in Egypt.

Generally speaking, food is a unique component of cultural capital due to its inherent fluidity. As Professor Barbara Kirshenblatt-Gimblett notes, unlike other types of cultural capital that "can be built and left to stand, food is perishable, ephemeral" and constantly renewed by people in their kitchens.[3] This malleability is part of the reason food deserves special attention in connection with remix Judaism. As Jewish cookbook author Leah Koenig has written, "Jewish cuisine is at once profoundly global, deeply regional, and eminently adaptable."[4]

But there is more to food when it comes to remix Judaism. As already discussed, remix also entails starting with an authentic base, and retaining aspects of this base throughout the adaptation process. In the case of food and Jewish tradition, the basis for authenticity derives from the Jewish dietary laws, known as the laws of *kashrut*, established initially in the Torah. Because Jewish law regulates extensively those foods that are permissible for Jews to eat, traditional Jewish cuisine differs from many others. Although the majority of American Jews do not keep kosher, these laws form a foundational element of the Jewish tradition and a critical backdrop for the application of remix Judaism in connection with food. In addition, although the main parameters of the dietary laws are largely fixed, the meaning or personal attribution one attaches to particular practices of *kashrut* can be highly variable.

The unique nature of the Jewish food tradition derives from its simultaneously fluid and stable nature. I believe this duality is largely the basis for a phenomenon known as "Kitchen Judaism." This term, used by Kirshenblatt-Gimblett, refers to cultural practices involving food that speak to what it means to be Jewish. Kitchen Judaism is a testament to the reality that Jewish food both reflects, and shapes, Jewish law and Jewish culture. In no small measure, Jewish food also reflects the cultures of the many host nations in which Jews have lived over time and space.

LINKING THE JEWISH PAST AND PRESENT WITH AUTHENTIC CUISINE

Food as a Link to a Personal and Shared Jewish Past

Today, there seems to be a substantial popular interest of global proportions in Jewish food generally (including kosher food) and Israeli cuisine in particular. In the United States, Israeli and Jewish themed restaurants are winning national awards and gaining increased visibility, and their chefs are becoming celebrities in their own right. Of course one would expect cities such as New York, Miami, and Los Angeles to have plenty of kosher and even nonkosher Jewish restaurant options. But even my baseball-enthusiast husband was surprised to learn that nearly half of the Major League stadiums have kosher concession food options.[5] And when Atlanta emerges as a haven for Jewish foodies[6] and an Israeli restaurant becomes wildly popular in the very Catholic city of New Orleans, something fascinating seems to be happening.

Nostalgia among American Jews may be a contributing factor toward the current popularity of Jewish food. Ted Merwin, author of *Pastrami on Rye: An Overstuffed History of the Jewish Deli*, observed that people seem to be waking up to the fact that something has disappeared from Jewish life and "there seems to be a wish to recapture it."[7] In 2016, a modern (and nonkosher) take on a traditional Jewish deli called Mamaleh's opened in the Boston area. Anyone with Yiddish-speaking parents or grandparents will instantly recognize that the name of the restaurant is taken from a Yiddish word that is a term of endearment for a young child. Upon perusing the restaurant's website, the retro motif is inescapable.

Equally interesting is the surging popularity of Jewish food among non-Jews, and the educational value this exposure has to an even broader audience. It cannot be denied that given the minuscule percentage of Jews in the overall American population, the more non-Jews who are interested in Jewish cooking, the stronger the prospects of keeping not only Jewish food alive, but also more broadly Jewish culture and tradition. For example, in Atlanta, the kosher BBQ Festival and competition draws more than 5,000 people, including many non-Jewish competitors. In 2017, one of these competitors was Jodie Sturgeon, a Lutheran chef who heads one of the biggest kosher catering companies in the city.[8]

This may seem surprising to some but the narrative of non-Jewish interest in Jewish food gets told in one form or another in many of the food articles in the Jewish and general media. According to an article in *The Atlantic*, the current popularity of Jewish cooking and food among both Jews and non-Jews is evidenced by "James Beard-sponsored seders, widely distributed community baskets of produce sourced from Jewish-run farms, and pop-up Shabbat dinners." This article emphasizes that through these food-focused mediums, "non-Jews are becoming more acquainted about who American Jews are, where they come from, and what's important to them."[9]

This interest in Jewish food is not limited to the United States or even Israel. A 2017 *Wall Street Journal* article focusing on the "Italian Jewish Rebirth" spoke of Jewish food, including kosher food, as "the clearest indicator of the strength and depth of Jewish popularity." Although Jews represent less than 0.1 percent of the total population in Italy, kosher food and wine are now regularly seen at national food fairs and are available at upscale stores throughout the entire country. According to Italian journalist Carla Reschia, "Regular people are selling and buying Jewish food precisely because it's Jewish."[10] Further to the north in London, Gefiltefest, the biggest Jewish food festival in Europe, had its busiest year yet in 2017, and Vienna also boasts a growing kosher scene.[11]

There is no question that the preparation and consumption of traditional Jewish foods, even with a modern twist, can be a highly effective pathway for cementing an intellectual and emotional connection to the past. Food can be the basis for a person's connection to their own personal Jewish past, as well as to the past of the Jewish people more generally. Perhaps even more significantly, food can be the basis for developing a powerful point of entry to a richer cultural, and even religious, Jewish tradition in the present.

Author and actor Rachel Shukert wrote about her emotions surrounding the annual Rosh Hashanah cakes she still receives from her mother. She confessed that the honey cake in particular was very emotionally freighted for her because the recipe was from her deceased maternal grandmother whom she had never met, but who had nonetheless influenced her in so many ways. Shukert would pore over the recipe card in her grandmother's handwriting, hoping for some insight into her character. Although Shukert still enjoys receiving these cakes as an adult, they also remind her of the negative experience of being trapped in Rosh Hashanah services for hours, "desperate for them to end." And Shukert hasn't seen the inside of a synagogue since she left home. [12] Yet, the last paragraph of her piece is particularly telling:

> Though I may have left these religious rituals behind, my mother's cake takes me back, reminding me of the passing of time, the need to take an honest accounting of my life and relationships, to think about what's working and what I can do better. They remind me of the person I was, and the person I have yet to become. [13]

Shukert may not be sitting in services during the High Holidays, but clearly the cakes of her childhood are prompting the very type of reflection that the Jewish New Year is designed to inspire. They are a link to her personal past as a general matter, but they also represent a bridge from her Jewish past to her present.

In some instances, the association of food with Jewish memories have brought people closer to Judaism. This is true for Derek Attig, who penned an article in *Tablet Magazine* about this aspect of his Jewish journey, even though the specific food linked to his Jewish memories is not one people would associate with being Jewish. Attig's parents both converted to Judaism and so even though he was born and raised as a Jew, he lacked a family history of Judaism. "Grandfather Dick," the rabbi of his synagogue, and "Grandmother Barbara," the rabbi's wife, were his godparents and the main source of his historical link to the Jewish religion. Every summer he would eat Froot Loops at their home before going to day camp at the synagogue. Attig recalls that eating this cereal every day before going to temple "seemed part of what it meant to belong, even partly, to a Jewish family." The lesson he learned back then, which he forgot for years when he became a teenager and young adult, is that "while food is central to Jewish identity, the ingredients themselves matter less than how and when we experience them." [14]

After Attig's godparents died, he began to drift away from Judaism. After more than fifteen years of disconnection, his interest in Judaism was reawakened through the holiday celebrations hosted by his fellow Jewish graduate students at the University of Illinois. Attig has written that these "messy, raucous, perfect gatherings" allowed him to re-examine what Judaism meant to him. And the food, both "traditional and the Froot-y," was again central to finding himself "at home as a Jew." [15] For

Attig, it seems as though his powerful association between Froot Loops and his Jewish memories created a bridge forging a link between his Jewish past and his personal Jewish present.

Jewish food can also help construct a bridge for some Jews to a shared Jewish past. Right now the Jewish Food Society is engaged in creating an online archive of Jewish recipes from around the world. Naama Shefi, the founder of the Society, decided to embark upon this project in 2005 after a *Shabbat* meal at the home of her now-husband's grandmother. Shefi observes that the flavors of this woman's cooking, reflecting time spent in Turkey, Greece, South Africa, and Israel, are "a vivid expression of disappearing worlds, and of bitter and sweet memories."[16]

Shefi's work illustrates that food provides a powerful lens through which to understand Jewish history more generally. An interesting narrative surrounding the first all-kosher grocery store in the United States, the iconic Hungarian Kosher Foods market in Skokie, Illinois, illustrates this same point. The store was the brainchild of Holocaust survivors Sandor Kirsche and his wife, Margit. For this couple, kosher food was how they connected with their families who died in the Holocaust. In their past world, "the rich fragrance of traditional foods like chicken soup and kreplach, paprikash with dumplings and homemade plum pie would fill the air on Shabbat and Jewish holidays." When they came to the United States, they initially filled their apartment with those same smells. Then, they opened a kosher meat market that they later turned into a complete kosher supermarket with separate sections for meat, dairy, wine, and all kinds of groceries, including a health food section in later years.[17]

An innovative food venture launched in 2012 called The Gefilteria also illustrates how Jewish food can be an important medium for connecting people with a global Jewish past. The Gefilteria is dedicated to reclaiming Ashkenazic culture and tradition through a remixed approach to Old World Jewish cooking, including its signature, gefilte fish. Even a quick glance at its website reveals that the co-founders of this venture are on to something huge given the myriad of catering and educational events in which they are involved. Co-founders Jeffrey Yoskowitz and Liz Alpern summarize their philosophy with the following observation: "Food is the vernacular of the day and Jewish is the language we speak."[18]

As these stories illustrate, memories of Jewish food can forge a link from a personal Jewish past to a Jewish present, and can also serve as powerful symbols of current Jewish identity. In a sociological study of Jewish identity among post-boomer American Jews, the authors report the story of Fran, who moved from a Jewish elementary school to a high school where Jews represented only about a third of the population. Now a minority among her classmates, Fran decided to invite forty friends to her home to prepare "traditional Jewish Ashkenazi dishes" such as challah, kugel, and rugelach (rolled pastries stuffed with different fillings). She found that this exercise in sharing her heritage enabled her to deepen her attachment to Judaism. Food became the medium through which Fran began to feel that "being Jewish is awesome."[19]

Jewish Food and Jewish Holiday Celebrations Go Hand in Hand

> There is nothing worthwhile for a man but to eat and drink and afford himself enjoyment with his means. And even that . . . comes from God.
>
> —Ecclesiastes 2:24

Writer Adam Rosen considers this passage from Ecclesiastes about enjoying food and drink as a gift from God as the trigger for his fascination with this biblical book more generally. In Rosen's words, "If this is Judaism—or religion in general—I'll take it, maybe."[20]

A work project provided Rosen with an initial reason for delving into Ecclesiastes, a book that is largely skeptical and grim. Rosen learned that despite its dark tone, Ecclesiastes is associated with the holiday of Sukkot, during which time Jews are commanded to be joyful. Eventually Rosen understood this connection:

> I've increasingly come to see Sukkot as the perfect holiday for skeptical but spiritually available Jews like me. Saluting the natural world doesn't require blind religious devotion, just an appreciation of the Earth's beauty and an acknowledgment of our smallness in the universe—regardless of whether its source is divine or accidental.[21]

In other words, the larger message of Ecclesiastes, as understood by Rosen, is inclusive—one does not need to be a "full-throated believer (or anything close to this) to connect in some deeper way." Rosen's story illustrates how the Jewish tradition's perspective on enjoying food and drink enabled him to reconnect with his religion. He ended his piece by saying that even though it has been a long time since he had visited a *sukkah*, the portable backyard structure traditionally erected on Sukkot, he planned on doing so that year and he had "faith" he would "find something there."[22]

Rosen's narrative about his connection to Sukkot through food began as an intellectual exercise, but for most people the association between food and the Jewish holidays is much more simple. As explored in the last chapter, food plays a huge role in the potential for joy inherent in the celebrations of many Jewish holidays. Personally, I do not eat meat and 95 percent of the year I serve either dairy or fish to our guests, but on Rosh Hashanah and Passover I always make a first-cut brisket with the same recipe I've been using for more than thirty years. I did experiment with a vegetarian Seder meal for a couple of years, and truth be told, this meal did not allow me to create the same type of celebratory atmosphere. For my family, my signature brisket plays an important part in helping us celebrate and perpetuate Jewish tradition during these holidays. Similarly, for many people, Jewish food facilitates celebration of Jewish tradition.

The current interest in Jewish food can translate into a way to educate Jews to observe Jewish holidays more authentically and consistently through foods and rituals that are becoming more widely familiar. This was true for Derek Attig, who described his Jewish holiday celebrations with his fellow graduate students years after his initial Jewish memories were created with Froot Loops. Attig observed that his "Judaism gets expressed and experienced in small moments—grating carrots, mixing batter, simmering matzo balls, sitting around a table, tasting honey . . . —as much as it does in the grand sweep of time."[23]

Another example of this idea can be found in Atlanta, where the interest in Jewish food spurred a "Sukkot farm-to-table festival" at the Jewish Community Center that drew more than 200 people in 2017. Also in Atlanta, the Jews of German descent have been eating *Shabbat* fried chicken since the nineteenth century. Today, the city's Jewish deli, The General Muir, continues to serve this dish only on Fridays. Although this deli is not kosher, its chef Todd Ginsberg claims that "Jewishness is woven into the deli's DNA."[24]

On a more organized level, the connection between the Jewish food renaissance in the United States and the celebration of Jewish holidays is evident at the Hazon Food Conference. This annual gathering, begun in 2005, brings hundreds of people together to explore the new Jewish food movement—and to celebrate *Shabbat*—with food, Jewish learning, and prayer. In 2017, many of the sessions focused on sustainability, pickling, and other types of food preparations popular among foodies. But the program also included different versions of *Shabbat* services ranging from Orthodox to Renewal, and a bidding farewell to *Shabbat* with the traditional *havdalah* service performed by a campfire. On Friday night, handmade, braided challah loaves baked by the participants played a prominent role in creating a traditional *Shabbat* atmosphere. The 2017 conference was held for the first time in the summer, and based on an account of the experience that appeared in *The Forward*, it sounded very much like a weekend of Jewish summer camp for foodies![25]

The traditional "break-fast" following Yom Kippur, the most holy day of the Jewish year, also palpably illustrates how Jewish food and observance of Jewish tradition are uniquely integrated. The majority of Ashkenazi Jews break their fast in the United States with bagels, lox, cream cheese, smoked fish, and other traditional staples of this genre. Yet, the stature this event has taken on in American Jewish culture is even more interesting than the actual food that is served during the break-fast. As Professor Jenna Weissman Joselit has observed, at least since the beginning of the twenty-first century this event has become "a national phenomenon."[26] She attributes its popularity to several factors, including that it is an easy way to acknowledge one's Jewishness and is amenable to inclusiveness and "radical hospitality," two values that resonate strongly with Jews and their non-Jewish friends and relatives.

Of course we all know that many, if not most, Jews do not believe kosher food has to be a part of their Jewish holiday traditions. In the greater Chicago area, for example, there are more than a few nonkosher restaurants that feature a traditional Rosh Hashanah or Passover menu, both for takeout and dining in. Every year, a popular bakery near my home markets macaroons and other baked goods during Passover that are not strictly kosher for Passover although they do not contain flour. People order their delicacies by the droves for their Seders.

Still, Jews who carve out the time to celebrate Jewish holidays with festive meals, especially when there is other Jewish content to these celebrations, can more effectively transmit Jewish tradition to their offspring. Through these celebrations, parents hopefully are able to create a home environment with a richer Jewish cultural capital that will not only create sweet memories but also help foster a desire in their children to replicate these celebrations.

My friend Robin has three young children. She hosts an annual Chanukah dinner celebration for her family and close friends. She goes all out in decorating the home with appropriate Chanukah decorations and does a special Chanukah charity project with her guests through a local Jewish organization. Even if scheduling requires her to host the dinner on the Sunday prior to the actual holiday, candles are lit and blessings are said. She typically serves traditional Chanukah fare such as latkes with applesauce, in addition to other Jewish staples such as brisket and challah. But since her home is not kosher, sour cream is available for the latkes.

I have been to Robin's home for this event and it is clear how much her three children love this special time of the year. Her celebration embodies the "remix" concept perfectly. She is taking hold of Jewish tradition in a way that works for her and her family and imbuing it with a sense of authenticity and personal meaning—even if her celebration does not align completely with Jewish law. I believe her children are likely to remember and treasure these Chanukah dinners.

But according to Jewish tradition, Jewish food is also kosher food. Although many of the restaurants and chefs who are currently involved in the Jewish food movement are not strictly kosher, even among this group some adherence to the dietary rules can be found. Those Jewish food providers who are not personally observant but still choose to embrace some version of these rules do so because they seek to produce a product that is authentic rather than out of a desire to observe Jewish law as a command.

Jewish Food and Authenticity of Tradition

Israeli-born Michael Solomonov has received several James Beard awards in recent years. In 2019, his Philadelphia restaurant Zahav won the prize for the best American restaurant; in 2017 he received the

James Beard Outstanding Chef Award, and in 2016 his Israeli cookbook *Zahav* was named cookbook of the year. According to an article in *Forbes* magazine, Solomonov "has become America's leading evangelist for Israeli cuisine."[27] In his cookbook, Solomonov writes that food and the story of his life are "inextricable." A particularly touching narrative in his book recounts how his Bulgarian grandmother Savta Mati taught him to make delicious borekas, flaky squares of dough filled with potato or cheese, even though neither could speak to one another in any language other than the loving actions that filled their kitchen during this instruction.

Solomonov spent most of his childhood in Pittsburgh but moved back to Israel for a while when he was eighteen. Upon his return, he found work in an Israeli bakery, and spent lots of time making "borekas in batches so large that it took four of us to lift the block of dough." He thought about his grandmother often during this time and "felt proud to be part of a tradition that she had brought with her from Bulgaria." And he loved working in a place that was so connected to the rhythm of Israeli life:

> On Friday mornings, we would arrive at 2 a.m. to start baking, mixing giant batches of challah dough that we'd braid into loaves that would soon grace Shabbat tables in every home in the village. When I came back to Israel, I had nothing. But when I left the bakery a year later, I felt that I had a home.[28]

Solomonov also devotes a page in his cookbook to explaining what keeping kosher means to him. He writes that although he does not keep kosher personally, in both his cookbook and his Philadelphia restaurant by the same name, he chooses "to honor the spirit of a few fundamental rules of kosher cooking." For example, he does not use milk and meat products in the same dish. He also does not use pork or shellfish. For Solomonov, these rules are important because they "help define the boundaries of Israeli cuisine." He observes that "without the influence of kosher rules, the notion of Israeli cuisine itself begins to fray."[29] Solomonov admits to having moments when he is cooking in his restaurant and secretly wishing that he could baste a particular piece of meat with butter, or add lobster to a dish he is preparing. But he refrains from doing this because he cares more about preserving the authenticity of his cuisine.

Of course what Solomonov says about Israeli cuisine is equally true about Jewish cuisine generally, including traditional Ashkenazi food. In a telephone interview with Liz Alpern, co-founder of the Gefilteria, she mentioned that the authenticity of Ashkenazi cuisine means that a bacon-wrapped matzo ball is simply a nonstarter. Although Gefilteria's packaged signature gefilte fish is certified strictly kosher, its pop-up catering services can more aptly be described as kosher sensitive. For example, if Gefilteria caters at a kosher venue, *kashrut* will be observed. With other venues, there can be more flexibility, although pork and shellfish products are never used. [30]

This concept of respect for the dietary laws as part of a more global concern for authenticity of cuisine, rather than religious observance, surfaces in articles about Jewish food more than one might expect. For example, The General Muir, the Atlanta deli serving the *Shabbat* fried chicken, does not serve any product with pork ingredients. [31] Significantly, the culinary authenticity theme even appears in connection with some strictly kosher establishments such as Zak the Baker's 405 Deli in Miami. Zak Stern grew up Reform and married a religious woman from Israel. His wife introduced him to the laws of *kashrut* and she was the reason he made his business a kosher bakery.

Stern is clear about what being kosher means for his cuisine: "We happen to be certified kosher, but that's not our identity." For Stern, kosher ensures the traditional nature of his food. In connection with his deli in particular, kosher status "brings a real authenticity": "If we're going to do it legit, it's got to be kosher, that's part of it. . . . European delis that catered to our great-grandparents would not have served melted cheese on their sandwiches." [32]

There is a fascinating similarity among the food narratives of cuisine artists such as Solomonov as well as food providers such as The General Muir, Zak the Baker, and the Gefilteria. All are adopting a remixed approach to *kashrut*. All are selecting, and consistently observing on an institutional level, aspects of *kashrut*. Zak the Baker is observing the letter of the law, but he is citing the attribution of authenticity, rather than Divine command, as his rationale. Although the others may not be dotting the *i*'s and crossing the *t*'s of *kashrut*, they too care enough about the authenticity of their cuisine to tap into Jewish tradition to varying degrees.

These stories play an important role in providing public education about Jewish tradition as well as aspects of *kashrut*. This educational function is particularly significant because the narratives of well-known chefs and venues have the potential to reach a wide audience through the popular media, not to mention popular cookbooks. The fundamentals of *kashrut* are important traditional Jewish knowledge that must be kept alive from both an educational and experiential perspective among more than the Orthodox community.

UNBUNDLING THE LAWS AND CULTURE OF *KASHRUT*

The Laws of *Kashrut*

The dietary rules in the Torah are unique among all the law collections of the ancient Near East. Most of these laws are concentrated in two separate passages in the Torah—one in the book of Leviticus and the other in the book of Deuteronomy.[33] As is the case with many of the commands found in Jewish tradition, the Torah provides the foundation but the rabbinic tradition added considerable guidance. As we will see, in the case of the laws of *kashrut* specifically, the people's cultural practices also had a significant impact in shaping how these laws are currently observed.

The Hebrew term "kosher" translates into English as an adjective equivalent to "fit." As applied to food, it describes food that is fit for consumption under Jewish law. There are many rules concerning this topic, some of which are generally well known and others less so. One of the most fundamental aspects of *kashrut* is the prohibition of the consumption of blood, which is seen as symbolic of life itself, and therefore belongs to God, who created life. All kosher meat is drained of blood during the ritual slaughtering process, and then soaked and salted.[34] Many people do not realize that the dietary laws require not only that foods be intrinsically kosher, but also that land animals and birds be slaughtered in compliance with *halakhah*, and the meat prepared in accord with the tradition.

Jewish law seeks to minimize animal pain and suffering in general, including when animals are killed as sources for food.[35] The law that details the process of ritual slaughter, known as *shechitah*, requires the use of an extremely sharp knife that is without nicks or dents, and a quick movement across the throat by a highly trained specialist known as a *schochet*. The *schochet* also recites a special blessing prior to slaying the animal.

A set of well-known rules concerns the prohibition of eating certain types of meat and fishes. As a general matter, it is prohibited to eat meat from animals that have disease or have died of natural causes. With respect to specific animals that are off-limits, most people, Jews and non-Jews alike, automatically think of the pig. This prohibition is so widely known that, from a cultural standpoint, the pig essentially symbolizes the very concept of *treif* (something that is not kosher). According to the Torah, however, there are many land animals that are prohibited because animals that are kosher must chew their cud and have a split hoof.

The Torah also specifies the type of birds that are pure, and thus permissible for food. As for fish, only those that have fins and scales are allowed. This law excludes shellfish, many forms of which are widely considered delicacies and important dining options.

Many people are also aware at some level of the prohibition on mixing meat and milk products. The origin of this prohibition is the Torah's command against boiling a kid in its mother's milk.[36] An understanding of what this language actually means in practice began to emerge in early Talmudic times when the sages concluded that cooking meat and milk required physical separation when these foods "give taste" to the pots in which they are cooked."[37] Professor David Kraemer has emphasized the lack of clarity regarding what it means to "give taste," and speculates that the language seems to reflect concern "for the transmission of the taste of one category of food to the other."[38] In general, however, the whole topic of mixing meat and milk was not a huge focus of rabbinic discussion until the High Middle Ages, probably because meat was not widely available in earlier times.

Professor Haym Soloveitchik has observed that "the traditional Jewish kitchen, transmitted from mother to daughter over the generations, has been immeasurably and unrecognizably amplified beyond all *halakhic* requirements."[39] Many of our current *kashrut* norms are not dictated by the Talmud and other early rabbinic sources, but instead are the result of more stringent rabbinic rulings that began to emerge in medieval times in Northern Europe.[40] These rulings codified the heightened observance level of the lay people who were influenced by the broader pietist movement, and whose behaviors exceeded that which was required by the then-existing law codes. In other words, the rabbis radically interpreted *halakhah* in order to accommodate the law to the lived reality of the people. By the middle of the eighteenth century, the practice of maintaining permanently separate dishes and utensils for meat and dairy was widespread.

Another interesting illustration of this pattern of enhanced observance is the evolution of the increased stringencies concerning the waiting period between consuming meat and dairy products (Jewish law allows eating meat following dairy without a wait, provided the mouth is cleansed and hands are washed). The Talmud provides relatively little guidance on the specific amount of time one must wait between eating meat and dairy.[41] Maimonides, the renowned medieval Sephardic authority, concluded in his Jewish law code that one should wait a period of time equivalent to eating another meal (about six hours), to give enough time for meat particles to dissolve between one's teeth.[42] Later Sephardic authorities adopted the six-hour wait as a matter of *halakhah*, and eventually this practice spread to Ashkenazi communities that had previously maintained only a one-hour waiting period. Today, most Orthodox Jews follow the six-hour practice whereas those Conservative Jews who keep kosher typically wait three hours, a practice originally followed by German Jews.

The Current Culture of *Kashrut*

The current system of kosher certification is an invention of the twentieth century, and was driven by modern technology. Simply put, when foods are prepared and served in any way other than in their natural state, they are vulnerable to violating the laws of *kashrut* because they can include additives. As a result, they require rabbinic supervision. Today, more than 80 percent of all food certified as kosher in the United States is certified by four mainstream agencies.[43] Kosher-certified products are made by A-list companies such as Kraft, General Mills, Coca-Cola, and Pepsi.

Although Jewish law prescribes the parameters of keeping kosher, the practices on the ground vary tremendously. They depend on one's denominational affiliation as well as one's geographic location. In recent decades, Orthodox communities in both the United States and Israel have been experiencing a significant "slide to the right" in both ideology and practice.[44] This shift also has impacted the culture of keeping kosher. There are increasing stringencies, known as *humras*, which are now characteristic of many Orthodox communities and homes given this shift toward increased religious observance among even Modern Orthodox communities. For example, in the 1970s, it was not unusual for Modern Orthodox Jews claiming to keep strictly kosher to eat a cold tuna salad sandwich in a nonkosher restaurant. Today this practice is frowned upon even though I personally know some self-identified Orthodox Jews who will eat not only uncooked foods but also cooked, nonmeat items in nonkosher restaurants.

Still, in many Orthodox communities today it is not considered appropriate to eat even a plain salad consisting of lettuce and other cold vegetables, without dressing, in nonkosher establishments because of the concern that fresh produce may contain undetected bugs that are not kosher and cannot be removed properly absent appropriate rabbinic supervision. In fact, in recent years some produce such as broccoli and strawberries have gone completely absent from kosher venues given the burdensome nature of checking for, and removing, these bugs.[45] Previously, *halakhic* authorities often were more lenient and accepted the view that if bugs could not be seen by the naked eye, they were not problematic. This view was based on the principle that if the kosher components of a given food or product are sixty times greater than the nonkosher ones, the nonkosher elements are annulled as long as they are removed if noticeable (known as *batul b'shishim*).[46]

Among non-Orthodox Jews, the culture of *kashrut* reveals a fascinatingly diverse spectrum. Of course many Jews keep absolutely no form of *kashrut* whatsoever. On the opposite end of the spectrum, some non-Orthodox Jews avoid all prohibited foods, including nonkosher meat. These Jews typically will eat in nonkosher restaurants but will refrain from eating meat and any products containing meat, or any other blatantly nonkosher ingredients. They maintain kosher homes with two sets of dishes, in addition to their Passover dishes, and will only buy food that is either kosher certified or made with seemingly kosher ingredients.

A group in the middle displays a huge range of remix. Some of these Jews avoid both pork products and shellfish but will eat nonkosher meat, either in restaurants or even at home. Some people in this group may also refrain from blatantly mixing meat and milk but will not necessarily inquire about the ingredients in foods that do not contain obvious dairy. Conversely, there are also Jews who will not overtly mix meat and milk, but will eat either pork products or shellfish, or both.

Other Jews eat everything except pork products. This trend was publicly documented as early as 1883 at the infamous Hebrew Union College Trefa Banquet where the first American Reform rabbis were ordained. At that meal, milk was mixed with meat, shellfish was in plain view, but nothing remotely connected with the pig surfaced. This event illustrates the well-known reality that in contrast to products derived from a pig, shellfish historically has been more acceptable on a cultural level. Perhaps the reason for this distinction is that in nineteenth-century America, various forms of shellfish were considered upscale fare and therefore popular among well-bred Gentiles whom the Jews sought to emulate.[47] Personally, I know more than a few people who fall into this particular category.

An even more liberal variation of the no-pig version of *kashrut* includes well-known exceptions for bacon and the pig products in Chinese food. I also know several people who fall into this group. The argument has been made that the renowned love among American Jews for nonkosher Chinese food is partially attributable to the fact that this cuisine slices and dices the nonkosher ingredients to the point where they are unrecognizable, and therefore, regarded as "safe *treif*" by nonobservant Jews.[48]

As these variations suggest, remix *kashrut* has had a long, venerable history in the United States. Professor Kirshenblatt-Gimblett has documented how most of the American Jewish cookbooks published before World War I were not kosher, but rather were "selectively *treif*."[49] But remix *kashrut* does not mean a complete rejection of the dietary laws. Rather, this element of selectivity often operated "according to well-understood, if unspoken, societal rules, themselves influenced by where one lives and with whom one associates."[50]

Kashrut presents an especially interesting paradox in twenty-first-century America. On the one hand, there are more available kosher, and kosher-compatible, food options than ever before. Special food needs characterize our current dietary landscape. Still, although the kosher food industry is booming, Jews who keep kosher and who intentionally buy kosher food represent only a small percentage of the population of American kosher food consumers. The majority of people who buy kosher food include people of other faiths who do not eat pork and other biblically prohibited animals, as well as vegetarians, vegans, and others who have issues with dairy and gluten, and therefore benefit from products that are marked as clearly containing or lacking these ingredients. Also, historian Roger Horowitz explains the burgeoning production of certified kosher processed foods as the result of reduced costs and the ability to incorporate kosher certification practices in "other manufacturing management systems . . . at minimal cost."[51]

But there is some evidence of a growing interest in *kashrut*, particularly among some Conservative and younger Reform Jews. On October 13, 2002, when Rabbi David Ellenson was inaugurated as President of Hebrew Union College, sponsor of the 1883 Trefa Banquet, the meal was entirely kosher.[52] In 2011, the Reform movement published a substantial volume called *The Sacred Table* that is devoted to exploring a meaningful Jewish food ethic and advocating for versions of *kashrut* for Reform Jews. The book's foreword, written by Rabbi Eric H. Yoffie, claims that the book represents a "historic event for Reform Judaism" as the movement opens "doors that have been closed for more than a century" and enters a "new era of . . . practice and belief." Although Yoffie notes that the number of Reform Jews interested in keeping some version of *kashrut* is "relatively small," he expresses the hope that this minority will grow.[53]

Even so, the resistance many Jews have to keeping at least some version of *kashrut* is still strong, as evidenced by the Trefa Banquet 2.0 held in San Francisco in 2018. At this controversial "remixed" event commemorating the 1883 banquet, Jewish chefs cooked up and served a bevy of *treif* items despite a local rabbi's recitation of a communal blessing that was an altered version of a traditional Jewish prayer.[54]

REMIX KASHRUT AND PERSONAL ATTRIBUTION

Any good health coach will tell you that food represents a freighted, emotional issue. For almost everyone, food can be a powerful pull, both for the positive and the negative, as it triggers very complex, and often irrational, processes involving desire and denial.[55] Kosher chef and author Laura Frankel told me that she believes for many Jews, kosher food still represents "the final frontier" of Judaism. During our conversation, Frankel stated that in her twenty-plus years in the kosher food industry, she has heard countless "confessions" of self-denominated "bad Jews" (some of whom are very publicly known) who don't keep kosher and who do not want to be told what they can and cannot eat. And this is not a new phenomenon. In 1937, Rabbi Abraham Heller observed that "we find a large number of our people deeply concerned with the problem of Jewish survival but with no significant interest in *kashrut*."[56]

There is a big difference between the approach of the Trefa Banquet 2.0, which actually celebrates *treif*, and a remixed approach to *kashrut* that instead embraces the importance of *kashrut* as a foundational element of Jewish tradition but does not strive for complete compliance. I fully understand that any version of *kashrut* is a very tough sell for many American Jews. But some degree of observance is not an impossible sell given the many rules of *kashrut* and their varied applications.

Significantly, the laws of *kashrut* are among the easiest to align with remix Judaism because they are extremely conducive to being explained through personal meanings that are very appealing to modern sensibilities. This reality likely explains the growing attraction of a personalized version of *kashrut* for some non-Orthodox Jews. In discussing the dietary laws, Professor Edward Greenstein has written that the many meanings "encoded" within the Jewish behaviors associated with eating are intended to "cultivate the ethical and spiritual dimensions" of those who observe.[57]

Also, it is not uncommon for people who ultimately choose to be fully committed to *kashrut* to begin their journeys with small steps that are taken for reasons unrelated to Jewish tradition. For example, Rabbi Mark Sameth began his *kashrut* journey years ago at an Argentinean restaurant when he realized that the mixed grill he ordered was "some poor animal's heart, brains, and other internal organs." That recognition prompted "an intuition that there were boundaries across which one should not allow oneself to pass," and it dawned on him that "the slice of bloody heart" on his plate was "one of them." Still, it wasn't until much later that he realized that his current level of dietary observance, which he calls "Jewish Ethical Vegetarianism," was shaped by the Jewish principles of showing compassion for others, caring for one's body, and searching for inner and public spirituality.[58]

Similarly, in *Tablet Magazine*, writer Liel Leibovitz penned a powerful description of his *kashrut* journey that began with his decision to get a handle on his health and weight. For some reason he still does not understand, he began by gradually starting to keep kosher. He candidly recounts that this choice was not based on religion but rather represented a way of forcing him to "stop and think before each bite."[59]

Developing a Respectful, Informed Approach to *Kashrut*

I vividly recall a story my father, who had been raised in a very Orthodox home, often shared with me as I was growing up. There was a *treif* hot dog stand near his elementary school that he always found very tempting. One day, he just gave in and bought a hot dog on his way home for lunch. That particular day, his mother fixed bananas, cottage cheese, and sour cream for his lunch, which he then had no choice but to eat because he did not want to tell her that he had eaten the hot dog. So my father's first infarction of the dietary laws not only involved eating nonkosher meat, but also mixing milk and meat by consuming dairy too soon after eating meat. He was probably seven or eight at the time, and by the time I was old enough to hear and understand this story, it was at least thirty-five years later. His recollection of the guilt he felt was still clear and further, he was able to communicate very palpably that sense of guilt to me. This story is all the more interesting because at that time, our home was not exactly kosher but more "kosher-style," and my father was not particularly strict about observing the dietary laws.

This story probably was my first introduction to *kashrut*. It was how I first learned both that certain meats are not kosher and that mixing meat and milk is prohibited. I also learned, even if not on a conscious level, that these rules represented a fundamental part of what it means to be Jewish. Even though my father was not keeping kosher when he recounted this narrative, he was very clear to me about how important being Jewish was to him, and that it should also be important to me. Although I cannot say for sure whether hearing this story repeatedly during my early childhood was a factor in my decision to begin keeping kosher shortly before my Bat Mitzvah, I do think it played a part.

When I decided to keep kosher, my mother accommodated me by dutifully changing over her kitchen so that the home would be completely kosher. So regardless of the fact that my parents were not strictly observant, the clearest message I received from both of them was that Jewish tradition was something that needed to be respected and passed down. They made joining a synagogue and sending me to Hebrew school a financial priority. They manifested respect, not ridicule, for Jewish tradition and gave me the necessary education to appreciate the beauty of the tradition. I like to say that my parents provided the ingredients for my Jewish journey, even though the recipe was my own. And when my observance surpassed theirs, they supported my journey.

The laws of *kashrut* occupy a prominent place in Jewish tradition. Jews who are not inclined to observe them even partially should at least be knowledgeable about these laws, given their importance as religious and cultural capital. They represent fundamental building blocks of Judaism 101. A respectful approach to these laws fosters education and avoids negativity. It embraces the concept of "educated choice" that it celebrated in *The Sacred Table*, even if full compliance is not a recognized goal for most people.

With some thought and education, it is relatively easy for parents and grandparents wishing to transmit a love of Jewish tradition to their offspring to approach *kashrut* in this way. Parents need to understand the basic principles of *kashrut* and share this knowledge with their children by emphasizing these laws as a fundamental aspect of Jewish tradition deserving consideration and respect. The framing of *kashrut* as an aspect of Jewish tradition that is positive, and still relevant, is critically important for families who are not living within the *halakhic* system. My parents' example taught me early on that people can exhibit a positive, respectful attitude toward elements of Jewish tradition even though they are not necessarily observing these elements to the extent required by *halakhah*. I fully understand that some people may consider such an approach hypocritical. On the other hand, how tradition is framed makes a huge difference when it comes to its transmission. Positivity, even without full compliance, sends a very different message from ridicule and negativity.

With respect to transmitting Jewish tradition outside of the *halakhic* system, I believe positive framing matters much more than the actual specifics that families choose to observe. As is the case with *Shabbat*

and the holidays, the key is to select, and observe in a consistent manner, distinct elements of the *kashrut* tradition. Also, with respect to
kashrut specifically, consistency of selected observances does not necessarily mean *always* observing the selected elements in *every* type of
environment. Consistency can mean one consistent standard in the
home and a distinct consistent standard when dining outside the home.
Jews who keep a degree of *kashrut* only in their homes have noted that
their practices still furnish a "daily reminder" of their commitment to a
specific community.[60]

Novelist Ellen Umansky provides an example of this approach in a
sweet piece called "Three Sets of Dishes."[61] Umansky recalls that when
she was growing up, her family originally kept two sets of dishes, one for
milk and one for meat. Outside the home, they ate nonkosher meat and
seafood, but never any sort of pig product or mixture of meat and milk
foods. Eventually, they embraced a system at home for keeping three
sets of dishes, with the third one, consisting of colored plastic plates that
she still contemplated as an adult, being used for *treif*.

As a child, Umansky struggled with what she perceived as her family's hypocrisy. I can relate to that struggle. For years, I could not understand how or why people drew certain lines with their *kashrut* practices.
Many years ago, I recall having to organize a luncheon program at my
school on one of the interim days of Passover, during which time Jewish
law permits one to work. There were many people going to be in attendance and there was no reason for anyone to think that there would be
kosher food available. I simply assumed that anyone who cared about
Passover *kashrut* observance, which entails a completely distinct set of
rules in addition to those observed regularly, would bring their own
lunch as I did. The food we served was, of course, not kosher.

But one of the attendees, who had absolutely no problem eating
nonkosher meat, was very upset with me for not ensuring that matzo
was provided at the luncheon. At the time I was so puzzled by her
reaction. Now I see things differently. The older I get, the more I see
the beauty of a system that lends itself to individual interpretation.

Umansky also came to see the wisdom of her family's choices. As a
married woman with children of her own, she continues her family's
pattern of no pork and no mixing meat and milk: "As I get older, the
logic of the way we kept kosher makes sense to me. We might not have

adhered to all the rules, but we were conscious of them. . . . And that awareness might not be everything, but it matters."[62]

Similarly, my experience raising a family has allowed me to understand more fully the value of a remixed approach to *kashrut*. Our daughters and their partners keep only some aspects of *kashrut*, and some more so than others. Candidly, when we were raising our children, they struggled with being restricted with food choices, especially when eating outside the home.

In order to help maintain a degree of clarity and consistency, my husband and I devised a family contract to help avoid some of the issues that were surfacing during the period of their late teenage and early adult years. This is the time when children often are eating out with friends or in college, and families lose whatever control they might have had earlier with respect to food selections. Our contract, which has become known as the "DODO" (our abbreviation for the Doctrine of Dining Out), essentially prohibits pork, shellfish, and blatant mixing of milk and meat during the same course when we dine outside our home together as a family. We wrote this out and had each family member sign the document (which I still have to this day). As our daughters began developing serious relationships and their partners were brought into the fold, they too participated in our family tradition when dining out with us. Of course, as each new partner appeared, the explanation of the DODO and its history took on an increasingly humorous quality. After all, children so enjoy making fun of their parents from time to time!

Still, we learned some important things as parents during our family's *kashrut* journey. First, although complaints may surface even now from time to time when we dine out, everyone essentially has accepted the DODO as our family's out-of-the-home standard. Second, the partners have been extremely respectful (sometimes even more so than our daughters!), and have willingly participated despite the fact that not all were raised with this degree of *kashrut*. Third, and perhaps most significantly, we are beginning to see that the attention we paid to *kashrut* while raising our daughters may be beginning to have an impact on their own personal practices and homes.

When our eldest daughter and her husband hosted their first Thanksgiving dinner in their home, they bought a kosher turkey and made sure that none of the side dishes my husband would be eating were prepared with dairy products. But my daughter told me in advance they would be having macaroni and cheese on the table with all the other food. I winced and pushed back on this a bit. At the time, she was pregnant with our first grandchild so I asked her how she was going to explain this to her children one day if she wanted them to take Jewish tradition seriously. She replied by pointing out that the original biblical prohibition against boiling a kid in its mother's milk does not expressly prohibit serving dairy with poultry. Her point to me is fair. The truth of the matter is that the Talmudic sages debated whether poultry should be considered meat, and although they concluded that it should, there was a discussion about this topic. Despite my personal preference for adhering to the established rabbinic tradition here, her response is a strong testament to the reality that for Jews who are not living completely within the framework of Jewish law, what most matters in terms of *kashrut* is education, respect, and selected buy-in.

In practice, most people are likely to adopt those aspects of *kashrut* that most clearly align with other values they prize, such as health, animal welfare, or mindfulness. When children are young, their parents' preferences will likely control these matters. As children mature and begin to develop their own views, their distinct sensibilities may help shape the family's overall Jewish food culture.

Contemplating Personally Meaningful Attributions

> A calf was being taken to the slaughter, when it broke away, hid his head under the Rabbi's skirts, and lowed [in terror]. "Go," said he. "For this wast thou created." Thereupon they said [in Heaven], "Since he has no pity, let us bring suffering upon him."
>
> One day the Rabbi's maidservant was sweeping the house; [seeing] some young weasels lying there, she made [efforts] to sweep them away. "Let them be," said he to her. "It is written, and his tender mercies are over all his works." Said they [in Heaven], "Since he is compassionate, let us be compassionate to him."
>
> —Bava Metzia 85a, Babylonian Talmud

As this passage from the Talmud illustrates, compassion toward animals is a prominent feature of Jewish tradition. The rabbi was punished when he lacked this compassion and rewarded when he had a change of heart. Other philosophies with a strong basis in Jewish tradition are worker welfare (*oshek*), caring for the environment (*bal tashchit*), and safeguarding one's own health (*sh'mirat haguf*). These philosophies not only resonate strongly in our current social climate, but they also can provide compelling reasons for adhering to aspects of *kashrut*.

Still, these philosophies are no longer associated just with Jewish tradition. Today they are regarded as universally appealing. In contrast, the laws of *kashrut* are particular to Jewish tradition. If preservation and transmission of Jewish tradition is a goal, it is not enough to focus just on these more universalistic elements of *kashrut*. The universal must be infused with some application of the particularities of traditional observance. But the marriage of selected elements of *kashrut* with these other Jewish-based, universalistic values can be a powerful force in cementing Jewish identity for liberal Jews.[63]

Compassion for animals is a highly important value for many people, including some who eat meat. One of my daughters is a huge animal lover. She volunteers at a local animal shelter and lives in an apartment with numerous pets. She is also a serious foodie. Recently she decided to eliminate meat from her diet (at least for now). To be clear, keeping kosher was not her motivation. On the other hand, compassion for animals has a strong pedigree in Jewish tradition, and by giving up meat, she will also be eliminating her consumption of nonkosher meat. I recently asked my daughter for her take on this idea, and she nodded approvingly and said, "So you are suggesting that I should one day tell my children that by being vegetarian, I am also keeping this aspect of a kosher diet, even if that wasn't my goal?" Exactly!

Recall how writer Liel Leibovitz began his exploration of *kashrut* because of health concerns. The perception that kosher food is healthier is common. Chef Laura Frankel told me that when she owned a restaurant in New York City some years ago, she would often look out the window and observe the activity in connection with two nearby hot dog stands, one kosher and one not. She observed that people from all walks of life would go out of their way to head for the kosher one, most likely based on a perception that kosher is cleaner and healthier, and that there is "another set of eyes on it." Hebrew National played upon this very theme in their iconic hot dog commercials emphasizing that their company answers "to a higher authority."

Similarly, Rabbi Mark Sameth frankly admitted that his decision to give up shellfish was based purely on health concerns about the dangers associated with eating crustaceans.[64] But Sameth emphasized that he was able to tap into these health explanations because he had already become more generally mindful about his eating practices given his experience with the mixed grill in the Argentinean restaurant.

In the same way, although Leibovitz began his exploration of *kashrut* to control his weight, he soon developed an appreciation for the benefits of a mindful eating regimen. He told me that after changing his eating habits, he developed a "strange sense of well-being" that he didn't "even begin to understand." When I asked Leibovitz whether his decision to begin keeping kosher impacted his connection to Judaism he observed: "There's no doubt that the decision has also deepened my connection, already plenty deep, to Judaism: in being mindful with every meal that I am a somewhat observant Jew and must make choices accordingly, the body . . . embodies this identity, and with it the soul."[65]

Mindfulness is an attribute with tremendous popular appeal in today's times. When I began writing this chapter, I wrote a post on Facebook inviting all of my friends (Jews and non-Jews) to comment on their perceptions of and experiences with keeping kosher. Althea, a young woman who went to Camp Ramah with one of my daughters, provided some interesting comments about the importance of mindful eating and *kashrut*:

> In my personal experience, Judaism and kashrut have been a part of my meaning making. Choosing my food, how it is prepared, and how it is consumed provide a rich experience that connects me to myself, my community/family, and the earth. . . . I have found that eating locally, looking at the sources of the foods (i.e., ethical and sustainable farming practices), and asking myself if the food in front of me will actually make me feel good provide much more meaning than adhering to a predetermined set of rules sanctioned by an entity external to myself.

Another Facebook friend, Maureen, who is the educational director at a Conservative synagogue in Florida, saw Althea's post and said it provides "an excellent narrative for *kashrut* (through mindful eating)" that she can use in her professional capacity as she encounters questions from less observant Jews who "have difficulty following a set of guidelines they don't inherently relate to." The idea of being mindful, aware, and conscious of what one consumes is also the same principle author Ellen Umansky emphasized as she reminisced about her family's three sets of dishes.

In connection with food, mindfulness does not just apply to contemplating what we put in our mouths. Judaism has a rich tradition that incorporates specific ways of expressing gratitude in connection with eating. These expressions of gratitude provide excellent examples of low-hanging fruit that can easily be incorporated in one's lifestyle to varying degrees. In *Real Life/Real Food: A Holy Moment at McDonald's*, Reform Rabbi Eugene Borowitz wrote about the spirituality he encountered at McDonald's on a day when he was particularly rushed and preoccupied.[66] He took a moment to pause, and recite the one-sentence blessing before eating bread, known as the *motzi*, before eating his fish sandwich. From a *halakhic* perspective this blessing should be said after washing one's hands in a specific ritual manner, but many Jews say it without the ritual washing. The *motzi* is short and sweet, can be easily memorized, and provides a daily opportunity to tap into Jewish tradition as a means of expressing gratitude.

In fact, Jewish tradition prescribes numerous blessings before eating all different kinds of food: non-bread foods made from different types of grains, fruits and vegetables, meat and dairy products, and of course wine. There are also different blessings that can be said after eating these distinct foods, as well as a somewhat longer prayer known as *birkat ha'mazon*, the prayer after eating a meal with bread.[67] The *birkat*, especially the first paragraph, lends itself to being chanted in a fun-filled way that is attractive to children and adults alike, even for those who do not understand the Hebrew words. Saying some of these food blessings consistently as a family, especially the *motzi* and *birkat*, whether at a daily meal or even just at *Shabbat* dinner, can create a foundation for a lifetime of practicing these unique aspects of Jewish tradition.

The recitation of traditional prayers of gratitude should not be seen as the province only of religious Jews who have a strong faith in God. Often I hear people say that they feel it is hypocritical to pray absent faith in God. But even those without faith in the Divine can be mindful of what they have, and take some time every day to express a sense of gratitude. The human ability to tap into our good fortune offers huge psychological benefits for all people.

Through the Jewish blessings related to food, those of us fortunate enough to be able to eat whenever we desire can express our gratitude on a daily basis. I receive an e-mail each day that provides a pithy, spiritually focused "thought for the day" called the Daily Lift, created and distributed by an Orthodox outreach organization. Sometimes the messages resonate with me more so than others, but this one really spoke to me:

> Every time you need to buy something and you have the money to purchase it, feel pleasure and gratitude that you have the money you need. When waiting in line in a grocery store, instead of focusing on how slowly the line is moving, focus on how fortunate you are to be able to buy the food you need. [68]

I try to remember this every Friday when I am always in a rush to get my shopping and cooking completed, and the checkout lines are much longer than I anticipated! Keeping this calming message in mind actually helps restore my patience and allows me to feel a sense of gratitude despite feeling pressured to finish everything I need to before the start of *Shabbat*.

One Day at a Time

Of course, liberal Jews also can embrace aspects of *kashrut* for reasons related directly to Judaism. For example, some people intentionally choose to give up pork products based on a desire to strengthen their Jewish identity. Reform Rabbi Peter Knobel has written that he initially decided to stop eating pork because doing so "immediately identified" him with the Jewish people and reminded him "that in times of persecution, anti-Semites often tried to humiliate Jews by making them eat forbidden foods, especially pork." [69] A while back my son-in-law Andrew told me that he would never order a ham sandwich (even if he would eat other types of pork) because he saw this as a way of "connecting with his religion." One New Year's Eve later on, shortly before our grandson was born, he surprised me by saying that his resolution was to try to avoid eating even other pork delicacies he had so loved.

Months later, I asked Andrew what made him desire to give up pork products. Initially, he pointed to our daughter and added that the decision really did not make him feel more connected to Judaism. I then asked him whether, given the then-impending arrival of his first child, he felt anything positive about his decision in the context of being a parent. He thought about this for a moment, and somewhat to my surprise, he acknowledged that he does see a benefit to his son growing up being conscious of this aspect of the tradition.

Many people in the Orthodox community see the first steps of *kashrut* as ideally the beginning of a pathway to full observance. I understand, and respect, that climbing up the ladder of observance is a key goal for the Orthodox community and this goal informs the way their religious leaders approach *kiruv*, outreach.

But full observance of *kashrut* specifically, as well as Jewish law in general, is just not a realistic goal for the majority of liberal Jews. It is more realistic to contemplate a pattern of practice that will enhance consciousness of Jewish tradition in order to maximize the ability to preserve and transmit. This approach emphasizes acquiring knowledge, showing respect, and engaging in some degree of practice. In other words, *kashrut* will never be an all or nothing proposition for most liberal Jews. It will entail picking and choosing—and choices being made often for reasons other than the desire to observe Jewish tradition. As is true of nearly all aspects concerning transmitting Jewish tradition, children understand and respond well to consistent choices that are identified clearly and framed positively.

Also, although consistency of practice is important, the process of developing one's personal *kashrut* practice should not be seen as a linear one. When contemplating one's *kashrut* journey, especially at the outset, it is helpful to think in terms of taking it one day at a time and not thinking too far ahead. People should not be afraid to try some measures of observance, even if they find that they cannot sustain them in the long term.

And sometimes practices that cannot be sustained at one point in time become easier later on. Many years ago, I began avoiding eating dairy or pareve foods that had been cooked in nonkosher pots. There is a technical justification for this practice according to *halakhah* that is based on absorption of particles during the heating process. This is a pretty limiting practice when eating in nonkosher restaurants, and for that reason, I started and stopped this practice several times over the years. Although I have managed to adhere to this standard for more than seven years at this point, I will on occasion allow myself a bit more leniency, especially when I am out of town for a prolonged time with little strictly kosher food available.

There is a compatible philosophy called MOOSHY that some Jews have adopted in connection with reducing their consumption of meat. This stands for Meat Only on *Shabbat*, Happy Occasions, and *Yom Tov* (designated holy days in the Jewish calendar).[70] MOOSHY taps into the concept that people can limit the amount of meat they consume, and mark whatever consumption occurs with special occasions. Of course this philosophy can be applied to the consumption of either kosher or nonkosher meat. The idea underlying MOOSHY is very helpful for those contemplating their personal *kashrut* journeys because it allows people to avoid thinking about a complete elimination of beloved foods.

Despite the importance of consistency, situational departures from our normative *kashrut* practices can be beneficial by renewing, and reinforcing, our commitment. Rabbi Mary Zamore, the editor of *The Sacred Table*, provided an interesting example in her own essay. Zamore's husband is a Jew by choice. She wrote about the process of education and compromise in connection with visits to his parents' home in Norway. Although her husband's parents are very supportive of their *kashrut* practices, kosher meat in Norway is not readily available. So only when dining in the home of her in-laws will they eat cuts of meat that are intrinsically kosher but that come from animals that have not been slaughtered in accord with Jewish law. This compromise also embodies a mindful choice reflecting their commitment to Jewish tradition.[71] Elsewhere in the volume, she wrote that sometimes she feels her Judaism even more when she is not in her own home as she pauses to scan a menu in search of choices that will support her *kashrut*. For Zamore, "pausing to think" before eating "is part of the exercise of keeping kosher."[72]

Similarly, my current *kashrut* practices require me to constantly compromise between the level of stringency I believe is appropriate for me personally, and what is practical for me as a member of my family and the Jewish community. The mindfulness that Zamore describes is something that is with me daily, and at a certain level, I too feel it enhances my overall commitment.

At the conclusion of his award-winning book *Kosher USA*, Roger Horowitz pens a fitting tribute to *kashrut*: "Kosher food, its triumphs and its limitations, our decision to observe or not, forces Jews to remember that even if we feel rived by differences, we remain connected, bound together by a history that we have never fully controlled and that we have managed as best we could, often magnificently." In his epilogue, Horowitz notes that throughout the many interviews he conducted as part of his research, he always presented himself as "a Jew for whom history and family defines" his Judaism. As an example, he notes that he only wore a *kippah* (head covering) if he entered the home of an Orthodox person, "out of respect for their beliefs."[73]

I suspect that many, if not most, liberal Jews would readily identify with Roger Horowitz's sensibilities. Kosher food is very much a part of the history and tradition of the Jewish people. Regardless of how widely Jews observe the entirety of the system of *kashrut*, it has a well-earned place in Jewish tradition. For this reason alone, Jews who care about transmitting Jewish tradition must grapple with the existence of *kashrut* and with the questions of whether and how a remixed approach to this aspect of the tradition might align with their Jewish journeys.

3

MARRIAGE AND FAMILY

If a man is newly married, he shall not join the army nor is he to be pestered at home; he shall be left free of all obligations for one year to cheer the wife he has taken.

—Deuteronomy 24:5

The institution of marriage is the foundation upon which Jewish tradition is built. A significant amount of Jewish law is concerned with the marital relationship, including the details governing sexuality. Indeed, historically, much of Jewish culture has been shaped by the norms of marriage and family life. In this respect, Judaism is not different from other major religious traditions that place spouses, specifically heterosexual couples, and children at the center of family life. Although Judaism has developed a rich legal and cultural tradition surrounding marriage that is particular to Jewish tradition, the types of challenges facing the Jewish family today are not unique to the Jewish religion.

That said, one thing that distinguishes Judaism from other major religious traditions is the comparatively small number of Jews throughout the world, including in the United States, where the largest Jewish population outside of Israel lives. For people who live in major cities such as New York, Chicago, and Los Angeles, it is easy to lose sight of this reality. But according to the comprehensive 2013 Pew Report of the American Jewish community, less than 2 percent of adults in the United States said they are Jewish by religion.[1] Given these demographics, and the overall increasingly negative attitudes in American society concerning marriage, family, and religious tradition generally, those who care about the perpetuation of Jewish tradition have reason for concern.

According to Jewish law, *halakhah*, Jewish marriage can only exist between a man and a woman, who are both considered legally Jewish (defined as born to a Jewish mother or having converted according to the legal requirements). As a result, the traditional position on Jewish marriage excludes gay and interfaith marriages. Yet, there is ample evidence that it is possible for parents who do not fit a traditional marriage mold to transmit Jewish tradition to their progeny. These parents include those who are gay, married to non-Jews, single, divorced, or who co-parent but choose to live together without a formal marriage ceremony. Conversely, experience teaches that Jews who do fit the traditional mold can still fail to instill a love of Jewish tradition in their children.

In the United States, the difficulties facing parents who do not fit the traditional mold are not all that different from the ones encountered by families that are made up of married, heterosexual parents who are Jewish according to *halakhah* but are not seriously observant. Transmission of Jewish tradition is especially challenging today because most American Jews believe that Judaism is about layers of personal choice and that Jewish identity represents only one of many aspects of self-identity. In this environment, people need a reason to choose to be Jewish, regardless of whether they or their partners are Jewish according to *halakhah*. Also, people must make this choice in a world of strong "others" that compete for their time, energy, and loyalty.

THE LAW, NORMS, AND GOALS OF JEWISH MARRIAGE

Marriage is a social construction and so it is expected that cultural norms will heavily influence the rules of the game concerning marriage within any particular group, including that of a religious tradition. When it comes to Jewish marriage, the laws and customs reflect a combination of social influences—especially perceptions about women, common in ancient patriarchal societies as well as the medieval and pre-modern periods. As is true for nearly all Jewish laws and traditions, the various geographic majority cultures in which the Jews have lived have also influenced the development of Jewish marriage.

One interesting example of how external cultural factors have influenced the law on Jewish marriage concerns polygyny, the most common and accepted form of polygamy, in which men have more than one wife. Under both Torah and Talmudic law, a man could have more than one wife but the ability to have multiple partners was not a two-way street. Jewish marriage has always considered a married woman to be exclusive for her husband and therefore off-limits sexually to any other man. Although virtually none of the rabbis named in the Talmud are explicitly mentioned as having engaged in polygyny, it was still legally permissible.

In contrast, Christianity prohibited polygyny and this reality impacted Jews living in Christian Europe in the Middle Ages. Ultimately, the medieval Ashkenazi authority Rabbenu Gershom issued a formal ban on polygyny, but his ruling only governed Ashkenazi Jews living among a Christian majority. Sephardic Jews living in Islamic countries where polygyny was practiced by the majority culture rejected this ruling, although the practice of having multiple wives still was not common even among these Jews. Interestingly, the State of Israel banned polygyny, but it allowed those Jews who arrived in Israel with more than one wife to keep them.[2]

The perspective of Jewish marriage that was prevalent in Biblical, Talmudic and pre-modern times may be difficult for many people to reconcile with our modern sensibilities, particularly in matters pertaining to women. The earliest codifications of Jewish law dating back to the first few centuries of the Common Era speak of a woman being "acquired."[3] Although the rabbis never intended that the acquisition of a wife be similar to the purchase of conventional property, we cannot escape the reality that this early conception of marriage was steeped in a set of cultural norms that are largely inapplicable to twenty-first-century Americans. When Jewish marriage is considered as a whole, both historically and even today in some communities, it is hard to escape the patriarchal roots of the Jewish tradition.

That said, there are some fascinating ways in which Judaism's historical view of marriage and women is surprisingly modern. For example, the tradition is very concerned that husbands pay close attention to the sexual needs of their wives, as demonstrated by the Torah's explicit statement that a groom should be exempt from the important work of defending the community for the first year of marriage so that he can rejoice with his wife. Also, Jewish law carefully regulates a man's sexual responsibilities to his wife in terms of both frequency and quality.

The tradition's regard for women's feelings is also particularly evident in the laws that require a woman's consent to a marriage. In what is perhaps the greatest love story in the Torah, the narrative concerning the patriarch Isaac and his wife Rebekah, the text explicitly states that Rebekah was asked for, and gave, her consent to be Isaac's wife.[4] Although the Mishnah, the earliest Jewish law code produced around 200 CE, does not require a woman's consent to marriage, later sources of the Talmudic era clearly do. The Babylonian Talmud contains a colorful narrative illustrating that flirtatious banter initiated by a woman in a public space, intensified by the man with an offer of betrothal that culminates in the woman's evading the proposal, does not constitute a woman's consent to a marriage proposal:

> A man was selling strings of beads. A woman came by and said to him, "Give me one strand." He said to her, "If I give it to you, will you marry me?" She said, "Give, give." Said Rabbi Hama: A statement like "give, give" has no legal validity.

> A man was drinking beer in a store. A woman came in and said to him, "Give me a drink." He said, "If I do so, will you marry me?" She said, "Give me a drink." Said Rabbi Hama, a statement like "give me a drink" has no legal validity.

> A man was throwing dates from a palm tree. A woman came by and said, "Throw me two dates." He said to her, "If I do so, will you marry me?" She said, "Throw, throw." Said Rabbi Zevid: A statement like "throw, throw" has no legal validity. (Qiddushin 9a, Babylonian Talmud)

According to Professor Judith Hauptman, these passages are "about as contemporary as a Talmudic anecdote can get." They show an enlightened perspective for this period and even more so in our day and age when the concept of "consent" in sexual encounters is so heavily contested. Some passages in the Talmud actually go even further than simply requiring a woman's consent for marriage by discussing women actually initiating marriage.[5]

We can learn much about the Jewish tradition's view of marriage by examining more closely how the tradition historically views the purposes of marriage. These purposes include companionship, economic protection for women, regulation of sexual activity, and procreation.

Companionship

> It is not good for man to be alone.
>
> —Genesis 2:18

With these words, the Torah explicitly recognizes the fundamental truth that human companionship is a necessity. The importance of companionship as a fundamental goal of Jewish marriage is illustrated by two of the seven blessings of the marriage ceremony that are recited under the *chuppah*, the wedding canopy. These blessings speak of the bride and groom as friends and companions. Interestingly, these blessings stress companionship but not procreation since they must be applicable to every married couple, rather than only those who are able to procreate.[6]

Economic Protection for Women

At my law school, I have taught a course called Family Law and Jewish Tradition, which covers many aspects of Jewish marriage and divorce. Molly, a former student with whom I keep in touch, is a staunch Catholic but was drawn to this course in light of her love of learning about religious tradition. After her graduation, Molly attended the wedding of a close Jewish friend and wrote to me immediately afterward about the ceremony. She was particularly struck by the following commentary the rabbi gave before reading from the *ketubah*, the Jewish marriage contract: "Before women's marches, before the glass ceiling, before women's suffrage, the Jewish people first believed in women's rights and the *ketubah* is evidence of that." Molly chuckled as she heard these words, remembering our class discussion about the origins and purpose of the *ketubah*.

Although it is possible that some type of marriage contract was used in biblical times,[7] the rabbis devised the *ketubah* during the early centuries of the Common Era to protect women in the event of unwanted

divorce or their spouse's death. According to Hauptman, during this
time marriage evolved into "a kind of 'social contract' entered into by a
man and a woman, albeit with him dominant and her subordinate." As a
result of this contract, women acquired a wide range of rights and
protections that were, in the Talmudic era, really quite remarkable. For
example, the *ketubah* explicitly provided women with a monetary sum
in the event that the marriage was terminated by divorce or the husband's death. According to Hauptman, these benefits afforded women
as well as their children the equivalent of "a complete insurance policy."
Should a woman predecease her husband, her sons inherited her *ketubah* money. Should a woman outlive her husband, both she and her
unmarried daughters were entitled to be maintained from the husband's estate.[8]

As discussed in the book's introduction, the legal protections furnished in the *ketubah* are largely irrelevant today. During medieval
times, Rabbenu Gershom issued a ruling that in effect prohibited a
husband from divorcing his wife without her consent. As a result, the
legal need for the use of a *ketubah* was substantially reduced because a
woman in this position could withhold her consent until she received a
satisfactory financial settlement. By that time, however, the *ketubah*
had become such a fixture in Jewish marriage that its continued use was
assured.[9]

This attraction for the *ketubah* still prevails given its cultural significance as a symbol of Jewish marriage, but in recent decades its use, and
the concept of Jewish marriage more generally, has also been chal-
lenged in some quarters on the grounds of sexism. The basis for this
view is that according to Jewish law, the man must be the one to dissolve the marriage by providing the woman with a *get*, a Jewish writ of
divorce. Without this formal document of dissolution, remarriage in a
Jewish ceremony is prohibited.

In light of the many women throughout the ages who have been
trapped in their marriages as a result of this aspect of Jewish law, some
modern rabbis question the continued use of the *ketubah*. They advocate instead documents such as *shtar*, essentially a Lovers' Covenant,
that allow for a completely egalitarian type of marriage and divorce. But
the Conservative and Reform movements have found other ways of
sidestepping the problematic issues generated by the tradition's requirement of the *get*. By and large, Reform rabbis will remarry individ-

uals without a *get*.[10] The Conservative movement instead recommends the insertion of language in a *ketubah* that levels the playing field by allowing either partner to summon the other to a Jewish court of law so that going forward "each will be able to live according to the laws of the Torah."[11]

But strong anecdotal evidence suggests that as a practical matter, the sexist origins of Jewish marriage are overlooked, or even unknown, to many couples. According to Rabbi Vernon Kurtz, a Conservative rabbi who has performed hundreds of marriages over the course of a forty-year career, couples typically do not focus on the meaning of the Aramaic text or history of the *ketubah*. Many couples enjoy writing their own English versions, or finding meaningful English texts, that can be printed on the document and read during the marriage ceremony. Most couples also spend time and energy on the artistry of the physical document because they plan to hang it in their homes as artwork. These types of activities related to the *ketubah* illustrate how remix operates to imbue tradition with an ongoing relevance and personalized meaning.

These modern developments in the culture of Jewish marriage have facilitated the enduring popularity of the *ketubah*, both as a symbol of Jewish marriage and as a tradition enormously capable of personal attribution. As a result, it has become popular even for intermarried and same-sex couples to have a *ketubah* as an element of their formal marriage ceremony, even though its use is not valid according to Jewish law unless both the bride and groom are Jewish. The popularity of the *ketubah* is affirmed with just a quick look at the ketubah.com website, which offers numerous categories of the document, including ones specific for the major Jewish denominations as well as for interfaith, same-sex, and secular humanist ceremonies.

Regulation of Sexual Activity

One of the most interesting purposes of Jewish marriage is to properly direct male sexual impulses *and* to ensure adequate sexual satisfaction for women. When I covered this material in my Family Law and Jewish Tradition class, virtually all of my students were pleasantly surprised by how solicitous the Talmudic sages were with respect to women's sexual needs. This topic illustrates the positive ways in which Jewish tradition has embraced female personhood from a very early period.

Not surprisingly, Jewish tradition sees male sexual desire as a threat to the family and society in general, and therefore as something that must be appropriately channeled. The Talmud contains a passage illustrating this point: "A man who has reached the age of twenty years and has not yet married a wife spends all his days in sin. In sin? Do not actually think so, but rather say [he spends all his days] in thoughts of sin" (Qiddushin 29b, Babylonian Talmud).

The rabbis believed that although women desired sex as much as men, their modest and internal nature generally precluded them from directly asking to have their needs met. As a result of these interesting dual perceptions, the rabbis structured Jewish law so that men are *commanded* to satisfy their wives sexually (an obligation known as *onah*),[12] and also to procreate. In other words, the rabbis fashioned the law so that it would link the man's need for sex to the two distinct commands of sexually satisfying the wife and procreating.

We get a wonderful sense of the specificity of Jewish tradition on the topic of mandated sex in the following Talmudic passage: "The times for conjugal duty prescribed in the Torah are: for men of independence, every day; for laborers, twice a week; for ass drivers, once a week; for camel drivers, once in thirty days; for sailors, once in six months" (Ketubbot 61b, Babylonian Talmud).

I have spoken about this subject at several synagogues over the years and have encountered more than a few women who commented that their husbands must be camel drivers or sailors! The Talmud also provides that Torah students are obligated to satisfy their wives once a week, preferably on Friday night, the eve of the Sabbath. It cannot be denied that this attention to women's needs and sensitivities is rather astonishing for the rabbis of this era.

Consider how the rabbis not only felt it necessary to prescribe specific quantities of sex for married couples, but also to vary the quantity according to the husband's occupation. Undoubtedly, the rabbis provided an adjustable timetable because it was understood by both men and women that a husband's occupation would impact the amount of time and freedom he had to satisfy his wife. Thus, the Talmud contains the following colorful statement in commenting on the men of independent means who must satisfy their wives every day: "They are like the decadent residents of Eretz Yisrael [the land of Israel] who wallow in food and drink and are therefore robust and have great strength for sex" (Ketubbot 62a, Babylonian Talmud).[13]

The Talmud also contains diverse views on whether the required times for sexual activity represent a minimum or a maximum.[14] This diversity of opinion continued throughout the centuries.[15] In a series of *responsa*, legal opinions, written between 1959 and 1985, Rabbi Moshe Feinstein, regarded by many Orthodox Jews as the leading legal authority of his time, ruled that the once-a-week Talmudic requirement for scholars should be changed to twice a week to accommodate the reality of increased female desire given the current social climate.[16]

Despite the rabbis' characteristic male voice, they were remarkably sensitive to women's sexual needs and approving of appropriate sexual activity. According to Jewish tradition, sex is not dirty or sinful when properly channeled. Rather, sex is seen as an expression of human intimacy and love. Consider the following passage by the renowned medieval Talmudic commentator Rashi:

> Rabbi Hisda said to his daughters—When your husband caresses you to arouse the desire for intercourse and holds the breasts with one hand and that place with the other, give him the breasts [at first] to increase his passion and do not give him the place of intercourse too soon, until his passion increases and he is in pain with desire. Then give him [the genitals]. (Rashi on Shabbat 140b)

In this passage, Rashi is interpreting advice given by Rabbi Hisda to his daughters, which appears in the Talmud as a "lesson in prolonging foreplay."[17] Between husbands and wives, sexual enjoyment is not only acceptable but also encouraged, as long as it does not include the male wasting semen, a clearly prohibited activity.[18]

Jewish law also forbids a man from raping his wife. The Talmud teaches that "a man is forbidden to compel his wife to the *mitzvah* (commandment) of *onah*."[19] In other words, a man cannot force his wife to have sex. Subsequent authorities also embraced this prohibition. In fact, the entire issue of "consent" in Jewish tradition is extremely progressive—not only for its time, but even by today's standards. According to the Jerusalem Talmud, coerced sex constitutes rape even if the woman came to enjoy it eventually:

> A woman once came to Rabbi Yohanan and said to him: "I have been
> raped." He said to her: "And didn't you enjoy it by the end?" She said
> to him: "And if a man dipped his finger in honey and stuck it in your
> mouth on Yom Kippur (a fast day), is it not bad for you yet enjoyable
> by the end?" He accepted her. (Sotah 4:4, Jerusalem Talmud)

In our day, the definition of consent has become extremely contested,
particularly with respect to the legal meaning of passive consent. Yet,
nearly two thousand years ago, the rabbis seemed to have had a very
clear notion of when consent is lacking.

Another significant way in which Jewish law regulates sexual activity
between spouses is through the laws of family purity. These laws are
complex, but they essentially forbid sexual relations during the time of a
woman's menstruation and for up to a week after the conclusion of her
period. Afterward, a woman must immerse herself in a *mikveh* (ritual
bath) before resuming sexual relations with her husband. Given the
operation of these laws, the couple's return to sexual activity normally
coincides with ovulation, and therefore favors the chances of conception.[20]

Although I know a small number of non-Orthodox women who observe the family purity laws on a regular basis, for the most part they are
of practical relevance to Orthodox Jews. The *mikveh*, apart from its use
in connection with the family purity laws, is significant because both
men and women are required to immerse upon conversion to Judaism.
But in recent years, a renewed interest in the *mikveh* has surfaced
among a wider spectrum of Jews. These individuals are not necessarily
interested in observing family purity laws but rather are attracted to
ritual immersion to mark a variety of milestones such as divorce, being
cured of a serious illness, or even transitioning to a different gender.[21]

Mayyim Hayyim, a *mikveh* that opened in a suburb of Boston in
2004, is the prototype establishment for those who seek to use the
mikveh for various types of spiritual renewal. From the beginning, the
staff sought the help of both artists and medical professionals to create a
space where significant life changes could be aligned with the process
of immersion. Aliza Kline, the first executive director of Mayyim
Hayyim, captured the imaginative possibilities for *mikveh* use when she
stated, "*Mikveh* is our model, but it's a paradigm for helping people find
meaning in a ritual they haven't felt is theirs."[22] The extension of the

traditional use of the *mikveh* to mark a symbolic personal milestone for individuals illustrates yet another meaningful example of remix.

Procreation

> Be fertile and increase, fill the earth.
>
> —Genesis 1:28

According to the Torah, the command to "fill the earth" was given by God to the first male and female, Adam and Eve, but they were not Jewish. Marriage as a prelude to children has been the historic norm in many cultures, despite recent indications that an increasing number of people in the United States are electing to have children outside of marriage.[23] As discussed, according to Jewish law, Jewish men (not women) are obligated to procreate. The reason for making this command incumbent upon men rather than women may be based on the rabbis' probable assumption during Talmudic times that women have an innate desire to have children, and therefore do not need to be commanded to procreate.[24]

Readers may wonder how men are supposed to fulfill their obligation to procreate if, as a couple, they are unable to have children. The Talmud does contain a discussion that requires a man to divorce his wife if they have remained without children for ten years.[25] Not surprisingly, however, this was not generally enforced if the couple wished to stay married. I know a number of Orthodox couples that have been married for many years even though they were unable to have children.

The topic of procreation as a goal of Jewish marriage leads directly into an area that is a main focus within the American Jewish world today—the escalating rate of intermarriage among non-Orthodox Jews. Procreation is important to Jewish marriage for the same reason it is important to other religious traditions—the continuity of the tradition. Because an increasing number of children are being born to couples where one parent is not Jewish, and there are relatively low birthrates among the Jewish population outside of Orthodoxy,[26] a burgeoning discussion in the American Jewish world is taking place about how these developments will impact the future of American Judaism.

ADDRESSING THE IMPACT OF INTERMARRIAGE

Before 1970, only 17 percent of individuals in the American Jewish community who married chose to marry non-Jews. According to the 2013 Pew Report of the American Jewish Community, this percentage climbed steadily during the last three decades of the twentieth century, reaching 58 percent of individuals who married in 2000 or beyond. It is hard to predict whether this trend is leveling out or will continue to rise. Significantly, Pew also found that among non-Orthodox Jews who married between 2000 and 2013, 71 percent are intermarried.[27]

More recent sociological studies reveal that extremely large numbers of non-Orthodox Jews are unmarried, intermarried, childless, and/or not raising their children as "Jewish-by-religion." A 2017 sociological study about Jewish continuity published by the Jewish People Policy Institute (JPPI) found that among American Jews between the ages of twenty-five and fifty-four who are not ultra-Orthodox, about half are unmarried, and only 21 percent have a Jewish spouse or partner. Further, only 39 percent of these 25–54-year-olds have children at home, and only 19 percent have children at home who are being raised in the Jewish religion.[28]

Of course, the tendencies to refrain from marriage and marry at a later age are also reflected in the broader American society. Relying on Census Bureau information from 2014, the authors of the casebook I use for my general Family Law class observe that the structure of the American family "has changed dramatically over the past century as individuals live longer, marry at a later age (if at all), have fewer children, and, more than in the past, separate marriage and parenthood."[29]

According to Jewish law, children have the religious status of their mother rather than their father. This position is known as the matrilineal principle and it first appears in the Mishnah. A simple explanation for the adoption of the matrilineal principle by the sages is that it was always possible to identify the mother, unlike the father. Even so, based on his exhaustive research, Professor Shaye Cohen concluded the existence of the matrilineal principle is likely the result of a variety of rabbinic motives.[30]

The matrilineal principle remained unchallenged until 1983, when the Reform movement adopted the Patrilineal Resolution, providing that all children of mixed marriages are presumed to be Jewish as long as they publicly manifest a positive and exclusive Jewish identity. This resolution, which governs only North American Reform Jews, changed the "who is a Jew" criteria for all children of mixed marriages. First, it allows children with Jewish fathers but not Jewish mothers to be considered Jewish if they are raised with a positive, exclusive Jewish identity. Second, this ruling requires children with Jewish mothers, who have historically been considered Jewish just by virtue of the circumstances of their birth, to also display a positive and exclusive Jewish identity in order to be considered Jewish.

Reform's Patrilineal Resolution was controversial at the outset and remains so to this day among some Jews. It continues to create complexities not only for some Jews in the United States, but also in Israel where Jews face a distinct set of political issues surrounding the topics of citizenship, membership in the Jewish people, and conversion.[31] Regardless, Reform's policy is strongly entrenched.

The oldest children born after the adoption of the Patrilineal Resolution are now well into their thirties. Studies provide ample evidence that millennials who grew up with intermarried parents show an increased tendency to be raised and to identify as Jewish,[32] and the positive results that can be achieved with educational experiences geared to college-age youth. For example, *Millennial Children of Intermarriage*, a 2015 study sponsored by the Cohen Center for Modern Jewish Studies at Brandeis University, demonstrates that Jewish college experiences such as participation in Birthright Israel trips and Jewish groups based on campus have a profound impact on the Jewish observance and identity of millennials raised in homes with intermarried parents.[33] Another study by the Cohen Center published in 2016 shows that intermarried couples wed solely by a Jewish clergy officiant are more highly engaged than other intermarried couples, more likely to join a synagogue, and based on early data concerning childrearing, significantly more likely to raise their children as Jewish.[34] These studies provide support for pushing back on the negatives of intermarriage and focusing instead on the opportunities that can be gained with appropriate support and policy initiatives.

But these studies, and others, also clearly demonstrate that intermarried families, by and large, are less ritualistically observant and less Jewishly engaged than families whose parents are in-married. Children of intermarriage have a smaller range of Jewish experiences—such as formal Jewish education, Jewish camp, and celebration of Jewish holidays—than children of in-married couples. Similarly, compared to in-married couples, even intermarried couples married by a sole Jewish officiant are less likely to raise children as Jewish by religion, select a Jewish preschool, have a special meal on Shabbat, attribute importance to keeping kosher, discuss Israel and Judaism with friends and family, and donate to Jewish or Israeli causes.[35]

The 2013 Pew Report also provides evidence of the disparities between in-married and intermarried couples. It shows that whereas 96 percent of in-married Jews are raising their children as Jewish by religion, this is true for only 20 percent of intermarried Jews. Instead, intermarried Jews are more likely to be raising children as partially Jewish (25 percent), Jewish but "not by religion" (16 percent), or not Jewish (37 percent). The Pew Report also shows that there is a strong tendency for children with intermarried parents to also marry a non-Jew.[36]

The 2017 JPPI study, which represents a secondary analysis of the earlier Pew data, also shows that there are profound differences between those parents raising their children Jewish by religion and those who are not. These differences include not only ones related to ritual observance but also to matters such as membership in Jewish organizations, giving to Jewish charity, and adoption of cultural non-Jewish symbols such as a Christmas tree in the home.[37]

Sociologists, commentators, and clergy may disagree about the necessary measures to be taken by those involved in setting policy agendas for non-Orthodox American Jews.[38] One thing that does not engender disagreement, however, is that intermarriage is a permanent reality for the American Jewish community. But the salient issue for all families who are concerned—even to some extent—with transmitting Jewish tradition is how to organize their lives so that they can create a thicker Jewish culture that provides sufficient space to create a meaningfully positive Jewish identity. As one of my good friends remarked shortly after our first child was born: the days are long but the years go by quickly. This succinct bit of wisdom, though not made in the context of assisting with transmission of Jewish tradition, is also relevant to this issue. For the majority of non-Orthodox Jews, the parental choices relevant to creating this space are made in competition with many other demands on their time and energies. Although the days may be long, there is usually not enough time in the day for parents to meet the demands of childrearing, homemaking, and work.

Yet, the years go by quickly. Parents who may theoretically care about transmitting Jewish tradition may not always find themselves in a position—with respect to time, money and even interest—to take certain steps that are important to achieving this goal. It is easy for religious education to take a back seat to public school and even sports. Carving out time for Jewish holidays, let alone adult Jewish learning, usually is not the top priority in our fast-paced world.

These realities confront all parents, not just those who are intermarried. In many cases, the differences between in-married non-Orthodox families and intermarried families are more about *the degree* to which outside influences crowd out the time and space for Jewish tradition rather than the existence of multiple priorities. All too often I hear stories of two Jewish parents who resent that their children have rejected their Jewish roots, and even intermarried, even though they themselves did not seem to care all that much about perpetuating Jewish tradition while raising their children.

Novelist Jessica Grose appeared on the "Have Yourself an Unorthodox Little Christmas" episode of the *Tablet Magazine* podcast *Unorthodox* in December 2016 to discuss why it is okay for Jews to have Christmas trees.[39] For me, the most interesting aspects of the conversation centered on why and how transmitting Jewish tradition had become a critical issue for her. Grose, who is married to a non-Jew and is the mother of two young daughters, is part of that group that is raising their children as "both." But because her two daughters look so much like her husband, she now feels more pressure to "prove their Jewish blood!" In other words, more so than previously, Grose is confronting, front and center, how to figure out her daughters' Jewish identities as well as her own.

The hosts of the *Unorthodox* podcast remarked to Grose that perhaps she would not even be facing a Jewish identity crisis at this point in her life had she married an ordinary, assimilated Jew. Their general point was that, in her case, marrying a non-Jew might actually have caused her to think through what Judaism means to her at an earlier point in her marriage. Of course her story is pretty typical to the extent that parents often feel differently about religion once they have children, regardless of whether they are in-married or intermarried.[40]

At the outset of a courtship and marriage, taking the time and putting in the effort to contemplate the relative importance of transmitting Jewish tradition is a productive exercise of self-reflection for *every* couple. Those parents who attempt to think through not only whether but also *why* Jewish tradition matters are likely to come up with meaningful answers sooner rather than later. This exercise is important for all Jewish parents, regardless of whether or not they are married to someone from a different religious, cultural tradition. Interestingly, when I followed up with Grose by e-mail after listening to the podcast, she mentioned to me that, for the first time in her adult life, she remembered to light Chanukah candles seven out of the eight nights.

But in thinking about transmission of Jewish tradition specifically in the context of intermarriage, there are two important points that call for candid discussion and reflection. First, not all intermarriages can be lumped together. Each situation is unique. Second, most marriages between a Jew and a non-Jew are not really "interfaith" marriages. Rather, they are intercultural marriages, and Jewish tradition clearly represents the minority culture in the United States.

Intermarriage Is Not a One-Size-Fits-All Proposition

When I co-founded a center for Jewish law and Judaic Studies at my university, one of my primary goals was to bring together Jews from a variety of denominations and backgrounds for programming that would be of mutual interest. One year, we sponsored a program on intermarriage.

One of our speakers was a Reform rabbi who really drove home the point that we cannot equate all intermarriage when it comes to the question of whether intermarriage hinders transmission of Jewish tradition. In her experience, those couples who sought out a member of the Jewish clergy to officiate, and who went through a period of counseling with their rabbi, have a much higher success rate with transmission than intermarried couples who chose different options to celebrate their wedding.

Of course it would make sense that Jews who are marrying outside the religion but still seeking a rabbi to officiate at their wedding would care more about raising their children with some tradition than Jews who intermarry under other circumstances. To be sure, there are many families where the non-Jewish spouse provides support—sometimes even more support than the Jewish spouse—by taking the children to Hebrew school and helping in other ways to facilitate a home environment that is friendly to Jewish tradition. These committed non-Jewish spouses are actively involved in raising their children as Jewish even if they themselves do not convert.[41] In other cases, the non-Jewish partner does not present barriers to raising the children as Jewish but is not an active participant.

When it comes to intermarried couples committed to raising their children as Jewish, there is considerable, and growing, support among the non-Orthodox movements for greater inclusion. Recall that Reform's Patrilineal Resolution embraced this perspective as early as 1983. Conservative rabbis are prohibited from performing intermarriages but in 2018, the movement's Committee on Jewish Law and Standards determined that its rabbis are allowed to attend interfaith weddings. In addition, several years ago its rabbinic leadership created and publicized a nonmarital ritual ceremony for interfaith couples pledging to create an exclusively Jewish home and raise their future children as Jews.[42] This ceremony, called *Hanukkat Habayit*, is designed to take place in the couple's home and involves reciting some prayers in Hebrew and English and an address by the rabbi to the couple and their guests emphasizing their pledge to create a Jewish home together. The core element involves placing a *mezuzah*, the quintessential sign of a Jewish home, on the doorpost of their home. In early March 2017, the Conservative movement went even further in extending a welcoming hand to intermarried couples. The United Synagogue of Conservative Judaism, the organization governing the movement's synagogues, overwhelmingly approved a new standard allowing individual synagogues to grant membership to non-Jews.

Around the same time, a prominent unaffiliated New York synagogue, some of whose clergy were ordained in the Conservative movement, announced its new policy of performing intermarriages as long as the couples commit to creating a Jewish home and raising their children as Jewish. The synagogue also emphasized that it would be continuing to uphold the matrilineal definition of Jewish identity, so that children with non-Jewish mothers will have to immerse in a *mikveh* and officially convert.[43] Around the same time, Rabbi Amichai Lau-Lavie, ordained as a Conservative rabbi, publicized his carefully considered decision that he would begin to officiate at interfaith weddings only for couples interested in creating Jewish homes and raising Jewish children.[44] A rabbi I know who was ordained in the Conservative movement adopted a similar policy several years before these developments and told me his purpose was "to save the next generation."

Although this level of inclusion is virtually nonexistent in Orthodox circles, Rabbi Avram Mlotek, ordained at the most liberal Orthodox seminary, Yeshivat Chovevei Torah, has suggested "it's time we revisit our tribalistic approach toward intermarriage and our highly divisive conversion practices."[45] Although he did not clearly spell out the practical meaning of his words, he suggested that both Orthodox and Conservative communities should be more welcoming toward intermarried couples. In response, Chovevei Torah took the opportunity to clarify that intermarriage is prohibited and poses a "grave danger" to Jewish continuity.[46]

At the same time, recall that according to Pew, 37 percent of intermarried Jews are not raising their children as Jewish at all. Undoubtedly some of these Jews are raising their children exclusively within a different religious faith. The childrearing patterns of these intermarried couples present a stark contrast to those who pledge to create Jewish homes and raise their children as Jewish.

There are also intermarried families in the middle of the spectrum who are claiming to raise their children with exposure to the religious traditions of both parents. Susan Katz Miller, an author and consultant on interfaith family issues, offered her perspective on what these couples want from rabbis and other community leaders. Miller writes that they want their rabbis to help them "forge bonds of affection for Judaism in our children," and celebrate their life cycle events, including co-officiating at life cycle ceremonies.[47] They also want Jewish institutions "to educate our interfaith children, whether or not we are raising them in monofaith households." Similarly, Edmund Case, the founder of InterfaithFamily, urges liberal Jewish movements to embrace a "truly audacious" level of hospitality for interfaith families who want to "do both" when it comes to raising children.[48]

I suspect the group that wants to "do both" presents the most complexity for clergy and professionals in the Jewish community. Those intermarried couples not interested in raising their children as Jewish in any way are likely off the radar screen completely. In contrast, it is relatively easy for many progressive Jewish communities to be warm and welcoming to intermarried families who are pledging to raise their children with an exclusive Jewish identity. But sharing religions is seen as a completely different matter, and one that many Jewish professionals are far less likely to support.

Is this distinction justified? For Jewish professionals and others who see Judaism as either a religion, or as both a religion and a culture, it is clearly understandable why raising children in more than one faith is troublesome. The reality, however, is that the majority of Jews see being Jewish as a matter of ancestry or culture.[49] When these Jews marry people from other religions with distinct cultural traditions, they often find it more natural and comfortable to raise their children with both.

Most Mixed Marriages Are "Intercultural," Not Interfaith

We usually hear about interfaith marriages, especially in the popular media, during the time intermarried couples face the "December dilemma." The typical discussion centers on how to craft a meaningful family celebration of both Christmas and Chanukah. This discourse is largely about the cultural trappings of both Christianity and Judaism at this time of the year. Rarely, however, do we hear about how intermarried couples seek to bridge theological differences. One must wonder whether this is because in most cases, there are no theological differences to bridge for most couples who intermarry.

Raising children in an intermarried home where the parents have strong theological differences is likely to be a huge challenge. As any parent knows, it is always best when parents give their children consistent messages. Probably for this reason, it is not uncommon for clergy of different faiths to recommend to couples contemplating intermarriage that they pick one religious theology for the home.[50]

In general, though, I suspect most couples from different religious backgrounds are not likely to have distinct faith-based or theological beliefs. The majority of intermarried couples are more likely to share different religious, cultural traditions. For this reason, the term "interfaith" marriage is really not descriptive of their reality. These marriages really are, from a religious standpoint, "intercultural." To be clear, I would not use the term "intercultural marriage" to refer to couples where one spouse is raised Jewish and the other is a Jew by choice, the term used for people who have converted to Judaism (even if the Jew by choice is from a distinct religious or ethnic background).

In this country, the majority of intercultural marriages involving Jews will involve another person who was either raised Christian, or raised in a secular home where cultural traditions associated with Christianity were celebrated. This reality has tremendous implications when it comes to couples in intercultural marriages seeking to transmit Jewish tradition.

The United States is a Christian culture. Even in geographic areas with large Jewish populations, Jewish Americans are not naturally exposed to the rhythm of Jewish life on a daily basis. The overall Jewish cultural context in the United States does not afford American Jews anything close to the same point of entry as Israelis. For example, a level of awareness exists in Israel for almost every Jewish holiday, even those that are relatively unknown among most American Jews. As a result, parents seeking to transmit any Jewish tradition must work harder to create a thicker religious, cultural tradition. This is a point that Jewish clergy who officiate, and co-officiate, at intercultural marriages need to take seriously when counseling couples.

One way or another, nearly all American Jews grapple with living as a cultural minority. But for intermarried couples, particularly those who wish to raise their children with exposure to the cultural, religious traditions of both parents, successful transmission is even more difficult. If these parents want to expose their children to a meaningful appreciation for Jewish tradition, they need to be prepared to do more heavy lifting. Hosting a Passover Seder and lighting a menorah during Chanukah are not, without more exposure, likely to provide their children with enough Jewish cultural capital to compensate for a world where the Christian cultural trappings are so pervasive and even alluring. To be clear, this is not an issue that just affects intermarried couples, but the degree of difficulty is more pronounced when there is another cultural, religious tradition in the home.

The difficulties presented by the allure of Christian culture are compounded by some portrayals of Jewish tradition as less than appealing. Perception, as they say, is reality. In 2016, the Bravo channel's sassy, snappy comedy *Odd Mom Out* featured an episode that illustrates this problem. The show is a spoof of family life on the affluent Upper East

Side of New York City. Its leading character, Jill Weber, is married to an Episcopalian but trots out her Jewish identity and culture at every turn.

The episode focused on Yom Kippur, the holiest day of the Jewish calendar. Weber does not embody a character that is merely culturally Jewish. In this episode, she spends a good portion of her time in synagogue and acknowledges her determination to fast on Yom Kippur. In fact, her difficulty fasting in this episode accounts for some of the show's funniest moments. Still, Weber tells her children, who are understandably resistant to spending a day in synagogue praying and fasting, that *if they want to do Christmas, they have to do Yom Kippur.*

If mainstream America's primary exposure to Judaism is as a religion featuring stringent and unpleasant traditions, people who do not have the education or experience to know otherwise will continue to reject its potential. Could Weber have threatened her children with taking Chanukah away rather than Christmas? Sure, but this dialogue would not have resonated as well with the majority of Americans, Jews and non-Jews alike, who know that Christmas takes top billing in our culture.

The dialogue in *Odd Mom Out* raises the question of how these types of conversations can be reframed in a way that makes the playing field more level. Access to quality Jewish education is important for anyone wanting to learn more, but the most important exposure to Jewish tradition for children are the experiential components that only home and community can provide. This exposure can produce children who will readily understand that because Chanukah is also special and fun, its loss is also a significant punishment.

The good news is that today, a larger diversity of Jewish learning and experience is available to a broader spectrum of the Jewish population than ever before. This diversity is particularly beneficial for intermarried parents, including those wishing to raise their children in both cultural, religious traditions. For example, PJ Library provides more than 250,000 North American families with monthly supplies of children's books and other resources concentrating on Jewish themes. According to a 2016 survey, more than a quarter of the PJ Library families have intermarried parents and of this group, 94 percent reported that the materials they receive have increased their confidence in engaging with their children on Jewish topics.[51]

With respect to learning that is community based rather than centered in the home, there are a growing number of start-up organizations and communities catering to intermarried and other people who have not yet found the right fit within more established Jewish institutions. These groups include independent prayer groups, start-up congregations and spiritual communities led by rabbis, as well as non-prayer-focused communities providing opportunities for intermarried couples and Jewish people generally to socialize and pursue mutual interests and experiences.[52]

Intermarried couples can also take advantage of Honeymoon Israel, which provides groups of intermarried and in-married couples who live in the same city with subsidized, immersive trips to Israel. The founders of this program have been monitoring its participants from the outset and report that although the trip itself is a "powerful trigger experience," the post-trip community building has even more potential for a deeper "and more sustainable impact."[53] They also report these positive outcomes are even more pronounced for interfaith couples.

I readily understand that some intermarried couples, particularly those who wish to raise their children in two cultural, religious traditions, feel as though they are still unwelcome even in certain liberal synagogues and religious education programs. Speaking for this group, Susan Katz Miller and Edmund Case have called upon Reform Judaism, in particular, to be more inclusive of families with intermarried parents, particularly those who want to raise their children in two religious traditions.[54]

Of course the level of "audacious hospitality" Miller and Case recommend simply will not be possible for every type of Jewish community. Recently, one of my non-Jewish colleagues confided to me that her husband is Jewish and it is important to her to provide some exposure to Judaism for her children, as she is unable to teach their children about Judaism. She told me she went to a Chabad synagogue and when the rabbi learned she is not Jewish, he told her that her children could not be part of the Hebrew school program. Although he was kind and respectful, she walked away feeling rejected.

Of course, this came as no surprise to me and I spent some time explaining why this boundary exists in this particular community. As my friend is a lawyer, she was able to understand the legal framework that provided the basis for his decision, especially when I discussed the

Reform movement's Patrilineal Resolution and its application to her situation. I then connected her with a Reform rabbi whose synagogue would be a much better fit for her family.

But even some liberal Jewish communities still struggle with what it means to be warm and welcoming in the context of an intermarried family, especially one that is raising the children in both cultural, religious traditions. In this day and age, no one wants to be part of a community that is not considered warm and welcoming. On the other hand, as already discussed, the challenges of preserving Jewish tradition are substantial when Jews live as the minority culture, and Jews must work harder to transmit this tradition. So how can parents prioritize Jewish tradition in a way that matches their lifestyles?

JEWISH TRADITION AND THE TWENTY-FIRST-CENTURY AMERICAN FAMILY

> One day Honi was journeying on the road and he saw a man planting a carob tree; he asked him, "How long does it take [for this tree] to bear fruit?" The man replied, "Seventy years." He then further asked him, "Are you certain that you will live another seventy years?" The man replied, "I found [ready grown] carob trees in the world; as my forefathers planted these for me so I too plant these for my children."
>
> Honi sat down to have a meal and sleep overcame him. As he slept a rocky formation enclosed upon him which hid him from sight and he continued to sleep for seventy years. When he awoke he saw a man gathering the fruit of the carob tree and he asked him, "Are you the man who planted the tree?" The man replied, "I am his grandson."
>
> —Ta'anit 23a, Babylonian Talmud

This beautiful Talmudic *aggadah* (narrative) has a simple but essential message that is as relevant today as it was hundreds of years ago when this narrative was recorded. The elderly man's point is that one should not live life just thinking of the here and now. He is telling Honi that it is the responsibility of one generation to prepare the path for the next generation.

We all know that parents have a responsibility to their children to provide them with the tools they need to survive and thrive. Readers of this book are likely to be interested in how to provide a love and appreciation for Jewish tradition among these tools. In fact, Jewish tradition can be analogized to the carob trees in this *aggadah*. Many Jews still want to see the world continue to have carob trees, even if they yield fruit that may look or taste somewhat different from earlier trees.

Fundamental Ingredients: Tradition, Education, and Connection

Throughout this book, I discuss ways to introduce Jewish tradition into family life in a way that can work for families that are not living—completely or at all—within the system of Jewish law. I emphasize the importance of careful selection of Jewish traditions, performing these traditions with consistency, attributing personal meaning to these traditions, and making sure to emphasize the particularly joyful aspects of Jewish tradition. As discussed in the chapter on *Shabbat* and holidays, nearly every Jewish holiday, including Yom Kippur, has a joyful element. Above all, it is important to remember that Jewish tradition is experiential and the home provides the best and the most available venue for showcasing the joy of Jewish tradition. Children who grow up with positive experiences in connection with Jewish tradition are far more likely to want to duplicate these experiences for their own children.

It also goes without saying that formal Jewish education, treated more fully in the following chapter, represents a fundamental ingredient in the overall recipe. A strong network of Jewish connections outside the home also is vital. The JPPI study provides compelling evidence that there is a circularity between personal Jewish relationships and Jewish engagement and connectivity: "More Jewish personal relationships nurture more Jewish engagement; and the more Jewishly engaged develop and sustain more Jewish personal relationships."[55]

When it comes to instilling a love for Jewish tradition, other types of personal relationships can be important in addition to that of the parent-child. As grandparents are especially significant, they merit a separate chapter in this book. Much of the discussion in that chapter also is applicable to special aunts and uncles who function in some ways like surrogate parents.

Other important personal relationships can be forged within the confines of a synagogue community. Although synagogue affiliation is declining, there are important reasons to think carefully about seeking out a prayer community that is comfortable for your family. First and foremost, these communities provide parents and children with an important source of spirituality. According to author and clinical psychologist Lisa Miller, greater spirituality has been linked to significantly stronger mental health in adolescents.[56] Communities that are spiritually centered can help parents instill religious tradition into their daily lives. Also, it is important not to underestimate the role that quality clergy can play in a family's life. Sermons, for example, can often offer memorable, thought-provoking life lessons that include both storytelling and Jewish learning. Indeed a rabbi, religious school educator, youth group director, or other Jewish professional at a synagogue can become one of the most significant people in the life of an individual or family.

Personal relationships can also be developed in other types of Jewish institutional settings, and overnight Jewish summer camp provides one of the most effective ways to strengthen Jewish identity in children. Camp allows children to forge significant Jewish relationships with their peers, as well as with older Jewish children who can serve as role models, and with professional Jewish educators. The benefits of Jewish overnight camp in developing and strengthening Jewish identity have been well documented over the years. For example, the JPPI study demonstrated that attending an overnight camp with Jewish content significantly increases the chances of marrying a Jewish partner and raising one's children as Jewish.[57]

My husband and I are both academics and because we were usually home more during the summer we did not readily embrace the idea of sending our daughters off to summer camp for eight weeks. At the time we were raising our family, we belonged to a traditional, Conservative synagogue whose rabbi strongly pushed Camp Ramah, the Conservative movement's official international camp. None of our daughters were the homesick type, and all very much wanted to go to overnight camp when they reached the appropriate age. We gave in reluctantly with our eldest, and much more eagerly with our younger two once we saw how much our oldest daughter enjoyed and benefited from the experience.

We soon learned that, despite the emphasis we placed in our home on Jewish tradition and observance, there were educational and social benefits that overnight summer camp offered our daughters that were unlike anything they could get at home. One example is the intensive community *Shabbat* experience Ramah provided our daughters. Although we always celebrated *Shabbat*, sometimes with other families, camp *Shabbat* was different. The peer and counselor relationships, and the group dynamics, created an atmosphere that was unique to that particular environment and very much prized by all of our daughters. It seems as though a special kind of magic happens when the observance of Jewish tradition is combined with a communal experience, particularly in the formative years.

Although our daughters had relatively minimal interest in most of the ritual side of the camp, they loved the social environment. All of our daughters are still in touch with some of their Ramah friends, and one of my youngest daughter's friends from Ramah, who is now studying to be a rabbi, actually officiated at her wedding. Also, now that they are all in their late twenties and early thirties, we are beginning to see that their appreciation for Jewish ritual was enhanced by their camp experience. Still, although Ramah probably is as religious as a non-Orthodox camp gets, the overall success of Jewish overnight camp in deepening connection to Jewish tradition and identity does *not* depend on creating intensive religious norms among the campers. It depends on providing children and teenagers with an immersive, cultural Jewish experience that presents Jewish content in a fun and memorable way.

In a similar vein, a young mom I know sends her daughter to a Reform overnight camp for a few weeks every summer. I once asked her daughter Lilly what she liked most about camp and one of her responses was *Shabbat*. When I pressed Lilly further about this, she told me that on Friday nights they used white paper tablecloths and after eating, the campers had fun throwing all the leftover food on the table before the tablecloths were collected and discarded. My son-in-law Andrew's experience at Jewish overnight camp is also illustrative. He spent numerous summers at Beber Camp in Wisconsin, first as a camper and then as a counselor. He remembers singing in Hebrew *birkat ha'mazon*, the prayer after eating a meal, a special source of fun and joy for him because the campers included "off-script" insertions that made its recitation fun. The camping memories Lilly and Andrew shared with me embody the type of consistent, positive experience with Jewish tradition that creates enduring memories for a lifetime.

Still, for many families the expense of overnight camp is daunting, especially on a yearly basis. I was unable to attend overnight camp because this simply was not financially feasible for my parents. But one summer I won a scholarship to a Jewish teen tour of the United States, sponsored by a Jewish youth group, which enabled me to spend eight weeks in a somewhat similar type of environment as Jewish overnight summer camp. This tour provided me with an opportunity to experience Jewish tradition in a community of peers for a sustained period of time. It was a formative experience for me both Jewishly and socially. In fact, Jewish youth groups in general are a very effective means of cementing Jewish identity in teenagers and are much more affordable than overnight camp. All the major Jewish denominations have associated youth groups, and nondenominational alternatives also exist.

Of course, neither Jewish overnight summer camp nor Jewish teen tours and youth groups will guarantee Jewish observance, identity, or marriage later in life. Also, even these experiences are far less likely to have an impact unless the home environment is conducive to instilling Jewish tradition. But there is much evidence showing that formative Jewish experiences with peers during the teen years can go a long way toward shaping Jewish adults who care about Jewish tradition. For this reason, if parents are in a position to consider overnight camp or other summer experiences for their children, options with Jewish content can be very helpful in transmitting Jewish tradition.

It's All about Communication—Both the How and the What

I want to return to the subject of intermarriage, given that this topic is one that many non-Orthodox Jewish parents will continue to face. I fully understand that not everyone believes that marrying someone Jewish is important, and that some people who believe raising Jewish children is a priority still may question the need for two Jewish parents. Also, some people claim that labeling intermarriage as a problem is off-putting and can jeopardize the possibility that offspring will be raised

Jewish.[58] I do understand these positions, both intellectually and emotionally.

On the other hand, there are people who may not be living within the system of Jewish law but who still strongly believe that their children should marry other Jews. In fact, it is sometimes the case that people who themselves have intermarried still hope their children will choose a Jewish partner.[59] Parents who feel marrying Jewish is a priority for their children should absolutely communicate their feelings to their children. In my experience, though, there are ways of communicating this message that are more likely to be effective. The key is that communication about intermarriage must be part of an overall communication strategy that allows for mutual listening and sharing.

Adina Bankier-Karp's research on Australian Jewry shows that "an ongoing strong, warm and meaningful relationship with parents contributes to young adults' adoption of a Jewish identification and connectedness which strongly resembles that of the home in which they were raised."[60] I suspect the significance of her findings in this regard is pretty much universal. They suggest that both the tone of the home as well as the nature of parents' relationship with their children in their young adulthood make a real difference in transmitting any message, including the importance of Jewish tradition.

It is also important for children to believe in the authenticity of the messages parents communicate to them. For this reason, if parents feel that in-marriage is a preferred choice, they must first and foremost demonstrate a rich cultural, religious tradition in the home and actively teach the importance of preserving this tradition. Parents also need to be direct about this preference. I have several friends who tell me they do not discuss their preferences because they feel their children know how they feel. But on any topic of importance and sensitivity, there is no substitute for honest discussion. It is also important to be prepared to support one's view on this matter with reasons that will make sense to your children given their overall environment. For some families, those reasons will center squarely on the importance of preservation of tradition. For other families, the emphasis will be more on the reality that marriage in general is hard but it helps to have a more common background.

In our home, I frequently articulated the message that it was important for our daughters to marry Jewish partners because I felt any other choice would compromise the preservation of Jewish tradition. My husband tended to focus on the more practical benefits of having a partner from a similar background. The combination probably was helpful in the long run. Even so, all of our daughters dated non-Jews periodically, sometimes even for an extended period.

Another component of effective communication is recognizing when your messages need to be tailored differently to different children. As an only child, I could never understand how two siblings raised in the same household could turn out so different. I now have a better understanding of this. When it came to intermarriage, and virtually all other topics, I often framed things somewhat differently depending on which daughter I was addressing. And when the content of the messages at times needed to be tweaked for one, I usually made it clear to the others why I was departing from my norm. My daughters all understood this because they also know that they are different people with different perspectives and sensitivities.

Still, even if parents feel strongly about their children's marrying other Jews, if their children make a different choice it is in everyone's best interest to accept this decision and be as welcoming as possible. Given the high involvement many parents have with their grandchildren today, parents often get a second chance to transmit some degree of Jewish tradition to another generation. But before turning to this topic, the following chapter explores the critical subjects of Jewish education for children and the iconic coming of age ceremony known as the Bar or Bat Mitzvah.

4

CHILDREN'S JEWISH EDUCATION AND THE B'NAI MITZVAH EXPERIENCE

> On another occasion it happened that a certain non-Jew came before Shammai and said to him, "I will convert to Judaism, on condition that you teach me the whole Torah while I stand on one foot." Shammai chased him away with the builder's tool that was in his hand. He came before Hillel and said to him, "Convert me." Hillel said to him, "What is hateful to you, do not do to your neighbor: that is the whole Torah; the rest is commentary; go and learn it."
> —Shabbat 31a, Babylonian Talmud

This well-known Talmudic *aggadah* (narrative) showcases the differing approaches of the two great sages, Hillel and Shammai, who represented the first two major schools of thought concerning Jewish law at the dawn of the first century of the Common Era. The point of Hillel's remarks is that Judaism—at its essence—is about treating others with the same dignity and respect as we wish to be treated ourselves. And all the rest is commentary. But the reality is that while Hillel's message is completely universal, the "commentary" to which he refers is extremely particular to the Jewish tradition. And the question of how to best package and disseminate knowledge of this commentary has become extremely complicated, and remixed, in modern America.

Despite how life has changed for the majority of American Jews over the past century, the importance of Jewish education for transmitting Jewish tradition cannot be sufficiently emphasized. Jewish education is critical for disseminating knowledge about Jewish tradition, both with respect to particular aspects of practice as well as the fundamentals concerning law, history, and culture. My friend Marilyn once described Judaism as a rich broth of minestrone soup filled with lots of delicious vegetables. As with any recipe, the specific ingredients can change somewhat over time across cultures, and even from time to time in the life of a particular cook. But the essence of minestrone must maintain a noticeable consistency if it is to remain a distinct type of soup. The same is true for the Jewish religion, and education provides the means to keep the recipe for the Jewish tradition consistent, and yet malleable when necessary.

Jews are known as the "People of the Book" because of the importance that reading and education historically have played in Jewish life and culture. Those working in the field of Jewish education have remarked that generally speaking, more people are learning about Judaism now than at any prior time in American history. And pride in being Jewish, which can be taken as a sign that most Jews believe at some level that Judaism is worth transmitting, remains very strong among American Jews.[1] These are very positive aspects of the American Jewish community.

At the same time, among non-Orthodox Jews in twenty-first-century America, the ability to transmit Jewish tradition is compromised by numerous competing life priorities that often win out over Jewish learning and practice. Also, for many Jews who care, at least in theory, that their children obtain some exposure to Jewish tradition, the motivation often is the Bar or Bat Mitzvah. This reality is a double-edged sword. On the one hand, it is a very positive sign that many parents still want their children to experience this cultural rite of passage steeped in Jewish law. On the other hand, it is problematic that in many cases, both parents and children see the need for Jewish education as a short-term means to this end, rather than as essential for their child's long-term growth and development.

Another complicating factor is that parents of children and teenagers often have little time for, and possibly interest in, expanding their own Jewish knowledge. But lack of knowledge and interest in learning often makes it more difficult for parents to instill a love of Jewish tradition in their children in their most formative years.

At the moment, in non-Orthodox communities, synagogues probably still remain the primary source of Jewish education for both children and adults. Although some children in these communities attend Jewish day school, the majority of non-Orthodox children receive their Jewish education through supplemental after-school programs traditionally known as Hebrew school.[2]

Anecdotally, there is good reason to believe that in the past far too many youngsters whose parents required them to attend Hebrew school were turned off to Judaism as children and grew into Jewishly apathetic and unaffiliated adults. Hebrew school was widely perceived as boring and the last thing children wanted to be attending after a long day at school. Fortunately, in recent years there have been many calls for change in Hebrew school education, and promising, successful programs are beginning to emerge across the country. These programs can be considered the epitome of a remixed approach to Jewish education. Still, most supplemental programs provide children with very limited hours of exposure. Also, in many places, financial constraints and limited networking outlets continue to pose a barrier for the attainment of quality instruction.

It is also unclear whether the synagogue model for supplemental school education will continue as the primary norm as the twenty-first century marches on. Studies show a current decline in non-Orthodox synagogue affiliation across the country, as well as in supplementary Jewish school enrollment.[3] We are also witnessing the emergence of new models of Jewish education for all ages that are not dependent on synagogue membership. Jewish education currently is being provided on many diverse levels and by many types of organizations, and these new models include digital content and virtual communities.[4] In short, when it comes to Jewish education, remix is the operative concept.

JEWISH EDUCATION AS AN IMPORTANT FAMILY GOAL

Parents who value transmission of Jewish tradition are fortunate today because they have the ability to choose from an increasingly large variety of educational models for their children. But no program of education can replace the need for parents to engage in some degree of observance in the home as well as careful thought about their Jewish aspirations for their children. According to the late Jewish education scholar Jonathan Woocher, "Institutions and educators have rarely engaged parents" in these types of conversations (or engaged children in talking about their own aspirations).[5] Yet, these discussions are important for all families who want Jewish tradition to continue as part of their family story. The particulars of these aspirations may differ from family to family, and educational options should be selected accordingly. But contemplating your family's Jewish journey early on, even if only in theoretical terms, is important so that when it is time to make decisions you are not starting from ground zero.

Also, whatever a family's Jewish aspirations may be for themselves and their children, realistically these aspirations will not materialize automatically. Judaism is a minority, cultural, religious tradition in the United States, which means that the deck is stacked against transmission absent some degree of proactive engagement. The nature and quality of this engagement will differ, of course, from family to family. But families who want their children to become Jewishly engaged adults must themselves be Jewishly engaged, and must communicate the importance of this engagement to their children.

This means that parents must strive to communicate and demonstrate to their children that religious education is as important to their future growth and development as any other activity in which they are involved. A strong ethos of family commitment can exist in connection with an educational program affiliated with any, or no, denomination but this commitment must be authentic and palpable—for both the parents and the children. If parents view part-time religious education as a low priority, even children who are enrolled in a program will be quick to pick up on this and embrace this same attitude.

My friends Jerry and Elyse have one child, a high-functioning autistic young man now in his twenties. Elyse is Jewish but classifies herself as a religion rebel. She married Jerry, who formally converted to Judaism. Elyse felt that religion was always forced upon her and she didn't want that same path for her son. In fact, despite feeling very connected to her Jewish roots, she always insists on having a Christmas tree to symbolize her frustration with how she was raised.

But when their son turned eleven, they gave him the option of Jewish education, which he fully embraced. This resulted in an increased family commitment, including attending Friday night services every week. Their son had a Bar Mitzvah, joined a Jewish fraternity in college, worked during college on staff at a Jewish overnight camp, and has been to Israel twice. Although their son made the choice, their commitment to his Jewish education was clearly communicated to him all along the way.

In an insightful article titled "Why? The Continuing Struggle for the Soul of Hebrew School,"[6] Rabbi Paul Steinberg fittingly captures how the black-and-white world in which we live impacts the thinking of many parents when it comes to how they feel about Jewish education: "Many believe in the 'either-ors' of the worldly success, such as, either their kid gets into Yale, or they will be doomed to life of janitorial service." With this mind-set, it is easy for parents to feel that the most important thing they can do to ensure their children's future success is to hone their secular studies and extracurricular talents as much as possible. The idea is that by the time children are applying to college they will at worst be seen as well rounded and versatile, and at best, superstars in one or more highly prized area such as academics, athletics, or music. In a world where this mind-set prevails, religious education will never get top billing. Even if children are enrolled, many parents are not inclined to prioritize Jewish education over other activities when a conflict exists.

I wish to offer a counter narrative as food for thought. Despite this cultural push to have children participate and excel in a myriad of academic and extracurricular activities, most parents know that realistically, their children will not become professional athletes, musicians, or actors. Of course it is important to encourage children to take their academic studies seriously and do their very best, as well as to expose them to a variety of extracurricular possibilities. But investing in a child's spiritual and emotional health is one of the most important decisions a parent can make for that child's long-term well-being. The story of Jerry, Elyse, and their son is a beautiful illustration of this point. As a parent of daughters who are now grown, I see the wisdom of Rabbi Steinberg's observation that it is "communal and spiritual health that is actually going to anchor and sustain parents and children through the challenges of the hour."[7]

CHANGES IN PART-TIME JEWISH EDUCATION MODELS: A WORLD OF REMIXED OPTIONS BUT STILL A WAY TO GO

Parents who are planning to raise their children as Jewish, fully or even in concert with another religious tradition, need to be aware that the Jewish education landscape has changed significantly in recent years. Young parents are likely to find many of the current options more appealing than their own experiences, and more in tune with their generational and religious sensibilities. But it can be challenging for parents to navigate their way through these choices.

The Synagogue Model Still Reigns

Despite a changing landscape, the synagogue model of supplemental Jewish education appears to remain the most common and the first recourse for many parents. But for the majority of non-Orthodox parents, synagogue membership probably will not even be on the radar screen until their children are old enough to be enrolled in a Jewish education program. In many cases, this timeframe will be just a couple of years away from the time their oldest child approaches the age of thirteen, the age at which most children celebrate their Bar or Bat Mitzvah.

Although many families do opt to send their children to a Jewish preschool, which often are affiliated with or housed in particular synagogues, this practice does not necessarily translate into synagogue affiliation, either simultaneously or later on. Most Jewish preschools located on the premises of synagogues do not require the families of their students to become synagogue members. Also, there are many Jewish preschools that exist independently of synagogues. As a result, even those synagogues that maintain a preschool do not necessarily draw large numbers of new members from this source.

But for those families who do affiliate, eventually the quality of their synagogue's education program can substantially impact the entire family's Jewish journey. So what does the current research show with respect to developments in part-time Hebrew school? Jonathan Woocher concluded back in 2012 that the then-current environment of part-time Jewish education was shifting away from a provider-centered model to one that was learning-centered.[8] Consumers of this education are more accurately labeled as "prosumerists" given their desire to both consume and produce (or co-produce) the educational end product. This shift mirrors the documented trends of customization and privatization characteristic of the millennial generation's Jewish identity.[9] The result is that many part-time Jewish education programs provide both a more flexible schedule and content that offer families far greater options than was the case previously. These types of "disruptive innovations" represent remixed developments in Jewish learning that depart from the conventional frameworks.[10]

Also, it goes without saying that innovations based on technology are critical to successful education in the twenty-first century. One example of successful technological innovation involves a multi-year professional development program sponsored by the Jewish Federation of Greater Houston. This program connects nearly four hundred Jewish professionals to one another and to innovative technological tools and techniques, with the goal of making every consumer of the Hebrew schools in the area a lifelong Jewish learner.[11]

A survey conducted in late 2016 among Hebrew schools affiliated with Reform congregations shows that although innovation is popular, most congregations innovate within the structure of a more conventional model. This survey included responses from more than two hundred congregations out of a pool of more than six hundred.[12] But this survey, as well as other anecdotal evidence, underscores that change still is happening.

Disruptive innovations can be found even in the most traditional supplemental school programs that maintain a focus on teaching prayer, Torah reading, and Hebrew language skills as well as Jewish law and history. My friend Alicia has been the Director of Education of supplemental religious schools affiliated with the Conservative movement for more than twenty years. Her current school is affiliated with a traditional Conservative synagogue in suburban Illinois. But the remix trend is alive and well even in her program. After several years of discussion, her school went from three fixed days of Hebrew school to two days—Sundays and the option of either Tuesdays or Wednesdays based on the family's choice. The school also revamped its program to incorporate required family *Shabbat* services (separate from the regular services); updated technology allowing students to engage the material on their terms (largely the result of generous donations); and six-week, small-group sections focusing on content designed to appeal to a wide spectrum of children. This approach represents a sea change from the established Conservative Hebrew School model that mandated three days a week and offered a standard curriculum lacking any options for choice on the part of the students.

The content at Alicia's school still stresses a traditional skill set and knowledge base, reflecting the norms of this particular synagogue. For example, children have the option to begin learning how to read from the Torah as early as second grade. But she also incorporates some unique project-based learning that allows students more diverse educational experiences: Her school participates in the international competition My Family Story in which students are required to prepare a 3-D presentation of the histories of both sides of their families going back three generations. Alicia's students have been consistently named among the forty annual winners of this competition. The prize includes a trip to Israel where students receive their awards at the Museum of the Jewish People in Tel Aviv.

Other part-time Hebrew schools are even more experimental with the content of their curriculums. These schools offer content that is substantially project-based and experiential. This "applied Judaism" approach is concerned with how Jewish content meshes with the global Jewish development of children and their families. In other words, the emphasis is on a connection between the classroom experience and Jewish life in the trenches. These experiential models avoid a focus on conveying detailed information to students and instead concentrate on subject matter that is learning centered and connected to the students' life experiences. Teachers are more appropriately seen as facilitators who provide students "with the tools and resources needed to advance their learning."[13]

Project-based learning generally facilitates student absorption of knowledge and skills through extended work on a project that interests them because learners perceive it as relevant to their lives. One Conservative Hebrew school in Michigan embraced this model for a more hands-on approach to learning about the Jewish holidays. For example, before Sukkot students were required to build their own kosher *sukkah* (meaning they had to comply with the legal requirements for construction of the temporary outdoor structure that is required for observance of this Jewish festival). But students could choose whatever theme they wanted for their *sukkah* project. Students had to take ownership of their project and, as a result, they became co-creators of their learning experience. Given that the intricacies of observance still were being stressed, this experience also embraced some traditional learning.[14]

Another advantage of the type of project-based learning such as this *sukkah* project is that it has greater potential for more effectively integrating a congregation's Hebrew school into the fabric of the synagogue as a whole. This approach is beneficial because it results in the educational program's having increased visibility among all the synagogue members rather than just the parents of school-age children. As a result, there is a reduced perception that the Hebrew school is a self-contained unit with minimal relationship to the overall synagogue community.[15]

In recent years, some Hebrew schools are changing not only the content of their programs but also their operational structures to incorporate a more informal summer camp–like atmosphere rather than a conventional classroom model. Evidence suggests, however, that although the camp format may be more marketable, the actual substance matters much more than the form. In a comparative study of two Midwestern Reform congregations, one with a conventional Hebrew school and the other a camp format, the author concluded that a school's success depends mostly on the program's quality of instruction and selection of content.[16]

The synagogue model of Jewish education, while still the most popular, is not the only option in an increasing number of places. There are a growing number of independent enterprises that combine Jewish education and after-school care, as well as individual tutors whose instruction completely replaces the Hebrew school experience. These remixed models represent especially significant disruptive innovations to the conventional Hebrew school method of education.

Non-Synagogue Models for Children's Jewish Education

The independent after-school program that provides both Jewish education and after-school care for elementary school-age children is a relatively new development. In 1992, an after-school Jewish education program called Kesher was founded in Boston, and this program has been credited as the inspiration for many of the twenty-first-century programs. [17] One of the earliest of these programs is Edah, established in 2010 in Berkeley, California, by a group of parents and Jewish education professionals. Similar programs have since surfaced all over North America. Typically, these programs offer flexibility in terms of attendance, a focus on conversational Hebrew, a substantial project-based or experiential style of education, and a balance of allotted time for play, Jewish learning, and secular school homework. Transportation from schools to the facility's location is often provided. [18]

These new ventures are supported by the Nitzan Network, a collaborative enterprise that facilitates a sharing of information and resources among those involved in these new models of Jewish education. According to founder Rena Dorph, Nitzan seeks to challenge at least two foundational assumptions: (1) that synagogue affiliation is necessary for supplemental Jewish education; and (2) that supplemental Jewish education cannot be high quality. The programs affiliated with Nitzan typically emphasize inclusiveness and embrace families from all denominations. Both Nitzan and many of its affiliated, part-time programs receive funding from local Jewish Federations and other sources of philanthropy. [19]

Not all of these independent after-school programs compete with synagogue Hebrew schools, but they can present significant potential for disruption. Rabbi Laura Novak Winer did a study of three members of the Nitzan Network and a representative sampling of the synagogues in the neighboring areas of these programs. She found the potential for tensions between the Nitzan programs and the neighboring synagogues "when the afterschool programs see themselves as an alternative to the congregation, a place where families can live out their Jewish lives in full." [20] These tensions will undoubtedly escalate to the extent these programs broaden their reach to include middle school children preparing for their Bar/Bat Mitzvah. Still, Winer doubts after-school daycare models, given their relatively small number and the presence of other types of educational innovations in synagogue supplemental schools, will ever totally supplant the conventional synagogue part-time Jewish educational model. [21]

Some parents opt out of formal Jewish programmatic education altogether. In the past, private tutoring was the norm mostly for Bar/Bat Mitzvah preparation, usually in connection with a formal synagogue program including Hebrew school. Today, however, a growing segment of parents do not participate in any organized Hebrew school and instead hire a tutor to supply all of their children's Jewish education. This choice provides what seems to be the ultimate remixed Jewish education experience.

One Sunday morning, I was writing in a coffee shop and noticed a woman sitting with a child with binders containing Jewish-related content. I tried not to eavesdrop but I just couldn't help myself. When I got up to use the restroom, I asked her whether she was tutoring her own child. As it turns out, the woman is a private Jewish education tutor whose name is Leah.

Subsequent to our initial meeting, I interviewed Leah so I could learn more about her tutoring business. She started out working for a synagogue as a Bar/Bat Mitzvah tutor, but needed to make a change for personal reasons. When she left the synagogue, a large number of families followed her and requested that she continue teaching their children. Now she has a following of about seventy students a year, and all come to her through word of mouth.

Leah's curriculum covers Jewish holidays, Israel, life cycle events, and Hebrew prayers. As the children inch closer to their Bar or Bat Mitzvah, she also serves as their tutor for the ceremony. She meets with her students for a half hour each week and does not assign any homework except when it comes time to practice for the Bar/Bat Mitzvah. All of her students are from families who are either affiliated with Reform congregations or are unaffiliated. She confessed to me that virtually all the parents have minimal Jewish knowledge and little interest in formal observance. About half of the families are intermarried, and about 40 percent still belong to synagogues. By her account, she provides her services to families that are minimally engaged with Judaism.

When I asked Leah what she hopes to accomplish with her students, she told me that she does everything in her power to "turn her students into Jews." Sometimes, in fact, her students do end up being more interested in Jewish observance and this rubs off on their parents. Each year about twelve of her students visit Israel, and over the years, she has even had a few students who have made *aliyah* (moved to Israel).

Leah was very clear with me that private tutoring goes against her grain because she strongly believes in the importance of Jewish community and synagogue membership. In fact, she actively encourages all of her families to affiliate with a synagogue, even if they find individual tutoring to be a preferable educational option for their children.

Leah is honest and thoughtful about her work, and I have no doubt that she has a tremendously positive impact on her students. Clearly, for some students, private tutoring is a more effective option than part-time group instruction. And for any student, even a half hour of quality Jewish education each week is better than none at all.

On the other hand, by opting out of organized, after-school Jewish education, parents are depriving their children of an opportunity to forge bonds with other Jewish children in a Jewish environment. These types of bonding experiences are important for building Jewish identity. And while youngsters can receive comparable benefits through over-night Jewish summer camp, or even Jewish youth groups, children of less Jewishly engaged families are not usually likely to be involved in such activities. Leah told me that in any given year, only one of her students attends overnight Jewish camp, although many go to other types of camps.

Given the growing options and complexities of part-time Jewish edu-cation, families are bound to be confused about what choice is best for their individual children and their families as a whole. In an ideal world, part-time Jewish education would be available in a well-run and enjoy-able synagogue Hebrew school that is part of a warm, welcoming, nur-turing congregation reflecting the family's religious sensibilities and lo-cated close to home. But many families do not live in the ideal world.

The Whole Jew and the Happiness Factor

> The task that devolves upon the Jewish religious school is to cultivate in the child a sense of warm intimacy with the Jewish people, with its life and its institutions, . . . and to implant within the child a sense of high ambition to contribute his share toward the perpetuation and enrichment of its spirit.
>
> —Mordecai Kaplan[22]

With its limited number of contact hours, the overall success of part-time Jewish education is likely to be reflected more by the positive feelings toward Judaism that it engenders in students rather than by the amount of content that students master. Rabbi Mordecai Kaplan's description, more than a hundred years ago, of the function of Jewish education for children still resonates today. Kaplan, the pioneer of the Reconstructionist movement, suggests that the goal of education is to develop a strong feeling of attachment to the Jewish people and sense of participation in their destiny.

Anna Marx is the Director of the Shinui Network for Innovation in Part-Time Jewish Education, a group of communal agencies that support the development of innovative part-time Jewish educational models. When I interviewed her, she told me that recent years have brought a shift in the underlying discourse of Jewish education generally, including supplemental school education. Whereas previously education discussion centered on the best ways to ensure Jewish continuity in the future, today the focus has shifted to how Judaism can help make people's lives better in the present. This current model is steeped in the discourse of positive psychology and focuses on thriving or flourishing rather than continuity.

I believe the most important function of any children's Jewish education program is to spark feelings of joy, pride, and connection on the part of the students, and to create positive, happy memories of the educational experience.[23] Today Jewish educators also talk about the importance of programs that instill happiness in the sense of fulfillment: "enabling young people to flourish by helping students feel like they are putting forth the best version of themselves."[24]

For most part-time religious school programs, the small number of hours and competing demands of life simply are not conducive to learning any type of deeper substance. Recently I attended the private rabbinic ordination of a good friend who had taught Talmud at a Jewish day school. Some of her former middle school students spoke at her ordination and I was struck by how the substance of what they learned in her class had influenced them in their daily lives. But this level of knowledge acquisition simply is not realistic for most students in any supplemental school, even those that have a more rigorous curriculum. Rather, the goal should be to set students up to be lifelong Jewish learners so that as they mature both their knowledge and their desire to learn grow.

And learning more about Judaism—even for the majority of Jewish adults today—does not necessarily mean familiarity with the intricacies of Jewish law. But it does mean having a working grasp of Jewish tradition and practice, and understanding how our tradition can, in the words of author and Jewish education guru David Bryfman, "empower people to thrive in today's world."[25] This type of approach focuses on the "whole person" rather than just the "Jewish part," and includes a focus on multiple components such as emotional, moral, spiritual, and "real world problem solving."[26] Theoretically, this is just the type of learning that Hebrew schools at their best can accomplish even with a few hours a week. Practically, however, challenges remain as to how this remixed approach can be implemented successfully.

Are We There Yet?

In my discussion with Anna Marx of the Shinui Network, I learned she believes that the positive psychology model has considerable potential, but also that there is no consensus on the best way to implement the insights of this discipline in the context of part-time Jewish education. She also cautioned that a unified vision of what success means is lacking. Specifically, with respect to both the goals and modalities of part-time Jewish education, success will be envisioned and measured differently by students, parents, educators, and rabbis.

Marx also emphasized that an absence of sufficient training for part-time Jewish educators presents another set of challenges. In addition, although the expectations many parents have of these educators are high, the amount of money and time they are given to work their magic is low. As a result of these factors, many programs still fall short despite the innovations part-time Jewish education has made in recent years. This reality is confirmed by both the literature in the field as well as anecdotal evidence across the denominational spectrum.[27]

My friend Wendy is the mother of two boys, one of whom celebrated his Bar Mitzvah a couple of years ago. Her family joined a very liberal Reform congregation when they moved to the Chicago area. Wendy came from a relatively strong Conservative Jewish background, but her Jewish husband was raised with little Jewish tradition. She is a thoughtful, devoted parent who also has a very demanding job, as does her husband. Given their busy schedules, geographic convenience weighed heavily in their choice of Jewish education for their sons.

After her older son's Bar Mitzvah, she confided in me that despite his very positive Bar Mitzvah experience, which included excellent tutoring and sufficient contact with the rabbi to facilitate a satisfying and successful outcome, the Hebrew school experience was negative and a waste of time. Wendy told me that the program was too "one size fits all" in nature and focused on activities such as art projects that were not of interest to her son. Based on her description, this program seemed more stuck in the historic model of Hebrew school education rather than being reflective of the "prosumer" orientation allowing modifications to meet individual needs. More recently, she informed me that her younger son appears to be having a similar negative experience. She also said that her family's experience was pretty similar to many of her friends, both locally and elsewhere.

Wendy is a credible source when it comes to educational quality and so I found our conversations on this topic quite discouraging. In light of my research documenting many of the newer approaches to part-time religious school, I was saddened to hear that these innovations were not yet impacting schools across the board.

My conversations with Wendy brought back less than happy memories about the Hebrew School education of our own daughters. I wanted our daughters to have a good Jewish education but I needed this education to fit seamlessly into our lives. I did not wish to spend endless time conversing with those running the Hebrew school about issues and concerns. In our case, none of our daughters loved Hebrew school but one in particular had a fairly negative experience that still haunts me to this day. In one of her last years of the program, she had a very strict, rude teacher with whom she just did not get along. She complained bitterly about him to me on a regular basis, and her complaints escalated as the year wore on. But I was busy with her teenage sisters, work, and other life issues, and I just wanted—and needed—something to be simple so, whenever she complained, I pretty much told her to deal with it. If I had to do things over I would have summoned up the energy to address my daughter's concerns more promptly and effectively. After her Bat Mitzvah I persuaded her to attend a Hebrew high school program in a different local synagogue with a class taught by a user-friendly rabbi, but even today I think it was too little too late. I am not sure how much this experience influenced her rather long anti-religion phase that seemed to last until her early adult years, but it certainly didn't help matters.

On the other hand, as was the case with Wendy's son, the Bat Mitzvah experience of all three of our daughters was very positive. The type of learning that generally is required for a Bar or Bat Mitzvah is distinct from the content of most Hebrew schools, and more conducive to individualized instruction. So for many children the experience can be much more satisfying and can have a lasting positive impact on their Jewish identity.

THE LAW AND CULTURE OF B'NAI MITZVAH

Jonathan Woocher posited that despite the issues associated with Jewish education, "the pull to have one's child educated Jewishly, even if only minimally, remains strong" largely due "to the enduring popularity of Bar or Bat Mitzvah."[28] Leah, the tutor I interviewed, confirmed this observation, confessing the "Almighty Bar Mitzvah" is the draw for her tutoring services for the majority of families.

The term "Bar Mitzvah" means "son of the commandment" ("Bat Mitzvah" means "daughter of the commandment"). Although people commonly say that someone was "bar mitzvahed," it is technically incorrect to use this term as a verb. Bar or Bat Mitzvah (B'nai Mitzvah in plural) refers to the status of being obligated to observe the religion's commandments. In popular usage, people also typically refer to the ceremony itself as a Bar or Bat Mitzvah.

According to Jewish tradition, a boy automatically becomes a Bar Mitzvah at age thirteen, and a girl becomes a Bat Mitzvah at twelve.[29] The age difference is due to the association of religious obligation with the onset of puberty, and the reality that girls tend to mature physically more quickly than boys.[30] In truth, the very concept of B'nai Mitzvah as it exists today can be considered a remix from a historical standpoint because the ceremony that is familiar to most American Jews was not a product of the Talmudic era, but rather traces its origins to Germany in the Middle Ages.[31] By the late nineteenth century, immigrant Jews in the United States were having Bar Mitzvah ceremonies for boys. The Bat Mitzvah is even more of a remix given that the first one was not held in this country until 1922, when Rabbi Mordecai Kaplan performed the ceremony for his daughter Judith.[32] The Bat Mitzvah ceremony still is not universal in Orthodox communities.

Although the Bar/Bat Mitzvah is based on the age at which young people become obligated to observe *halakhah*, Jewish law, this event has become a foundational element of Jewish culture in the United States. This cultural significance is reinforced through frequent depictions of these ceremonies on television and even movies. Also, in areas with sizable Jewish populations, many non-Jews become familiar with this ceremony given their personal experiences as guests and, with greater frequency these days, as family members.

The most well-known B'nai Mitzvah rite involves the adolescent being called to read from the Torah and to recite a specific blessing before and after sections of the Torah are read. The tradition of reciting these blessings is known as receiving an *aliyah*. In many congregations, the child also chants all or a portion of the *haftorah*, the weekly reading from the Prophets.

According to normative *halakhah*, women are not eligible to receive an *aliyah* or to read publicly from the Torah.[33] In contrast, non-Orthodox synagogues do not adhere to this traditional practice and allow greater female participation in the service. As a result, in Reform and most Conservative congregations today, boys and girls typically celebrate their B'nai Mitzvah in a similar fashion without any gender distinctions.

Some have questioned whether the skill of reading Torah should be such a foundational part of the B'nai Mitzvah experience given that it requires a tremendous investment of time and effort to learn how to do this properly.[34] To do a credible job, one must essentially memorize the Hebrew words and their exact pronunciation since there are no vowels in Torah scrolls. As if that isn't enough, there are musical tropes whose melodies must be learned and then matched with each word. The particular tropes that appear in any given section of the reading also must be memorized since, just like vowels, they do not appear in the Torah scrolls. In less traditional congregations, students often are just expected to read the words from the scroll rather than sing them with the corresponding musical tropes. This practice reduces the amount of preparation time and effort.

A good argument exists for retaining the Torah reading as the centerpiece accomplishment for the majority of B'nai Mitzvah ceremonies because this is a uniquely Jewish practice. Adults who know how to read from the Torah usually say that this is an extremely spiritually satisfying endeavor because it enables the reader to connect with the narrative and the history of the Jews in a visceral, compelling manner. Of course, one may question how many thirteen-year-olds have the emotional maturity to appreciate the spiritual significance of reading Torah.

On the other hand, even if a typical thirteen-year-old cannot appreciate the spirituality of reading Torah, there can be appreciation for the accomplishment that goes along with learning a new skill and sharing it with a community of family and friends.[35] And most children also can understand that reading Torah represents a time-honored tradition that marks this celebration in a uniquely Jewish way. Reading even a short passage from the Torah can have considerable symbolic significance, the memory of which will be retained for life.

Adolescents, and their families, will largely get out of their B'nai Mitzvah experience what they put into it. Although Tyler, my friend Wendy's son, chanted more than ten verses from the Torah portion for his Bar Mitzvah, he and his family also did many other things in preparation for the event. The seriousness with which the entire family approached their responsibilities not only guaranteed a successful outcome on the day of, but also laid the groundwork for a continuing embrace of Jewish tradition at a level comfortable for their family.

Wendy told me that her son spent six months preparing for his Bar Mitzvah and that it truly became a part of him. His *d'var Torah* (speech) required him to contemplate what it means to him to be a Jewish adult, and she was grateful for the structure that having to prepare the talk created for him. She and her husband also embraced the opportunity that Tyler's Bar Mitzvah provided for them to reflect on the role of Judaism in their lives. In addition, they participated in a *tzedakah* (charity) project as part of their overall preparation that entailed feeding those in need in their town. Overall, as a family, they felt very invested in the process and "invigorated" by both the process and the ultimate product.

In some ways, Tyler's Bar Mitzvah looked very different from the ones our daughters celebrated at a very traditional Conservative synagogue. Given that girls at our synagogue were not allowed to lead prayers, and that none of the children gave a speech during the service, the only ways in which they could participate was by chanting Torah and their *haftorah*. Also, since our synagogue's practice was to read the entire weekly Torah portion (rather than a third of the weekly portion that is customary in many Conservative synagogues), all three of our daughters read a large amount of the weekly portion.

One of our daughters never really mastered the skill of decoding Hebrew, and so we anticipated that Torah reading would be more challenging for her. Although she had to rely completely on her memory when she did her Torah reading, she somehow was able to flawlessly master more than thirty verses. As parents we have harkened back to this experience over the years when she has expressed concerns about the difficulty of coursework. For example, we confidently told her that taking biology and chemistry for her nursing degree would be no problem given how much Torah and trope she was able to memorize for her Bat Mitzvah!

In general, an especially visible complexity in connection with B'nai Mitzvah at many congregations today is the nature of participation by non-Jewish friends and relatives, particularly parents of the child. This topic entails a considerable degree of creative remix on the part of more liberal congregations. Scholar Patricia Keer Munro did a study of the B'nai Mitzvah ceremony in the Bay area, one of the most liberal Jewish geographic regions in the country. This area boasts an intermarriage rate than exceeds the national norm, and the impact of intermarriage on B'nai Mitzvah was one of many areas she examined closely. Munro found that although the high rate of intermarriage has fostered new ways of acknowledging non-Jewish members of Jewish communities, inclusion in connection with public Jewish worship still presents challenges even for liberal communities. She discovered a basic consensus around certain norms that avoided participation by non-Jews in activities such as reading sacred texts in Hebrew and reciting prayers that allude to the nature of obligations that are incumbent just upon Jews.[36] Other types of participation in the services were fairly common. As one might expect, Munro found that the more liberal the synagogue, the more additional and remixed avenues of participation are open to non-Jewish family and friends.

In large cities such as New York and Chicago, there is an emerging trend for a complete remix of B'nai Mitzvah by removing its traditional location from the synagogue to other venues such as homes, country clubs, and even yachts—any place other than the synagogue.[37] Of course, it has always been a popular choice to hold the after-service party outside the synagogue. And celebrating B'nai Mitzvah in Israel also is not uncommon. But this particular remixed version, known as the "DIY" B'nai Mitzvah, is different. It typically eliminates any synagogue involvement and therefore requires parents to hire a rabbi and perhaps other Jewish professionals who provide their children with what they see as the appropriate training to prepare them for these celebrations. Recall that this is the B'nai Mitzvah option of choice for many of the students of Leah, the tutor whom I interviewed, given that a significant number of her students are not from affiliated families. Some synagogues have also made the decision to allow parents to hold B'nai Mitzvah off premises even if their children attend the Hebrew school.

The perceived benefits of the DIY approach include the ability to create an event that showcases what the family wants rather than a prescribed service. As a result, these ceremonies can be seen more as a celebration of the child and their interests rather than as a ceremony with a traditional, intended meaning. For example, one account of a DIY Bar Mitzvah in the media discussed how a special prayer book was created for the occasion that featured a cover with basketballs and soccer balls, things of strong interest to the young man.[38] The article noted that the guests walked away with a strong understanding of the Bar Mitzvah boy. In our day and age, most non-Orthodox families want the ability to individualize, and remix, both the process and product of a B'nai Mitzvah celebration, at least to some degree.

The DIY B'nai Mitzvah trend is driven by larger social forces such as the Internet generation's generalized preferences for customization and personalized experiences across the board—everything from clothing to media. Of course, any family in our largely secularized society deserves much credit for facilitating the celebration of a B'nai Mitzvah for their child. But by taking the ceremony, rather than just the reception, outside of a synagogue, this model may fuel the already declining appreciation for the benefits of Jewish community.[39] Given that Jewish community has always represented the heart and soul of Jewish tradition, and that synagogues represent the traditional means of forging these communities, the emergence of the DIY B'nai Mitzvah model can be seen as a cause for concern.

The Bar Mitzvah of the son of my good friend Sasha demonstrates that individualization can also be accomplished through a more traditional process for willing secular families. I got to know Sasha many years ago when she was a student at my law school. At that time, we lived in the same town, and she graciously offered to drive me home after our evening class. During our car rides together, we talked a lot about our common Jewish heritage, although we had very different backgrounds when it came to Judaism. She grew up in the former Soviet Union in the 1970s and came to Chicago with a newborn son when she was in her early twenties. Like many Jews from the Soviet Union, she is not conventionally religious.

At the time I met Sasha, her son Eugene was about twelve and studying for his Bar Mitzvah with an Orthodox rabbi. Apparently an Orthodox work colleague made this connection for Sasha, and she was happy to have a more traditional orientation for her son's Bar Mitzvah given her own lack of knowledge regarding Judaism. The goal was not for her son to become more observant, but rather to become more knowledgeable. Eugene chose to continue his studies, which included Bible, Talmud, and Hebrew, with the rabbi through high school.

Eugene, who is now a physician, told me recently that his studies caused him to appreciate how important it is for him to continue to have a strong Jewish identity, and how important this identity is to his parents, despite their relative lack of observance. Although I did not ask Eugene about his plans for marriage, he volunteered that although he has dated non-Jewish women, he definitely plans to marry someone Jewish because he feels that is the best way to ensure that his strong Jewish identity is passed down to his children.

Overall, there is no doubt that a Jewish education and B'nai Mitzvah experience that is appropriate for a particular child and family can have a positive, long-lasting impact regardless of denomination, educational setting, or type of ceremony. Although Tyler and Eugene had different types of B'nai Mitzvah experiences, both young men benefited from parents who were thoughtful about the Jewish education process and deliberate with the messages they sent to their children. The goal was not just to celebrate the Bar Mitzvah as a one-day event, but instead to situate the ceremony as a milestone rather than a capstone to their child's Jewish education.

JEWISH EDUCATION AND B'NAI MITZVAH AS A STEPPING STONE TO LIVING JEWISHLY

Shortly after Tyler's Bar Mitzvah, Wendy confessed to me that she was concerned about whether it would be possible to maintain the Jewish momentum given that her son's Bar Mitzvah and accompanying preparation were activities that represented a very "carved out" experience from their normal secular world. She wondered whether they would still be able to integrate Jewishness into their essentially non-observant lifestyle.

My immediate response was that she should consider incorporating some low-hanging fruit into their weekly routine, such as lighting candles on Friday night and saying the blessings together over challah and wine. Upon hearing this suggestion, she looked a bit perplexed. Not being someone terribly interested in the culinary arts, she asked, "But can we still order Chinese?" I responded "of course" and taking the liberty only a close friend can, jokingly added, "But maybe no pork!"

Several months after this conversation, Passover rolled around. In prior years, Wendy's father led their Seder but her parents were unable to come in to town that year due to some health issues. And then the magic moment occurred. Her son Tyler asked whether now that he had his Bar Mitzvah, he could lead their family Seder in place of his beloved grandfather. Fortunately, the following year her parents were able to come in for the Seder and grandfather and grandson led the Seder together.

Tyler's asking to lead the Passover Seder, and his continued leadership with his grandfather, show that he absorbed the message that becoming a Bar Mitzvah means taking on the responsibilities of a Jewish adult. It is not just about the day of the celebration. The B'nai Mitzvah brings a new Jewish status that forever remains, and binds someone to a people whose traditions have endured throughout the centuries.

The significance of this status can easily get lost in life's busy shuffle, even for the most well intentioned parents. It has to be actively nurtured at home and in communal settings that are conducive to living Jewishly. These settings include synagogues and other institutions of Jewish learning, volunteering opportunities with Jewish related themes, Jewish youth groups, and Jewish summer camp. With respect to education, the sociological evidence demonstrates that Jewish education that extends into the teenage years translates into the probability of Jewish engagement in later years.[40] But all of these settings represent diverse ways of helping families transmit Jewish tradition down the line.

At the end of Patricia Keer Munro's book about B'nai Mitzvah, she discusses her practice of attending *Shabbat* services on Saturday mornings with her two small grandchildren. Munro, a self-denominated "serious, liberal Jew," expresses excitement about the prospect of her grandchildren beginning to prepare for their B'nai Mitzvah in due course.[41] It was interesting to me that she chose to conclude her book on this note, since it also serves as an implicit reminder that grandparents can be an invaluable resource for advising their adult children on feasible ways to transmit Jewish tradition to their grandchildren. The next chapter explores this important topic.

5

THE GRANDPARENT FACTOR

Life Stage Matters

May you . . . live to see your children's children.

—Psalms 128:5–6

During many Bar/Bat Mitzvah ceremonies, particularly those associated with the Reform movement, a Torah is physically handed from the grandparents to the parents to the child. This symbolic gesture is intended to highlight the importance of passing tradition down through the generations. Tyler's Bar Mitzvah, discussed in chapter 4, included this popular custom. In fact, my friend Wendy told me afterward that she believed Tyler's Bar Mitzvah was among the highlights of her parents' lives and that it added a powerful new dimension to what they had experienced at her own Bat Mitzvah.

Wendy's description of her parents' views concerning Tyler's Bar Mitzvah makes perfect sense. As parents, we juggle a large number of responsibilities and usually do not have the luxury of time. Grandparents, on the other hand, may have more discretionary time and they may also have a keener sense that time itself is not infinite. As such, they can feel a stronger need to make their mark, both in a general sense and specifically on their descendants. These feelings can also give rise to a deeper examination—or even a re-examination—of one's feelings about the importance of religious tradition.

> So he [Jacob] blessed them [his grandsons Ephraim and Manasseh] that day saying, "By you shall Israel invoke blessings, saying: God make you like Ephraim and Manasseh."
>
> —Genesis 48:20

Rabbi Berel Wein notes that Jacob's blessing of his grandsons is "one of the most memorable human scenes portrayed in the Torah." His blessing serves as an instruction to later generations to concentrate on the grandchildren because "the three-generation cord is the certain key to Jewish survival and success."[1]

The Talmud also builds upon this concept:

> R. Parnak said in R. Johanan's name: He who is himself a scholar, and his son is a scholar, and his son's son too, The Torah will nevermore cease from his seed, as it is written, As for me, this is my covenant with them, saith the Lord; My spirit is upon thee, and my words which I have put in thy mouth, shall not depart out of thy mouth, nor out of the mouth of thy seed, nor out of the mouth of thy seed's seed, saith the Lord, from henceforth and forever. . . . What is the meaning of "from henceforth and forever"?—R. Jeremiah said: From henceforth [i.e., after three generations] the Torah seeks its home. (Bava Metzia 85a, Babylonian Talmud)

According to a footnote explanation, "the Torah seeks its home" means that the Torah "becomes hereditary in that family."[2] Perhaps surprisingly, though, Jewish law has relatively little to say about the extent and types of obligations grandparents owe to their grandchildren, and vice versa.[3] But as Rabbi Gerald Skolnik has observed, when Jacob blesses his grandchildren, he still is actively engaged as a parent to Joseph, their father, and his actions "must be understood as consciously directing his grandchildren's destiny."[4]

Sociologists of the American Jewish community are focusing serious attention on the influence of Jewish grandparents on the upbringing of their Jewish, and partially Jewish, grandchildren. As baby boomers continue to age, they represent a generation that will have an unprecedented amount of time, wealth, and longevity. In addition, today's Jewish grandparents differ from their predecessors in that they were mostly born and raised in the United States and, therefore, share more similar educational and other formative experiences with their grandchildren than was the case in previous generations. These factors facilitate their ability to influence the lives of their grandchildren in a potentially deeper way than was the case in earlier times. According to Professor Jack Wertheimer, who has studied and written about the influence of Jewish grandparents, today those who are interested in actively participating in the lives of their grandchildren are poised "to become almost equally active great-grandparents."[5]

Recently, a grassroots organization called the Jewish Grandparents Network has surfaced and grown with rapid pace. Co-founded by Lee M. Hendler and David Raphael, this organization is dedicated to advocating for more effective ways for Jewish organizations to utilize the time and talents of grandparents. It also seeks to create opportunities to help grandparents develop strategies for sharing their family stories with their families and deepen their own Jewish journeys so they can more effectively help transmit Jewish tradition to their grandchildren.[6] David Raphael explained to me that one of the main reasons he wanted to start the network was his recognition of the reality that "having grandchildren raises the stakes and not everyone knows how to go about transmitting Jewish tradition to the next generation."[7]

Between late 2018 and the first part of 2019, the Jewish Grandparents Network developed and administered a survey for baby boomer grandparents. The survey quickly spread across the country as a growing network of partner organizations disseminated the questionnaire to their constituents. By the end of the timeframe for completion, around 8,000 people had filled out the survey and taken advantage of this opportunity for Jewish grandparents to supply information on their family stories and grandparenting practices, including the Jewish components of these stories and practices. Clearly one lesson of this survey is that it is relatively easy to get people to talk about their grandchildren and how they interact with them.

This chapter explores the ways in which grandparents operating outside of the Orthodox world can harness their influence to enhance the Jewish identity and engagement of their grandchildren. The concept of remix can be an invaluable tool for grandparents desiring to exert this type of influence, though grandparents schooled in a more traditional perspective may need to adjust their expectations and approaches in order to maximize their opportunities for influence. But influence clearly is possible under the right circumstances. Both the literature and substantial anecdotal experience suggest that grandparents can have a major impact on the Jewish journeys of their grandchildren, and this is true with respect to grandchildren who are the products of in-marriage as well as intermarriage. For this reason, Wertheimer believes grandparents represent "American Jewry's great untapped resource!"[8]

During the time I was writing this book, my husband and I became grandparents for the first time. When our daughter was pregnant, and even for a time before, all we heard from our friends who already had grandchildren was how wonderful it is to be a grandparent. We were repeatedly told that the grandparent experience far surpasses the high expectations everyone has. It is not that we doubted what seemed to be this universally shared truth. But the intensity and consistency of the feelings on this matter still surprised us.[9]

We quickly discovered the reality lives up to the hype. From the moment Sander arrived, we were smitten! Before his arrival, I spent a good deal of time thinking about what grandmotherly appellation I wanted to use. Apparently this isn't uncommon, and numerous articles have surfaced in recent years discussing this very topic. According to a 2016 article in the *Wall Street Journal*, more people are gravitating toward unique grandparent designations that suit their personality and reflect their particular identity as a grandparent.[10] Ultimately, I settled on Bibi, a derivative of my nickname "Bobbi."

The level of involvement with grandchildren among nearly all of our friends and acquaintances who are grandparents is rather astounding. It exists among grandparents who are still actively involved in their careers and among grandparents who do not live in close proximity to their grandchildren. My colleagues who are law professors all spend time caring for their grandchildren. My friend Ava, a doctor, devotes every Monday to watching her grandchildren. Our friends Stephen and Ellen continually travel from Chicago to Connecticut and Minnesota to spend time with their two sets of grandchildren, even though Stephen still maintains an active law practice. Our friends Larry and Ellie care for some combination of their five grandchildren nearly every day of the week, and tell us this is their greatest joy.

One the other hand, some observers of the grandparent scene have reported that it is also common to hear that grandparents do not want to be as involved as their predecessors in helping to raise their grandchil-dren. In an article in *Tablet Magazine*, Naomi Grossman wrote that female baby boomers raised in traditional Jewish homes are redefining what it means to be a grandmother by pursuing their own interests rather than being so involved with their grandchildren.[11] Wertheimer's study of twenty-four grandparents across fourteen states also indicated that some of his participants mentioned they had friends who felt this way.[12] But I am still not convinced this is the majority. Just for fun, I posted Grossman's article on my Facebook page with some commentary about my take being different from hers. One of my friends, a physician with a huge circle of patients and friends, agreed that nearly all of her patients in this age group "take their grandparenting very seriously."

Although the focus of this chapter is on grandparents who are alive and well, it is important to note that the influence of deceased grandparents—even those whom a grandchild has never met—can be significant, especially if the parent does a good job of keeping their memory alive. I have personal experience with this situation. My father constantly spoke about how observant both of his parents were, particularly his mother, with whom he was very close. In fact, I was named after her, following the Ashkenazi custom of naming children after deceased relatives to give them a merit.

I have never seen a picture of my paternal grandmother but I feel as though I know her well. My father always raved about how she was the most knowledgeable and religious woman in their synagogue, so much so that even the rabbi's wife would seek her advice on matters pertaining to Jewish practice. And as I discussed in the chapter on food, my first introduction to the laws about keeping kosher came from my father repeatedly telling the story of how guilty he felt about sitting down to the dairy lunch fixed by his mother after he had consumed a nonkosher hot dog for the first time. Although his father died when my dad was relatively young, he frequently told me how his father stopped smoking from sundown Friday until sundown Saturday because he would never light a flame on *Shabbat*. Given that I am an only child, I cannot attest to whether my father's verbal memories of his parents would have influenced other children. But I know that his stories made a huge impression on me and to this day they provide a strong foundation for many of my past and current patterns of Jewish observance.

Based on my research for this chapter, I reached the following conclusions about transmission of Jewish tradition and grandparenting, none of which are terribly surprising: (1) grandparents who live close to their grandchildren have a significant advantage, but distance can be overcome with time, effort, money, and technology; (2) it greatly helps when grandparents have a close relationship with the parents of the grandchildren (including the spouse or partner of their own child); (3) grandparents will be more successful facilitating transmission of Jewish tradition when their feelings about Judaism are perceived as authentic by their children and grandchildren; and (4) grandparents are more likely to be successful when they have taken the time to contemplate carefully their own Jewish journeys, including how and why they believe it is important for their grandchildren to be exposed to Jewish tradition.

As discussed in the chapter on marriage, the rate of intermarriage among non-Orthodox Jews is more than 70 percent. Not surprisingly, therefore, many of the grandparents I interviewed for this chapter have intermarried children. Most of these grandparents would have preferred their children marry Jews, and for some this preference is extremely strong. Still, many grandparents saw intermarriage as an opportunity to double down and strengthen the Jewish identity of their grandchildren as well as their children. On a related note, I spoke with many grandparents who expressed regret about some of their choices in connection with Judaism as they were raising their own children, and who also expressed the hope that they might get a second chance with their grandchildren. [13]

The need that some grandparents feel to "do better" Jewishly with their grandchildren is not necessarily one that they can easily explain. In the chapter on *Shabbat* and holidays, I discussed how my friend Sarah, a self-denominated cultural Jew, laments the fact that she did not formally acknowledge *Shabbat* on Friday night as her children were growing up, despite the fact that she always made a nicer family dinner that night to usher in the weekend. Now she wants the chance to do better with her grandchildren. During one of our more recent conversations, I pointedly asked her what caused this change of heart. She pondered my question and said, "Honestly, I'm not even sure. . . . Maybe it's just the wisdom I've gained by growing older." At the time we had this conversation, her daughter-in-law was pregnant with her first grandchild, a boy, and Sarah confided in me that she was already excited about hosting the *brit milah* (ritual circumcision).

Even in conversations with several grandparents whose families were not especially Jewishly engaged, I encountered expressions of hope that their grandchildren will be raised with at least some Jewish tradition. For example, Larry, a highly successful attorney whose son married a non-Jewish woman, talked nonstop about his two grandchildren, especially his grandson. Larry proudly announced that his son had assured him that his grandson will have a Bar Mitzvah but nothing has been said so far about his granddaughter. When I asked him whether he was okay with that result, his response was "I have to be happy with what I can get!"

As a parent, I always found it helpful to talk to other parents so I could learn from their experience and I feel similarly about grandparenting. The following three fictionalized narratives, based on numerous conversations, illustrate how grandparents can use a remixed approach to Judaism to effectively influence the Jewish practices and identities of their grandchildren without crossing boundaries set by their own children. They demonstrate how thoughtful grandparents who are good at communication can make a real difference in terms of instilling a positive feeling for Judaism despite the presence of some potential obstacles for successful transmission. These narratives also highlight why certain strategies can be counterproductive.

Jennifer and Gary

Jennifer and Gary are in their late sixties and have been married for more than forty years. They have two sons and a daughter, and all live in close geographic proximity. Their oldest son is married to a Jewish woman and has two daughters. Their younger son was married to a Jewish woman, but that marriage ended following the birth of their son. Afterward, he remarried and he and his non-Jewish wife also have a son. Jennifer and Gary's daughter is married to a Jewish man and they have a son and a daughter. So Jennifer and Gary have a total of six grandchildren, all under the age of ten.

Both Jennifer and Gary are highly engaged Jewishly and Gary's religious practices border on Orthodox. They are both very knowledgeable about Jewish ritual and Gary is especially learned. As a result of his rabbi's influence, Gary started to become more religious when his children were in high school, and this change caused a bit of tension given that a certain level of family observance had already been firmly established. But today they enjoy an exceptionally close relationship with all three of their children, their children's spouses, as well as their six grandchildren. So what is the secret of their success?

Jennifer and Gary are highly involved with the care and nurturing of all of their grandchildren on a daily basis. Talk to just about any grandparent who seems to have unlimited time with their grandchildren and you will find that they are spending a considerable amount of time helping their children care for their children. On any given day, Jennifer and Gary are watching some combination of their grandchildren for an extended period of time. Although often grandparents report being closer to the children of their daughters as opposed to their sons,[14] this is not true in Jennifer and Gary's case. To their credit, they have the same degree of access to all of their grandchildren, including their grandson who is the child of their son and his ex-wife. Jennifer attributes their strong relationship with this particular grandson to the significant efforts they make in being flexible, continually helpful, and very supportive in their interactions with his mother. As a result of their efforts, they have been able to overcome the existing convention that the divorce of the parents can negatively impact the children's relationship with the grandparents.[15]

Jennifer and Gary also defy existing data suggesting that it is more difficult for grandparents to transmit Jewish tradition when their child is the father, rather than the mother, of a child born into a mixed marriage.[16] Jennifer in particular has spent a significant amount of time thinking through how she and Gary can best influence all of their grandchildren, including Samuel, the grandchild born to their son and his non-Jewish wife. The intermarriage was particularly difficult for Gary given his level of observance. He had to come to terms with the reality that any grandchildren born from this union would not be Jewish according to *halakhah*, Jewish law, since their mother is not Jewish. It took some time, but eventually Gary grew comfortable with the idea that he had to approach Samuel exactly the same way in terms of Judaism as all of his other grandchildren. He knew that he had to teach him the same way and expose him to all the same rituals and customs. Some less observant people did not understand why this should have been so difficult for Gary but he needed to grapple with the reality that he was operating outside the bounds of Jewish law. This was not easy for him initially. Gary's willingness to adapt embodies a strong application of remix.

Of course Gary does harbor the hope that, one day, Samuel may choose to convert formally, but he knows that realistically this may never happen. He also knows that Samuel is likely to consider himself Jewish even if he never converts. Still, Gary's potential for embracing a remixed approach to Judaism was tested when Samuel was about a year old and his parents decided, with Jennifer's support, to have a Hebrew naming ceremony for him. According to *halakhah*, Jewish males are circumcised eight days after their birth, and they are given their Hebrew names during this ceremony. Samuel was circumcised in the hospital after he was born because it would not have been possible for him to have a ritual circumcision according to Jewish law.

Initially Gary was resistant to participating in a Hebrew naming ceremony because he felt that giving Samuel a Hebrew name would be a perversion of the tradition. But with Jennifer's encouragement, he eventually warmed to the idea. He came to believe that if Samuel has a Hebrew name just like all of his cousins, he might be more likely to regard himself as Jewish when he matures. Otherwise, Samuel would feel different, and possibly even excluded, and this would accomplish nothing from the standpoint of transmitting Jewish tradition in their lived reality.

For her part, Jennifer approaches her non-Jewish daughter-in-law, Kate, through their shared love for food and cooking. Kate is a wonderful cook and very interested in learning how to make special holiday dishes. This bonding over ethnic food is a common theme with many parents and the non-Jewish partners of their children. But the situation with Kate and Jennifer is unique in their family in that Kate always is the one working in the kitchen with Jennifer preparing for Rosh Hashanah dinner or the Passover Seder.

Jennifer and Gary know that part of the reason Kate is so involved in these activities is that she enjoys cultural tradition generally. Her fondness for tradition naturally also extends to her own religious, cultural traditions, particularly Christmas, although she is not religious. When Kate married their son, Jennifer and Gary knew that a Christmas tree in their home would be part of that picture. This was a very difficult adjustment not only for Gary but also for Jennifer.

Jennifer made up her mind that she would not focus on what her son and Kate were doing for the non-Jewish traditions but rather on what they were doing on the Jewish side. So when Kate discussed with Jennifer whether she should decorate the tree with blue and white stars and other Jewish-themed ornaments, Jennifer stressed the importance of keeping the traditions completely distinct. She advised Kate to set up a separate space in her home for the Jewish celebrations so their children would understand the distinctions.

By keeping their focus on what their son and Kate are doing Jewishly, Jennifer and Gary are able to help them create as rich a Jewish religious, cultural tradition as possible. They try hard to reinforce the positive Jewish decisions that are being made and refrain from complaining about the choices they are not as happy with. So far, this approach seems to be working well. And it is important to emphasize that their son and Kate are making important choices about Judaism for Samuel even if not all their choices are Jewish ones. For example, in addition to choosing to give Samuel a Hebrew name, they also send him to a Jewish preschool where his exposure to Jewish holidays and customs is reinforced.

Realistically, the situation facing Jennifer and Gary with respect to their intermarried child differs only in degree from their other married children. None of their children are particularly religious. They do not keep kosher homes and do not regularly celebrate *Shabbat* unless they are having *Shabbat* dinner with Jennifer and Gary. The situation in which Jennifer and Gary find themselves is a fairly common one in which the parents are far more observant than the children, and they must carefully navigate their desire to instill a strong dose of Jewish tradition in family units for whom this tradition is not nearly as high a priority.

In his study, Wertheimer noted that grandparents in these situations essentially have three choices: they can openly battle their children, avoid religion altogether, or try to negotiate a middle ground that consists of the grandparents exposing their grandchildren "to carefully calibrated doses of Judaism: Shabbat dinners, occasional visits to the synagogue, minimal instruction in Jewish perspectives."[17]

Jennifer and Gary essentially follow the middle ground approach but they enjoy several advantages that have produced very successful results. First, as noted earlier, they live in close proximity to all of their children and grandchildren. This geographical advantage is about more than just their time with their grandchildren. Because all the cousins live close to one another, Jennifer and Gary's home is often the "cousin hub." The ability to create these memories of collective family time, such as *Shabbat* dinners and other traditional holiday celebrations, provides ready-made opportunities to create not only Jewish memories but also close family bonds. In their case, the memories and the family ties go hand in hand with the Jewish content.

Also, both Jennifer and Gary have a visible, genuine love of Judaism that affords them another critical advantage: the ability to be perceived as authentic by both their children and their grandchildren. Gary insists that no one watch television or use the computer on *Shabbat* at their home. Gary explains that this enables the family to spend quality time together during *Shabbat* in other ways that the grandchildren find special and fun. From a young age, their grandchildren realized that when they come to Grandma and Poppa's home on *Shabbat* there is a consistent pattern that became familiar and comfortable. Their grandchildren often are with them on Saturday nights and the family bids *Shabbat* farewell by reciting the *havdalah* prayer, complete with a candle and fragrant spices. Not only is this ritual a very fun one for children, but also their grandchildren understand that after this prayer they can return to their video games and television.

Jennifer and Gary have tried hard to be accepting and nonjudgmental of their children's choices when it comes to Judaism. These qualities, combined with Jennifer's generally more flexible approach to religion and their mutual devotion to the care and nurturing of all of their grandchildren, have placed them in a very strong position to facilitate transmission of Jewish tradition to all of their grandchildren.

Carol and Robert

Carol and Robert have been married for almost forty years and have two children, Chelsea and Michael. They still belong to a Conservative synagogue and currently attend *Shabbat* services at least once a month. The Conservative synagogue was a compromise since Carol did not grow up in a religious home, but Robert's parents, Holocaust survivors, self-denominated as Orthodox. Still, they engaged in certain leniencies, such as using electricity and even working occasionally on *Shabbat*.

Robert became more lax than his parents as he matured, but certain aspects of the tradition still very much mattered to him. So Carol agreed to keep a kosher home when they married, although both she and Robert eat nonkosher meat outside the home and always allowed their children to do the same. When their children were growing up, they always had a family *Shabbat* dinner on Friday night, and usually attended services the following morning unless the children had conflicting activities. When it came to Passover, Robert required of his family a very high level of observance both with respect to the special dietary laws and the length and content of the Seders.

Carol is from the West Coast but they settled in a suburb close to where Robert grew up in one of the smaller Midwestern cities. Over the course of their marriage, there was frequent contact with Robert's family that was not always positive, particularly for Carol. Robert's parents were difficult on many levels but especially when it came to religion. Despite their own lack of consistency with respect to observance, their overall attitude was that their way was the only way. Carol found particularly annoying their view that women should not be able to participate equally in Jewish synagogue ritual. Carol always felt it was important for Chelsea to have the same opportunities for participation as Michael.

Since Carol is not as Jewishly knowledgeable as her husband, she concentrated on infusing the home with Jewishness through food and festivity. This approach meant preparing special family recipes for all the holiday meals, including ones that were kosher for Passover, and other special treats such as *hamantaschen* (tri-cornered pastries) for the festive holiday of Purim. Most of the religiously based heavy lifting was left to Robert and his family, and supplemented with their synagogue's mediocre Hebrew school. By the time their children were in their teens, Chelsea was already indifferent to Judaism and Michael was actively hostile. Undoubtedly the tensions with Robert's family played a role here but so did what the children perceived to be an overall dogmatic approach to Jewish tradition. Carol's culinary talents simply weren't enough to compensate for an approach to Jewish tradition that was seen as bereft of joy.

Chelsea married a local Jewish man who is also indifferent to Jewish tradition and they now have twins, a boy and a girl, who are approaching middle school. Like Jennifer and Gary, Carol and Robert see their grandchildren frequently and help out a good bit when it comes to watching them. Although Chelsea and her husband are raising their children Jewish—at least in theory—there is far less Jewish content to their home than the one in which Carol and Robert raised their children. They celebrate the major holidays with Carol and Robert but that is pretty much all they do. The twins did not go to a Jewish preschool and do not attend Jewish summer camp despite repeated offers by Carol and Robert to pay for Jewish camp. But the family recently joined a Reform temple in the area so the twins could begin to prepare for their B'nai Mitzvah. Carol and Robert are happy about this decision, but they still would like to see their grandchildren raised with more Jewish content.

Michael married Sharon, a non-Jewish woman, and they moved to Denver. Before their marriage, there was a great deal of drama since Robert's immediate family strongly disapproved of the intermarriage. None of his family attended the wedding, held in Nebraska, where Sharon grew up. A liberal Christian minister, one of Sharon's close family friends, performed the wedding and she made every effort to keep the ceremony nondenominational out of respect for Carol and Robert.

Michael's intermarriage was also very difficult for Carol and Robert, but they tried their best to be as welcoming as possible to Sharon. On the surface, they have a pleasant enough relationship with Michael and Sharon, but the dynamics with Robert's family left scars. Currently Michael and Sharon have a young daughter and son, both of whom were baptized in a ceremony that was more party-like than religious. Carol and Robert did not attend. Michael and Sharon are raising their children as both Jewish and Christian, but like many intermarried couples they are defining what this means as they go along.

A few years ago, Carol and Robert realized that, notwithstanding their circumstances, they still have a window in which they can attempt to provide a positive role model for their children and grandchildren when it comes to Jewish tradition. One decision Robert made after Chelsea gave birth to the twins was to be called *saba*, the Hebrew word for grandfather, rather than Grandpa. Carol decided to go with the Yiddish word for grandmother, *bubbe*. Although they made these decisions instinctively, and before their son married, they now realize there was much wisdom in these choices. The twins have already asked about why they selected these grandparent appellations and this gave them an opportunity to explain to them why Jewish tradition is so important to them as a family. They look forward to having similar conversations with their son's children when they get a bit older.

Carol and Robert know they cannot undo the past, but they made a joint commitment to rethink how the positive side of Jewish tradition can be presented to all of their grandchildren, children, and their spouses. For Robert in particular, this meant he had to be willing to let go of his tendency to frame Judaism according to his upbringing and instead embrace a remixed approach to Jewish tradition that can be made more appealing to his grandchildren.

Carol and Robert consulted some rabbis and other Jewish professionals and came up with a plan. Initially, they realized the need for a candid conversation with both of their children and their partners about *why* exposure to Jewish tradition is important for their respective families. They explained to their children that it is important to revisit all of their family history but particularly on Robert's side given how many relatives his family lost in the Holocaust.

Next, they decided to create a hard-copy journal for each of their grandchildren about why they both love Judaism. They considered doing a digital blog, but ultimately decided they wanted to create something tangible for each of their grandchildren that they can enjoy in the present as well as in the years to come. They also liked the idea of being able to tailor this journal to the current ages and interests of each of their grandchildren and adding more mature content as they grow.

Carol also decided to make more of an effort with both her daughter and her daughter-in-law to share not only Jewish culinary traditions but also other aspects of Jewish religious culture. On the food side, for years she has sent her homemade *hamantaschen* to both families as part of a Purim basket that, according to Jewish tradition, is sent to friends and relatives.[18] More recently, she has shared her recipe and offered to teach both women how to make them. Carol realizes she should have done this much sooner with Chelsea but she had little interest in this activity growing up. Carol hopes that she can interest Chelsea and her twins in learning how to make *hamantaschen* now. She has also offered to travel to Denver to teach Sharon and her children in person.

But Carol now realizes she needs to do more on other fronts of Jewish tradition. So she asked Chelsea and Sharon to join her on a

Shabbat retreat—either individually or together—and down the road, a women's trip to Israel—naturally, all on her dime. Although Chelsea has been to Israel twice, with a youth group and on a family trip, Sharon has never had an opportunity to visit the country. When Carol initially raised these ideas, she knew it would take time for any trips to materialize, but she kept talking about these possibilities and eventually both women joined her, separately, on a *Shabbat* retreat. Now they are more actively discussing the possibility of a women's trip to Israel or even a trip for the entire family. In fact, Chelsea and her husband are now open to considering some type of post–B'nai Mitzvah celebration for their twins in Israel.

Robert also made some efforts to take a trip with just Michael, which proved to be somewhat difficult to schedule given work and family responsibilities. But they were able to schedule a one-night getaway in Colorado, and the two enjoyed some quality time together. They were able to discuss Michael's religious upbringing and openly talk about things Carol and Robert might have done differently. Robert was also able to explain his feelings about why it matters to him that Michael's children have some exposure to Jewish tradition and they brainstormed ideas about how this could be accomplished within the realm of what would be acceptable to Michael and Sharon. The conversation is ongoing and has facilitated some communication in an area that previously was closed off.

Unlike Jennifer and Gary, Carol and Robert face the obstacle of distance that presents two associated negatives. The first, of course, is the inability to spend as much time with their nonlocal grandchildren as with those who live close by. Second, siblings who live in different places do not have the same opportunity to cultivate relationships between their children, the cousins, as is the case with siblings who live near one another. From the standpoint of transmitting Jewish tradition, these missed opportunities are also missed opportunities for creating family memories in connection with *Shabbat* and holiday celebrations.

Of course video-based calls through FaceTime and Skype provide grandparents, parents, and grandchildren a transformational opportunity for interaction, and perhaps this can also be helpful for older children who want to stay in touch with their cousins. With Michael and Sharon's permission, Carol and Robert initiated the practice of using

FaceTime every Friday afternoon to offer their out-of-town grandchildren the traditional *Shabbat* blessing.

But quality in-person time still matters. For this reason, Carol and Robert decided that it was important not only for them to make frequent visits to see Michael and Sharon, but also to pay for them to make return visits so that the whole family can be together. Carol and Robert always schedule these visits during Rosh Hashanah or the Passover Seders, rather than Thanksgiving, so that they can maximize the opportunities for Jewish content.

Carol and Robert stand firm on the importance of celebrating these holidays on their actual days, rather than on nearby days that may be convenient more generally. In contrast, a recent trend has emerged for families to designate a day that works for the family collectively, regardless of whether that day is the actual holiday.[19] Given Robert's background, this is one of the few lines in the sand they decided it was necessary to draw. They chose to deal with this decision by explaining their thinking to their children as best they could, and asking whether they could live with this one concession to them. But when it comes to the Passover Seder, Carol and Robert display much more flexibility in the length and content than when they were raising their children, as long as the major elements are included. They also try to include more content that is child oriented so the experience will be positive for everyone at the table.

Carol and Robert recently experienced some important validation to their approach with Michael's family. When both of their children married, Carol and Robert gave each couple a menorah and it has been their practice to send Chanukah candles to both families every year. Last year, Carol and Robert visited Michael and Sharon in December during a period that included part of Chanukah. When they all lit the menorah, Carol and Robert were delighted to hear their grandchildren chanting the blessings in Hebrew. Apparently Michael had been celebrating Chanukah with his children for the past couple years. Michael also confessed to his parents that this visit marked a significant sign of progress from his perspective because it was the first time they had visited in December, and they were able to be comfortable (at least outwardly) in the presence of the Christmas tree that also graced their home.

Like Jennifer and Gary, Carol and Robert work together as effective partners in their efforts to facilitate the transmission of Jewish tradition to their grandchildren. All four of these parents have a genuine interest in Judaism and raised their children with a good dose of Jewish tradition as a foundation. These positive factors are lacking in the situation presented by the third couple.

Jackie and Craig

Jackie and Craig are both Jewish but raised their two daughters with minimal religious tradition. Ten years ago, when their daughters were in their midtwenties, Jackie and Craig divorced. One of their daughters, Stephanie, is married to a religious Christian man. They are raising their three children in his faith, although Stephanie did not formally convert and is minimally involved in religious events at the church. Their other daughter, Beth, married a Jewish man but they are raising their two children with no religion. Still, they celebrate Christmas as a cultural holiday. The entire family lives in close proximity to one another.

Both Jackie and Craig are on good terms with their daughters despite their strained relationship with each other. After the divorce, Craig married a younger Catholic woman and she is raising her two children from a prior marriage in that faith. Meanwhile, Jackie has taken a growing interest in Judaism as a result of her personal connection with a warm, loving Orthodox couple who live near her and do *kiruv* (Jewish outreach). She has been to their home for *Shabbat* dinner several times and is now feeling as though she completely missed the opportunity to instill Jewish values and tradition in her daughters. It pains her very much that, although all of her grandchildren are Jewish according to *halakhah*, none of them are being raised Jewish. Jackie knows that she will never be as observant as her Orthodox friends, but she now wants more for her grandchildren than she gave her children. But when she has raised anything having to do with Judaism with her daughters, she encounters overt hostility,

Although Jackie remains on good terms with both of her daughters, she knows that this could easily change if she pushes too much on the subject of Judaism. Also, with respect to one set of grandchildren, she confronts the reality that they are being raised as devout Christians and there is virtually nothing she can do to change that reality. In truth, Jackie likes Stephanie's husband and believes he is a good man. She does not want to say or do anything that will cause friction for the couple.

Jackie scheduled an appointment with a local Reform rabbi who specializes in interfaith families. He advised her that if she wishes to be active in the Jewish journeys of any of her grandchildren, she must invest some time and effort in learning more about Judaism.[20] He explained to her that this education should be broad based to include not just religious practices but also Jewish history and narrative. He also recommended she take a basic class on Torah, the Five Books of Moses, since that is also a foundational text for Christians.

In addition to recommending some basic Jewish learning, the rabbi also suggested that Jackie learn more about her family's Jewish history. He shared some basic strategies for getting started on this type of genealogical research and explained that often, these personal Jewish narratives provide an important way for grandparents to share their families' Jewish stories "with confidence and joy."[21]

After this conversation with the rabbi, Jackie realized that she could share Jewish content with her grandchildren being raised Christian without being seen as threatening their religious upbringing. One of Jackie's friends suggested she meet with a Christian minister of the same denomination as her son-in-law to discuss this matter in more detail. During their discussion she learned that many religious Christians have high regard for the Jewish faith, even if they disagree with Judaism's theology. Armed with this knowledge, she decided to speak with her daughter and son-in-law about whether they would allow her to introduce a degree of exposure to the Jewish religion to their children. To her surprise, her son-in-law was open to this idea as long as Jackie promised to be respectful of their choices in how they are raising their children.

Meanwhile, her daughter Beth and her Jewish husband are more resistant than Stephanie and her husband. At first, Jackie could not understand why there was such a difference between her two daughters and their husbands regarding her desire to transmit Jewish tradition to her grandchildren. Eventually, though, Jackie came to understand that, whereas Beth and her husband view religion negatively, Stephanie's husband is coming from a place of respect for religion in general.

So Jackie decided to sit down with Beth and have a heart-to-heart talk with her about why Jewish tradition matters more to her now, and why she feels it is important that Beth's children have at least some exposure. She asked whether she could introduce Beth to the Reform rabbi she met with earlier and whether Beth would at least keep an open mind to hearing what he had to say, and even exploring his synagogue's religious school. Beth and her sister Stephanie are close and Beth is aware that Jackie has also been attempting to provide some exposure to Jewish tradition to Stephanie's children but with very clear boundaries. Currently Jackie and Beth are discussing whether some degree of limited exposure to Jewish tradition might be acceptable to Beth and her husband, and what that exposure might look like.

Jackie also has made substantial progress on her genealogical research and, as the rabbi predicted, both her daughters and all of her grandchildren have been very interested in her findings. Jackie is hoping that down the road, she might be able to persuade both daughters and their families to join her on a Jewish heritage tour to Europe so they can all see some of the places where Jackie's grandparents and ancestors lived. At this point, Jackie feels this trip might be a better sell to Beth's family than a trip to Israel. Not surprisingly, though, Stephanie's husband has expressed interest in a family trip to Israel.

Over the past year or so, Jackie has made Passover and Chanukah a particular focus with her grandchildren. For now, Beth and her husband have been more amenable to events at Jackie's home as opposed to any sort of Jewish celebrations in their own home. Jackie hosted a Passover Seder that everyone attended and she spent a lot of time coming up with child-friendly activities that were the focus of the celebration. With the permission of both of her daughters, she bought menorahs for the two families but she has not asked whether they have ever been used. This year Jackie hosted a Chanukah party at her home where everyone lit candles and sang a couple of Chanukah songs. She has yet to tackle a *Shabbat* dinner and she knows this may be more of a challenge given the weekly schedules of her grandchildren. But she is actively thinking about making her next birthday celebration a *Shabbat* dinner instead of the usual dinner in a nice restaurant.

Jackie admits that she would do things differently if she could go back in time, but given how things have turned out, she feels this is the best she can do given her circumstances. She is feeling more hopeful now that at least she can favorably impact her grandchildren's knowledge about Judaism. As Jackie expands her own Jewish horizons, she hopes she can continue to foster some degree of Jewish education in all of her grandchildren. She also hopes that this exposure will spur a desire in some of her grandchildren to learn more as adults, and maybe even for Beth's children to practice Judaism to some degree as they grow older.

Finally, Jackie has developed a relationship with her local Jewish federation, through which she devotes at least one day a month to volunteering in local soup kitchens. She recently decided to approach both of her daughters about joining her in this work from time to time, and including their spouses and all five grandchildren. Somewhat to her surprise, this request was met with approval from both families. Jackie also has explored some programming in connection with Grandparents for Social Action, a movement begun in Chicago that has spread across the country. She has learned much from their programming and monthly newsletter, and she believes this exposure will help her pass along Jewish values of social action to her grandchildren.

The receptivity of Jackie's whole family to social action affirms the universal appeal of this aspect of Jewish tradition. Indeed, social action is widely embraced by secular Jews as well as people of other faiths. The following chapter examines the benefits, as well as the limitations, of social action efforts in connection with preserving Jewish tradition.

6

TIKKUN OLAM

Judaism's Most Celebrated Remix?

A Jew must be sensitive to the pain of all human beings. A Jew cannot remain indifferent to human suffering, whether in other countries or in our own cities and towns. The mission of the Jewish people has never been to make the world more Jewish, but to make it more human.

—Elie Wiesel[1]

These words, penned by renowned author and Holocaust survivor Elie Wiesel, cannot help but move any reader. For many Jews, his sentiment also represents a lived reality. Jews can find ways to tap into the wisdom and meaning of Jewish tradition, including the ritual aspects of the tradition, as they also focus on the much-needed task of humanizing the world. Consider the narrative of Susan Rothstein, a consultant to nonprofit organizations, who found Judaism as an adult on a crowded bus in Uganda. Rothstein was raised in a Reform family that took social activism very seriously. But by her own admission, her "personal connection to the religious side of Judaism wore thin." Still, her innate drive to heal the world led her to volunteer for three months in Uganda with the American Jewish World Service as a strategic planning and fundraising consultant for an environmental NGO. During this time, she witnessed the installation of Uganda's first rabbi, Gershom Sizomu, followed by the very first *Shabbat* service led by a Ugandan rabbi. Rothstein wrote in *Tablet Magazine* that this *Shabbat* "was the most pure religious experience" she ever had.[2]

When Rothstein returned to the United States, she decided to "reclaim her Jewish self" by creating what she believed to be a real Jewish home and having a Bat Mitzvah. After a year of preparation and study, she became a Bat Mitzvah at the age of sixty-two. The ceremony took place in her Reform synagogue, the oldest synagogue west of the Mississippi. In describing this experience, she observed, "By standing before my family, friends and congregation in all my Jewish glory, I finally made myself whole. I had gone to Uganda to help heal the world, and the person most healed was me."[3]

I selected Rothstein's story as the entry point to this chapter because it situates the idea of *tikkun olam*, commonly thought of as "repairing the world," as a foundational element of Judaism, and one that can provide a pathway into greater involvement with the ritual components of the tradition. This is not an uncommon connection. Recently my friend Terrie, who grew up in a very secular Jewish home and is not particularly religious, confided in me that what she would miss most about her life in her current geographic location is her synagogue. Intrigued, I asked her why. She needed no time to reply with her reasons: the heavy activism of her synagogue community and its rabbi's dedication to social justice. This activism was the reason she joined. But, by being affiliated, she and her family have also grown in their appreciation for some of the ritual aspects of Judaism. They are more engaged with the Jewish holidays and Jewish community, and they have deepened their knowledge of Judaism. Recently they even went on a trip to Israel sponsored by their synagogue, which was Terrie's husband's first time in the country.

In his preface to a volume of essays dedicated to exploring *tikkun olam* from a variety of perspectives, Rabbi Martin Cohen wrote that this concept has morphed and developed in ways that would be seen as unexpected, "even perhaps foreign" to those who crafted its original formulations.[4] Today, the term *tikkun olam* is a regular part of the lexicon of many American Jews. Not surprisingly, Justice Ruth Bader Ginsburg, who is Jewish, touted her commitment to *tikkun olam* during a trip to Jerusalem when she was the recipient of the Genesis Prize Foundation lifetime achievement award. Even former president Barack Obama used this phrase in public addresses to Jewish audiences.[5]

For many Jews, the Hebrew phrase *tikkun olam* is synonymous with the concept of social action. According to Rabbi Vernon Kurtz, a story is told about an American Jew who, on his first visit to Israel, asks his Israeli cousin when he arrives at the airport to greet him "How do you say *tikkun olam* in Hebrew?" This story is funny precisely because it underscores the reality that some Jews may not even realize the phrase *tikkun olam is* Hebrew. The story's humor derives from the reality that although use of the term *tikkun olam* is quite common, knowledge of the term's history is not.

Although *tikkun olam* has strong roots in the Jewish tradition, the way most Jews think about the concept today is a fairly recent development in Jewish history, particularly in the United States.[6] When it comes to the role of *tikkun olam* in a remixed approach to Judaism, its current popularity is a double-edged sword. On the one hand, as discussed more below, the concept has an authentic basis in Jewish tradition. But on the other hand, because the application of *tikkun olam* has become so universalized, its role in transmitting a particularized Jewish tradition can become compromised unless Jews also are engaging in some other important foundational Jewish ritual observances.

Some commentators are critical of the current understandings of *tikkun olam* on the ground that they have little or nothing to do with the various ways in which the term was understood in the classical Jewish literature. Critics of the current perception also emphasize the negative effects of transforming the totality of Jewish identity and observance into a message that is essentially universal in nature. Although many people in this camp tend to be traditionally observant, there have also been criticisms of the use of *tikkun olam* even by self-denominated liberal Jews. Other commentators defend the current popular understanding of *tikkun olam* as representative of the core mission of Judaism. These observers believe that an emphasis on social action has deep roots in Jewish tradition and the concept is a very helpful one in providing a necessary path for Jews who are not conventionally observant to connect with their tradition. Commentators in the middle see merit in both positions and try to forge common ground.[7]

In 2018, these debates took center stage with the publication of Jonathan Neumann's divisive book *To Heal the World? How the Jewish Left Corrupts Judaism and Endangers Israel*. Neumann's discussion of *tikkun olam* in the context of advancing a conservative political ideology engendered significant controversy, further underscoring the sharp differences among American Jews not only religiously, but also politically.[8]

If *tikkun olam* is understood to embrace a commitment to social justice, it is difficult to see how anyone can argue that this is a bad thing in and of itself. I distinctly recall the enormous sense of pride I felt several years ago when I taught Family Law for the first time and learned the names of the two lawyers who represented Mildred and Richard Loving in the landmark 1967 Supreme Court decision outlawing state prohibitions of interracial marriage: Bernard Cohen and Philip Hirschkop. I think it is fair to say that most Jews—especially liberal Jews—are proud of their commitment to causes that fit within the rubric of *tikkun olam* as it is commonly understood today. In fact, the 2013 Pew Report, which identified nine potential elements of Jewish identity, provides ample evidence of this reality. After "remembering the Holocaust," the two most popular elements were "leading an ethical and moral life" and "working for justice and equality." In contrast, "observing Jewish law" came in second to last.[9]

But with respect to *tikkun olam*'s application to a remixed approach to Judaism, it is important to acknowledge that embracing *tikkun olam* absent any other elements of Jewish practice will not do much to preserve Jewish tradition. This position is underscored by the Pew data. Andrés Spokoiny, the chief executive officer of the Jewish Funders Network, framed one aspect of this issue extremely well when he encouraged *tikkun olam* advocates to clarify the difference between secular social activism and *tikkun olam* in order to ensure that "they are making a uniquely Jewish contribution."[10] Part of the challenge here can be met with more effective education, but also vital are larger conversations that center on the respective roles of *tikkun olam* and celebration of ritual in connection with preserving Jewish tradition.

THE EVOLUTION OF *TIKKUN OLAM* IN JEWISH TRADITION

Anyone with even a rudimentary knowledge of the Torah knows that it has much to say about treating people in a humane manner. The Torah portion in the book of Exodus known as *Mishpatim* (translated as "laws") provides a wealth of source material for today's *tikkun olam* enthusiasts. For example, although slavery is allowed, people are commanded to set their slaves free in the seventh year of their servitude, unless the slaves themselves wish to remain. It is also prohibited to mistreat widows, orphans, and strangers, and to retain overnight a neighbor's item of clothing as a pledge to secure a loan repayment because it may be his only covering and he will have nothing else in which to sleep. In addition, showing bias in a court of law is forbidden. This Torah portion also mandates concern for the poor by requiring that the land must rest in the seventh year and be available for the needy. Admittedly, these same passages also contain some content that does not sit well from a modern viewpoint, but the concern for society's underclass in the Torah is clear and visceral.[11]

Subsequent books in the Torah reflect a similar theme. For example, in the book of Leviticus, God commands the Israelites to refrain from reaping their harvest to the edges of the land and to leave the "gleanings" for the poor and the stranger. This theme is repeated in verses in the book of Deuteronomy, the final book of the Torah, that command Israelites to preserve portions of their harvest, olive trees, and vineyards for orphans and widows.[12] Also, once every three years, the Israelites are commanded to dedicate a second tithe of their fields for the benefit of the poor.[13]

> For there will never cease to be needy ones in your land, which is why I command you: open your hand to your poor and needy brother in your land.
>
> —Deuteronomy 15:11

Rabbi Jill Jacobs has observed that by using the term *achikha* (your brother) when speaking of the poor in this verse and elsewhere, the Torah is commanding resistance "of any temptation to view the poor as somehow different from ourselves." Chapter 15 of Deuteronomy also states that every seven years, all debts are to be forgiven. The reason for this law is to avoid the existence of a permanent underclass. This chapter also requires people to continue to give to the poor regardless of whether it is close in time to the seventh year. Taken together, these laws demonstrate that even as early as the era of the Torah, Jewish tradition demanded that people act against their own self-interest by providing a legislative path designed to care for the poor and minimize permanent poverty.[14]

Although the Torah does not use the term *tikkun olam*, the term is used in the Mishnah (the earliest Jewish law code, produced around 200 CE) in connection with a number of social policy laws designed to provide additional protections to those members of Jewish society who are potentially disadvantaged. The institution of the *prozbul* by Hillel is one of the more well-known examples of this type of legislation. In light of the Torah's ruling that every seven years all debts must be forgiven, Hillel was concerned that people would refrain from lending money especially as the seventh year approached. So he instituted this legal work-around by which lenders could authorize the court, which was not bound to forgive debts, to collect any debts that were owed. Although this maneuver circumvented the Torah's dictate because it allowed loans to be collected even after the seventh year, it safeguarded the community's economic well-being in a society that differed from the Torah era.[15]

The phrase *tikkun olam* also was mentioned in the Babylonian Talmud and other early rabbinic sources. The contexts of these usages leave little doubt that the "world" initially meant specifically the Jewish world. But by medieval times, there is evidence of a different meaning being associated with this term. During this period, the well-known *Aleinu* prayer, whose second paragraph contains a reference to *tikkun olam*, became part of the daily liturgy and is still recited by observant Jews three times a day. The term's usage here centers on repairing the world in a more universalistic sense through mankind's recognition of God's sovereignty. The use of *tikkun olam* in the *Aleinu* generally is understood to refer to the entire world rather than the Jewish world, and in this manner it departs from prior usage.[16]

Kabbalists in the Middle Ages used the term *tikkun olam* in their circles of Jewish mysticism to mean that by observing God's commandments, Jews, as a result of changes in God's essence in response to positive human actions, could repair not only their broken inner lives but also the larger cosmos. Rabbi Elliot Dorff has observed that this usage of the term undoubtedly brought comfort to Jews because it gave them hope that they could take action to make things better for themselves in a world in which the surrounding environment was hostile to them on so many levels. The use of *tikkun olam* in this context took the concept to a level that transcended its Talmudic origins because it emphasized the impact of human activity not only on the individual actor, but also on God's response.[17]

According to Rabbi Jill Jacobs, "the term *tikkun olam* more or less disappeared from popular usage between the sixteenth century and the 1950s, when the concept emerged within liberal Jewish communities as the new shorthand for 'social justice.'"[18] Although the term *tikkun olam* may not have been in vogue until fairly recently, the reality is that with the advent of the Enlightenment and the emancipation of the European Jews, the drive for social justice that had always occupied Jewish thinking from an internal perspective began to be directed in more outward terms. In the United States, this tendency fostered a liberal Jewish identity that centered on aligning with other oppressed groups— historically, African Americans. In the 1960s, Rabbi Abraham Joshua Heschel, a professor at the Jewish Theological Seminary, emerged as the face of civil rights activism within the Jewish community. The iconic photograph taken in 1965 of Heschel marching arm in arm with Dr. Martin Luther King Jr. in Selma, Alabama, cemented his status in this respect.[19]

Since the last decades of the twentieth century, *tikkun olam* has become an increasingly popular concept for the repair of people, animals, the environment, the economy, and many other causes, some of which have no direct connection to Jewish observance. But all of these newer applications are steeped in the fundamental concepts of *tzedakah* and *hesed*, cornerstones of the Jewish tradition.

> Rabbi Eleazar said: Whoever does deeds of charity (*tzedakah*) and justice (*mishpat*) is considered as having filled the entire world, all of it, with lovingkindness (*hesed*).
>
> —Sukkah 49b, Babylonian Talmud

Both charity and lovingkindness have the potential for tremendous universalization, especially in our modern world. But it is worth exploring here the Jewish roots of these concepts, known in Hebrew as *tzedakah* and *hesed*, in order to gain an appreciation for the unique perspective Jewish tradition provides in connection with these terms. *Tzedakah*, providing financial assistance to the poor, is mandatory according to Jewish tradition. For some people, it seems counterintuitive that someone who gives because they are commanded to is seen as worthier than one who gives voluntarily, but recall that Jewish law embodies an obligatory system. In fact, according to the *Shulchan Arukh*, the sixteenth-century code of Jewish law that still governs Orthodox practice today, even those who receive *tzedakah* may be obligated to give.[20] Despite this focus on obligation, the tradition also recognizes the benefits that people derive from giving financial support to those in need. According to an early homiletic commentary on Leviticus, "More than the wealthy person does for the poor, the poor person does for the wealthy" (Vayikra Rabbah 34:8).

The importance of *hesed* is emphasized in the famous statement by Hillel: "What is hateful to you, do not do to your neighbor," discussed at the beginning of chapter 4.[21] Consider also the following narrative about *hesed*:

> Our rabbis taught that deeds of lovingkindness are superior to charity in three respects. Charity can be accomplished only with money, while deeds of lovingkindness can be accomplished through personal involvement as well as with money. Charity can be given only to the poor, while deeds of lovingkindness can be done for both rich and poor. And charity applies only to the living, while deeds of lovingkindness apply to both the living and the dead. (Sukkah 49b, Babylonian Talmud)

Hesed is performed on an individual level and everyone has the ability to engage in acts of lovingkindness. Also, according to Jewish tradition, individuals are created in the image of God, and therefore must mirror God's lovingkindness to man: "Just as the Holy One is righteous, so you too must be righteous. Just as the Holy One is kind, so too you must be kind" (Sifrei D'varim, *Eikev*, on Deuteronomy 11:22).

The concept of God's *hesed* to man is a major theme in the Torah, running from beginning to end. In the book of Genesis, we learn that God showed lovingkindness to Adam and Eve by making garments for them to wear. Deuteronomy states that God buried Moses in the valley in the land of Moab.[22]

> "Follow the Eternal your God" (Deuteronomy 13:5). What does this mean? Is it possible for a mortal to follow God's Presence? The verse means to teach us that we should follow the attributes of the blessed Holy One. As God clothes the naked . . . you should clothe the naked. As the Holy One visited the sick . . . so you should visit the sick. As the Holy One comforted those who mourned . . . so you

should comfort those who mourn. As the Holy One buried the dead . . . so you should bury the dead. (Sotah 14a, Babylonian Talmud)

Early rabbinic sources also illustrate that Jewish tradition demands study as well as acts of kindness. This theme is vividly emphasized in a version of a Talmudic passage appearing in the traditional Jewish prayer book at the beginning of the daily morning service:

> These are the deeds which yield immediate fruit and continue to yield fruit in time to come: honoring parents; doing deeds of loving-kindness; attending the house of study punctually; morning and evening; providing hospitality; visiting the sick; probing the meaning of prayer; making peace between one person and another. And the study of Torah is the most basic of them all. (Adaptation of Shabbat 127a, Babylonian Talmud)

Jacobs fittingly captured this critical intersection between Jewish learning and action by emphasizing that "the rich Jewish tradition of law and narrative must be lived in the world." But she also rightly observes that American Jews involved in social justice initiatives largely keep "their Judaism quiet" when it comes to matters of religious observance. Additionally, she laments that "there has been little effort to think seriously about American policy through the eyes of Jewish law and tradition."[23]

Several years ago, when I was co-directing the Center for Jewish Law and Judaic Studies at my university, I had a telephone conversation with a very prominent law professor who remarked to me that Judaism colored virtually every aspect of his thinking about constitutional law. I was so struck by his remark that I decided our center should sponsor a conference exploring how the Jewish backgrounds of some of the nation's most renowned law professors influenced their thinking and writing. Our participants had a range of Jewish backgrounds—from those who were brought up in completely secular homes to those raised with significant Jewish tradition. Their current levels of observance also ran the gamut. Despite these differences, all of the contributors maintained strong Jewish identities and all believed these identities influenced their current work. From the standpoint of content and attendance, I feel this symposium was one of the most successful programs our center sponsored during the period of my administrative involvement.[24]

My good friend and DePaul colleague Professor Susan Bandes was one of our speakers. Much of Susan's professional life has revolved around public interest law and civil rights. She grew up in the New York area in a home that, in her view, lacked any significant Jewish content. Still, just by virtue of growing up during the 1950s and 1960s in this environment, Susan became what she called a "maven of cultural Jewishness" despite being "woefully ignorant about too much" of the religion. Susan decided to become a Bat Mitzvah at the age of 50. She "began to appreciate the power of ritual, or what it is that makes Judaism not just a system of beliefs but a religion."[25]

Although Susan learned to appreciate Jewish tradition later in life, this is not the case for all Jews who consider themselves social justice advocates. The relationship between *tikkun olam* and preserving Jewish tradition is complicated. One arguable aspect of this complexity relates to the history of *tikkun olam* concerning whether the concept applies just to the Jewish social order or to the world at large. Specifically, should the beneficiaries of this repair be only the Jewish people or all people? In writing about this dimension, Vernon Kurtz asks, "Is our greatest concern as Jews the condition of our collective and shared humanity, or are we meant to focus on the particulars of our own peoplehood?" Agreeing with the reasoning of Rabbi Lord Jonathan Sacks, the former Chief Rabbi of the mainstream Orthodox synagogues in Great Britain, Kurtz concludes there is no real conflict because Jews can be members of both our Jewish family and our greater human family. Yet Kurtz cautions that the concept of *tikkun olam* has the potential to become so universalized that it detracts from its specific Jewish meaning, "as understood by Jewish sources and sages throughout history." In his view, Jews must be motivated to create a better world order for *both* the Jewish and the non-Jewish world.[26]

Lack of knowledge is another complexity. Although *tikkun olam* has deep roots in Jewish texts, many Jews are completely unaware of these sources and connections. But this reality can be changed with appropriate education. For example, in 2019, the Israeli-based nonprofit organization Bina: The Jewish Movement for Social Change opened its first satellite operation in Palo Alto, California. This location was selected because of the perception that its residents were intellectually curious and interested in tradition, as well as in "innovating tradition." Bina, which means "wisdom" in Hebrew, embraces text studies, social action, and community. The organization's philosophy is to rely on sacred texts to support social action and community building efforts. Its nonreligious setting is designed to facilitate a learning process perceived as more egalitarian and user friendly to all, including non-Jews. According to Bina's philosophy, the instructional Jewish texts are inspirational rather than binding. The point is not to follow the laws but rather to understand the tradition.

But Bina's philosophy underscores another complexity that may represent the greatest challenge to defining the role of *tikkun olam* in preserving Jewish tradition. Caring about *tikkun olam*, participating in social action projects, and even understanding the relevance of the Jewish sources do not necessarily go hand in hand with observing Jewish ritual. An exclusive focus on the non-ritual aspects of Judaism can easily morph the practice of *tikkun olam* into a universalistic concept divorced from the richness and beauty of Jewish tradition, regardless of knowledge of the original sources. For this reason, I embrace the call by Jill Jacobs for an "integrated Judaism" that includes "the use of Jewish ritual within social justice organizations and activities," as well as "concerted efforts to bring engagement with the world into synagogue life."[27]

CREATING SPACE FOR *TIKKUN OLAM* AS PART OF REMIX JUDAISM

Tikkun olam differs substantially from most of the other examples of remix discussed throughout this book because it is readily capable of being divorced from any particularistic aspect of Jewish tradition and ritual. As a result, from the standpoint of its potential for preserving Jewish tradition as a whole, *tikkun olam* plays a different role than, for example, the Jewish holidays, the dietary practices, and the celebration of B'nai Mitzvah. For this reason, although *tikkun olam* may be the most *celebrated example* of a remixed approach to Judaism, it is better to think of it as a *significant component* of a remixed approach to Judaism. As Dorff reminds us, although "the tradition is clear about the essence and imperative of *tikkun olam*" it does not embody "the whole of Judaism."[28]

It is fair to say that for many liberal Jews, participation in social justice endeavors ranging from activism to monetary support is the primary, and often the only, way in which they encounter Jewish tradition. Recently, my middle daughter and I were having a conversation about observance of Jewish tradition. Or, to put it more frankly, we were having a conversation about her *lack* of observance at this point in her life when she is balancing a full-time job and going to nursing school part-time. During our talk she observed, "Mom, to me being Jewish is really about being a good person." Of course, she is not wrong about the importance of being a good person according to Jewish tradition. But as I explained—with the best balance of caution and advocacy I could muster—Jewish tradition is about so much more.

My daughter's sentiments are fairly widespread—and not only among her peers. Shortly after our conversation, my friend Steven gave the sermon in the lay-led, alternative *Shabbat* service my synagogue sponsors once a month. He began his talk by saying that over the years he has either been the only Jew, or the most observant Jew, in his professional environment and frequently he has been asked some form of the following question: "Would you agree that Jewish observance is not necessary to be a good person?" Steven told our group that over the years, he realized that this question really misses the fundamental point about Judaism. Specifically, Jews are not commanded to be *good*, but rather to be *holy*:

> You shall be holy for I, the Lord your God, am holy. You shall not insult the deaf, or put a stumbling block before the blind. You shall not render an unjust decision; do not be partial to the poor or show deference to the rich; judge your neighbor fairly. Do not stand idly by the blood of your neighbor. You shall not hate your brother in your heart. Love your neighbor as yourself. (Selected from Leviticus 19:2; 14–18)[29]

The prophet Isaiah imagines Israel as "a light unto the nations." This notion has a universalistic quality that was readily embraced early on by the Reform movement and foreshadowed how *tikkun olam* would later evolve. Interestingly, in 2017, Orthodox authorities also interpreted this phrase in universalistic terms as imposing an obligation "to contribute to humanity's appreciation for holiness, morality and piety."[30]

Many Jews today can relate to the idea of being holy and "a light unto the nations" regardless of how they understand the relevance of faith in God, a topic to which I will return in the epilogue. For purposes of *tikkun olam*, these concepts can be important markers of Jewish peoplehood, which has a broader appeal to many modern Jews than religious obligation. Also, the tradition's understanding that Jews should be holy and "a light unto the nations" is very much capable of personal attribution, and therefore easily amenable to a remix philosophy.

The view that *tikkun olam* should be understood as a significant part of a remixed approach to Judaism emphasizes the importance of maintaining the particularity of Jewish tradition as well as undertaking social justice types of activities. On many levels, *tikkun olam* by itself fits perfectly with the concept of remix as developed in this book. Recall that remix entails exercising individual choice concerning elements of ritual performance, infusing these choices with personal meaning, and practicing these choices with consistency and a degree of authenticity. For many Jewish Americans, social justice activities are a regular part of their lives, representing a consistent pattern of practice. Also, as is the case with so many of the other Jewish traditions discussed throughout this book, people can easily infuse their *tikkun olam* work with personal attributions, rendering these projects extremely meaningful for themselves and their families. As for authenticity, we have already seen that *tikkun olam* gets high marks given its strong roots in Jewish tradition.

> On three things the world stands: on the Torah, on the service (worship of God), and on acts of lovingkindness.
> —Pirkei Avot 1:2, Mishnah Torah (quoting Shimon the Righteous)

As discussed earlier, lovingkindness, *hesed*, has a unique Jewish history and application but the general concept is universally appealing and readily embraced today by liberal Jews. In contrast, many nonobservant Jews have difficulty with Torah and worship. But with the proper framing of these concepts, Jews who struggle with Torah and worship can develop an appreciation for how they can work together with *hesed* to form a solid basis for a meaningful form of Jewish tradition, including the performance of *tikkun olam*. Regarding Torah, the results of a recent survey of Jewish social justice leaders conducted by the Jewish Social Justice Roundtable are instructive. This survey demonstrated that Jewish tradition creates "a layer of meaning" onto the experiences that energize social justice workers and provides a fountain of wisdom that strengthens their operations.[31] These findings suggest that even Jews who are not traditionally observant can still look to the Torah for useful wisdom.

Worship can also have relevance even for Jews who struggle with prayer. Jews choose to participate in formal worship for many different reasons, including the opportunity to be part of a community or to experience a sense of quietude or disconnection from the daily grind. Recall my friend Terrie's experience with her synagogue. She would be the first to agree that the community bonds created by a synagogue with an active social justice agenda will inevitably impact its members' attendance at other types of functions, including worship. The larger point here is that Jewish tradition and ritual still provide valuable sources from which all Jews, regardless of their level of religiosity, can draw to sustain and strengthen acts of *tikkun olam.*

Given that Jewish tradition includes *tikkun olam*, it is clearly important to make room for a consistently utilized space in our daily lives for *tikkun olam.* Creating an individual and family culture of giving *tzedakah* and performing *hesed* allows *tikkun olam* to become an integral part of life. But it is also important to link *tikkun olam* to its Jewish roots by, whenever possible, pairing *tikkun olam* with specifically Jewish rituals and applications.

Regardless of whether one understands *tzedakah* as a binding Divine command or something that is important to do voluntarily because it is the right thing, there is no doubt that the concept is central to the Jewish tradition. There is also significant authority, including Talmudic sources, for the proposition that Jews should not confine their giving only to Jews in financial need. Rabbi Samson Raphael Hirsch, considered by many to have laid the groundwork for the current Modern Orthodox movement, wrote the following in the nineteenth century:

> Be just in deed, truthful in your speech, bear love in your heart for your non-Jewish brother, as your Law teaches you. Feed his hungry, clothe his naked, console his mourners, restore his sick, help his helpless, assist him with counsel and deed in time of need and sorrow—unfold the whole noble breadth of your Israeldom.[32]

But from the standpoint of transmitting Jewish tradition, it is important to direct at least some *tzedakah* and volunteering efforts to Jewish causes. Donating to Jewish causes not only reinforces the message that support for the Jewish community is an important element of Jewish tradition, but also helps model and strengthen Jewish identity. And with creative research, it is possible to identify charities that combine more secular themes with a Jewish application. For example, in his discussion of new models for giving to Israel, education expert Alex Sinclair mentions possibilities such as giving money to an Israeli dog shelter for animal lovers and the Israeli Cancer Research Fund for those with an interest in supporting cancer-related research.[33]

Our family's gift of choice for all newborn babies is a *tzedakah* box, and judging by the huge selection of beautiful options available on the various Jewish-themed gift websites, we know we are far from alone in making this choice. Many people keep *tzedakah* boxes in their homes, and traditionally Jews fill them right before the start of *Shabbat*. This practice represents low-hanging fruit for families wishing to infuse their *tikkun olam* endeavors with Jewish ritual. It is also customary to give *tzedakah* in connection with Jewish holidays such as Rosh Hashanah, Passover, and Purim. When *tzedakah* is emphasized as a central part of these holiday celebrations, children will readily make the connection between *tikkun olam* and the particulars of Jewish tradition. Making *tikkun olam* a visible part of Jewish holiday celebrations is an easy way for parents to model the type of integrated Judaism advocated by Jill Jacobs.

For younger families, practices of *tzedakah* and volunteering should be as routine and consistent as possible, even if they only occur periodically. Recall from the chapter about food that I discussed my friend Robin who always does a special charity project with a local Jewish organization in conjunction with her annual Chanukah dinner. Even though she may change the nature of the project from year to year, her children know that at the time of the year they celebrate Chanukah and receive gifts for eight nights, they are also doing something to help others who are less fortunate. These projects provide wonderful teaching moments that will likely have a lasting impact on Robin's children.

My husband and I also used *tzedakah* at moments of special joy in connection with Jewish life cycle events to teach our daughters the value of generosity. When we first moved to Chicago and I began practicing law, a Jewish senior partner called me into his office and asked me to contribute to the Jewish Federation of Metropolitan Chicago. He proceeded to tell me all about the organization's annual book detailing the contributions of every participant. As someone from a very modest economic background who had tons of student loan debt, I was shocked and even somewhat horrified that a book detailing every person's contribution would be publicly available. Today, decades later, I see things differently given my substantial experience in fundraising for two centers at my law school.

Over the course of time, the Federation became our family's banner charity. One of the many reasons we actively support the Federation is its efficiency and ability to satisfy the needs of Jews, and non-Jews, on local, national, and international levels. My husband and I became involved in different ways and learned to appreciate, and take pride in, our city's outstanding Federation. When our daughters celebrated their B'nai Mitzvah, we made a conscious decision to scale down their parties so that we would have sufficient funds to make meaningful additional donations and proudly announced this at each of the receptions. We strongly felt that our joy would not have been complete unless we did something to enhance the lives of those less fortunate. We also continued this tradition at the weddings of our two married daughters, and look forward to more opportunities for these special-occasion contributions.

When our daughters were young, we also asked each of them to donate a portion of their annual birthday party presents to less fortunate children. I had actually forgotten about this practice until I saw that our youngest daughter recently referred to it in a biography she submitted in connection with her own Federation work. We take a lot of pride in the fact that all of our daughters, and their partners, donate to charities of their choice, with Jewish ones well represented, even though they are still at fairly early stages of their careers.

But in writing this chapter, I realized it would have been even better if we had paired the occasions for our charitable giving with family study of some short and sweet Jewish texts about *tzedakah* and *hesed* such as those contained in this chapter. As discussed in the introduction, Jewish narrative, *aggadah*, is an especially useful way of teaching children the moral lessons you are trying to convey. Exposure to *aggadah* also promotes Jewish literacy by enabling children to absorb the unique content and context of rabbinic narrative in an age-appropriate manner. Providing children with opportunities to become familiar with

Jewish narrative from an early age, especially combined with a fun family activity, can provide an important impetus for lifelong Jewish learning. Plus this exposure bolsters the element of authenticity that is so important to a remixed approach to Jewish tradition.

On a related note, I also wish we had done more volunteering as a family when our daughters were younger. These occasions also could have served as opportunities for brief Jewish learning as a family. Before our children were born, my husband and I tutored disadvantaged children through a program sponsored by a Chicago church. It was very difficult work even though we are both educators. But after our first daughter was born, the combination of parenting, working full-time, and an absence of family in the area to help took its toll. As is the case for so many young parents, the days flew by and it was all we could do to juggle everything on our plates.

Fortunately, in recent years we have done much better on this score, largely due to the efforts of our son-in-law Jordan, who is heavily involved in the *Tikkun Olam* Volunteer Program. Jordan continually organizes family volunteer days for us at local soup kitchens. This type of work also creates a wonderful opportunity for family bonding time, particularly if it is paired with a family meal afterward. But going forward, I will be sure to prepare a short *aggadic* text we can read and discuss together to add a dimension of Jewish learning to our work. It is never too late to start!

In most of the local soup kitchens in which we have worked, we are asked either to help prepare the food or serve it. But the JUF Uptown Café, the only kosher soup kitchen in our area, also asks its volunteers to sit and speak with those who are eating, and if possible, share some of the prepared food. I realized the reason for this policy while writing this chapter. Jewish tradition demonstrates that *tzedakah* and *hesed* are not just about providing the means, physically and economically, to help the poor. An equally important aspect of these concepts concerns tending to human dignity. By asking the volunteers to sit and break bread with their Jewish and non-Jewish guests, this particular soup kitchen maintains a policy that seeks to maximize the comfort and dignity of those who are being served.

> And thou shall speak to all the wise-hearted whom I have filled with
> a spirit of wisdom that they shall make Aaron's garments to sanctify
> him that he may be a priest to me.
>
> —Exodus 28:3

Although the context of this verse from the Torah does not have anything to do with *tikkun olam*, it illustrates the importance of emotional
intelligence, a quality that is significant for performing certain acts of
tikkun olam. The verse actually relates to those whom God considers
appropriate to make sacred clothing for Aaron, the first Israelite High
Priest. The language is a fairly literal translation of the Hebrew that
uses the phrases "wise-hearted" and "spirit of wisdom." I believe a "wise
heart" is an emotionally intelligent heart. The verse is telling us that
only those with emotional intelligence are fit to fulfill the appointed
task of creating an environment of holiness.

Drawing directly from this passage of the Torah, we should learn
that striving to be "wise-hearted" also means developing our sense of
emotional intelligence and mindfulness so that we can be more present
for our family and friends. Although many people think of *tikkun olam*
in terms of activist-oriented social justice work that is organizationally
based, Dorff reminds us that there are certain types of social action with
strong roots in the Jewish sources that are "often omitted when contemporary Jews think about *tikkun olam*." He offers several suggestions
under the rubric of "communal forms of *tikkun olam*" such as fulfilling
the "duty to be present for people in their times of need or joy."[34]

Sometimes just the act of being a good friend, partner, child, or even
parent can embody the very essence of what repairing the world is
designed to do. The same can be said for showing kindness to a complete stranger. This is especially true in our fast-paced world in which
we often are not as present—both physically and emotionally—for others as we might like. I am particularly drawn to Dorff's sentiments
because they enable us to keep the principles of *tikkun olam* foremost
in our minds as we go through our days, helping us to pay more attention to how Jewish tradition can impact our behaviors, even with respect to the smallest of matters. Without intending to minimize the
importance of the various social justice causes that are typically associated with *tikkun olam*, it is important to remember that these personal
exercises of *tikkun olam* can operate as an important part of a remixed
approach to Jewish tradition.

In this vein, consider also the following Talmudic wisdom: "Tzedakah saves a person from death" (Bava Batra 10a, Babylonian Talmud; Proverbs 10:2). In a moving commentary on this short passage, Rabbi Laura Geller wrote how she only understood the meaning of this sentence at the end of her thirty-day period of mourning for her late husband. She discussed the custom of giving a dollar or two of *tzedakah* during the morning prayer service that Geller had been attending daily following her husband's death. On that last day, as she reached into her purse for money, she suddenly realized that this particular form of *tzedakah* symbolizes how these morning prayer communities literally save mourners from a "living death, a heaviness that makes life seem unbearable."[35] In other words, the *tzedakah* became a symbol of the entire prayer community.

Tzedakah is not just an important component of *tikkun olam*, but it also has a prominent place among the Jewish rituals relating to death and mourning. As Rabbi Geller's piece suggests, Judaism maintains a prescribed way of coping with these aspects of the life cycle. The following chapter explores the unique approach Jewish tradition takes with respect to death and mourning, and demonstrates the continuing appeal of these rituals for Jews of all levels of observance.

7

REMIX AND THE POWER OF JEWISH MOURNING

At this point, it is worth emphasizing that the concept of remix has always played a role in Jewish lawmaking. After the destruction of the Temple in 70 CE, the rabbis needed to resolve how the Torah could be applied in a completely new environment. Their reforms, which embodied a remixed approach, formed the basis for the religion Jews practice today. These reforms also laid the groundwork for the continual development and application of Jewish law to new contexts and surroundings.

Also, once the Jews were living in exile among Diaspora cultures, both the rabbis and the people were exposed to foreign influences that impacted many types of rabbinic laws as well as folk practices among the people. As discussed in the introduction, Jewish tradition includes both Jewish law and culture, as well as foreign cultures that have influenced the development of this tradition.

The topic of mourning makes an especially compelling case for remix. Initially, because death and mourning are universally relevant, this area is one that has been particularly influenced by outside cultures. For example, the sages of the Palestinian community surrounded by a Hellenistic influence were buried in containers with mythological Greek images, and they saw no contradiction between this practice and Jewish law.[1] Centuries later, as discussed more below, the persecution of Jews living in Christian European countries spurred the development of now familiar Jewish rituals to memorialize the dead, elements of which were taken from Christian practice.

In addition, many of the rituals surrounding mourning are capable of significant personal attribution, an important ingredient in a remixed approach to Judaism. I believe this reality contributes to the staying power of these traditions. People find these rituals meaningful and helpful for a variety of reasons, and therefore are likely to tap into these personal attributions at liminal moments when they need spirituality the most.

We all feel a deep absence of control when we are faced with the loss of a loved one. In these circumstances, Judaism provides a path for grieving and healing that many people find helpful, even if they do not follow all of the rituals as they are prescribed according to *halakhah*, Jewish law. When it comes to mourning the death of a loved one, I see strong anecdotal evidence of a widespread, genuine inclination to observe *some* aspects of the tradition, even among Jews who are not otherwise observant. Many Jews follow some of the mourning practices in a way that is consistent, or somewhat consistent, with the law, adapt others to suit their needs, and ignore those they do not find meaningful. These choices of partial compliance, adaptation, and even rejection are all part of a remixed approach to Jewish tradition.

More specifically, although nontraditional Jews often truncate the initial seven-day period of mourning, they almost always have some type of *shiva* (derived from Hebrew for the word "seven") following a funeral, even if the *shiva* is only for one day. Many nonobservant Jews will also make a point of reciting *kaddish*, the traditional mourner's prayer, for a departed loved one for some period of time following the death, as well as on the *yahrtzeit*, the anniversary of the relative's passing (which is based on the date of death according to the Jewish calendar).

My friend Kathy's experience mourning her husband is illustrative. She went to great lengths to celebrate her husband's unveiling, a gravestone dedication ceremony that takes place a year or so after the funeral. Neither Kathy nor her late husband could be considered remotely observant but marking this occasion in a traditional manner somehow was very important to her. Not surprisingly, Kathy had a lot of difficulty letting go of her husband and their life together. For her, the unveiling represented another way to honor her husband, keep his memory alive, and perhaps stay close to him.

The anecdotal evidence of widespread observance among liberal Jews of some Jewish mourning practices is supported by some scholarly work, as well as the quantity and enduring popularity of books written about this topic.[2] But little actual empirical evidence on this score exists.[3] Even the 2013 Pew Report, the most recent comprehensive survey of the American Jewish community, contains no questions concerning the degree of observance of rituals and traditions relating to mourning.[4]

I believe the staying power of the unique Jewish traditions surrounding mourning also plays a role in reaffirming Jewish identity. The idea that the traditions surrounding mourning can contribute significantly to one's Jewish identity actually makes sense given that Judaism itself is a religion focused on the living. The laws and customs surrounding mourning are designed to strike a balance between maximizing reverence for the dead and the mourner's psychological well-being.[5]

My perspective that Judaism approaches mourning in such a meaningful and helpful way has been shaped by my personal experience in mourning both of my parents. These experiences allowed me to directly experience the wisdom of Jewish tradition as a mourner, even as I remixed to some degree my observance of the laws and traditions through a combination of adherence, partial compliance, and occasionally rejection. During the separate one-year periods I mourned for my father and then my mother, I was deliberate about which rituals I chose to follow (and there were many) and which I chose to ignore or modify. Although my primary guide was *halakhah*, I did at times intentionally depart from prescribed practice or modified it to suit my own needs. And although there was a significant degree of consistency regarding my practices during both years, there were times that I allowed myself to engage in specific situational departures. As I explain in the narrative below, in many instances I also created a personal attribution for the rituals I followed. Sometimes my attributions were the result of a conscious effort, but other times they just seemed to come organically. For these reasons, even my rather traditional approach to mourning embodies a remixed approach to Jewish tradition.[6]

EXPECTING THE UNEXPECTED

My first experience dealing with the death of a close relative was when I was twenty-three and my maternal grandmother passed away fairly suddenly after suffering a stroke. Prior to this time, my only experience with Jewish mourning practices consisted of a few condolence calls at the homes of various friends who had lost their grandparents. Also, although my father's parents passed away before he met my mother, I don't recall him speaking about visiting their graves and I was never at a cemetery prior to my grandmother's passing. As a general matter, I think my parents were fairly protective of me when it came to the topic of death. As a result, although there were areas of Jewish practice with which I was well acquainted growing up, the traditions surrounding death and mourning remained pretty much a mystery to me until I was much older.

For most of my adult life, I did not live in geographic proximity to my parents. Shortly after my husband and I married and moved to Chicago, my parents moved to Florida, where they lived for many years. We saw one another a few times a year and spoke at least weekly, often more. But during most of this time, I found it relatively easy to avoid too much focus on my parents' mortality despite their occasional brushes with some serious health conditions. Eventually, however, I had to confront the reality that they needed to move closer to me so I could step up my level of involvement on a daily basis. They moved to Chicago about two years before my father passed. Not surprisingly, this was not an easy sell given the harsh Chicago winters.

I found a lovely retirement community, with graduated care for my parents, that turned out to be a wonderful choice. They began their tenure there in the independent living quarters and enjoyed their new environment and being close to us. But soon my father was diagnosed with Alzheimer's disease, and then my mother was hit by a car as she was crossing the street. I had to move my father to the nursing wing while my mother spent three months in the hospital and a rehab facility. Given the extent of her injuries and his progressing illness, my father needed to remain in the nursing section permanently.

Six months later, my father fell and broke his pelvis. His doctor predicted he had about a month to live given the nature of his injuries and the trajectory of Alzheimer's patients who experience this type of injury. He was 100 percent on target. In a way, I was relieved because I never wanted to see my father in the end stages of Alzheimer's. At the time he passed away, he more or less knew who I was and he could still communicate. When the call came, it was almost sunset on a wintry Saturday afternoon and I was home reading a book. Despite his doctor's prediction, the event seemed unexpected and was a shock. I learned what it meant to expect the unexpected.

My mother passed away six and a half years later, but although they both died at the age of 92, the circumstances were very different. She recovered as best as she could after her accident, but she was never the same physically. Although she returned to her apartment for several years, eventually she too needed the support of full-time nursing care. Her last years were difficult physically but I want to believe they were also somewhat emotionally joyous. She saw our family all the time and even got to meet our daughters' significant others and attend our oldest daughter's wedding.

The last time I saw my mother was a beautiful sunny day right before my husband and I left for a trip to Italy. It was a short but sweet visit and she seemed stable and in good spirits. I never expected this to be the last time I would see her, although that thought always crossed my mind whenever I traveled. But two days into our trip I got a phone call informing me that she had passed away. We were at breakfast overlooking the Amalfi coast, and I was just about to take a sip of a delectable Italian coffee. Again, another case of expecting the unexpected. No matter how old your parents are, and how infirm, it is often the case that one just does not expect to receive the news that they have passed.

In both instances, the structure provided by the Jewish mourning traditions provided me with tremendous comfort. I opted for a traditional process of mourning, which meant starting down a path that I knew would offer a simultaneous sense of direction and reassurance. For example, Jewish law requires burial in the earth, as soon as possible after death. This shortened time frame between death and burial not only is mandated by Jewish law, but also has become a distinguishing feature of the American Jewish culture surrounding death, contrasting with the predominant Christian practice of a longer interim period. By requiring as quick a burial as possible, Jewish tradition affords mourners a strong boost to their grieving spirit by facilitating a sense of closure. The interim period between a close relative's death and the funeral is extremely stressful no matter how many logistics are taken care of before a death.

My mother handled several significant aspects of their funeral arrangements when they moved to Chicago, which was an incredible gift to me that I still deeply appreciate. For the most part, I did not have to worry about determining their larger-scale wishes or making difficult choices. In the case of both of my parents, I had sketched out some ideas for what I wanted to say at their funerals long in advance, so I also did not have the pressure of having to come up with content after they passed. Even so, there still were some logistics to be handled, especially since my mother passed away while we were abroad. In both instances, I felt completely unhinged during this interim time and longed for the routine that I sensed the *shiva* would bring.

When my father passed away, my focus was largely on my mother and her well-being. She and I disagreed a bit about the specifics of the funeral that had not yet been determined. For example, I wanted my father to be buried in a white shroud without pockets, which is the customary tradition. This clothing requirement is designed to equalize all people in death, regardless of how much wealth they possessed while alive. The color white reflects the tradition's belief that death should reflect purity and innocence rather than sin and indiscretion.[7] My mother instead wanted my father to be buried in one of his suits.

Jewish law also prescribes that the deceased is not to be left alone during the interim period before the funeral, and so I wanted to hire a *shomar*, someone who watches the body during this period and recites selections for the Book of Psalms.[8] In addition, I wanted my father to undergo the traditional ritual process of washing and purifying the body, known as *taharah*, that is typically performed by the members of a local Jewish burial society, known as a *hevra kaddisha*.

I am told by people who work in the Jewish funeral industry that it is not uncommon for people to adopt all, none, or some of these practices. For example, some people elect to do *taharah* but do not hire a *shomar*. The variability here parallels the variability of Jewish practice in all other areas for people who are not governed by *halakhah*. Again, in non-Orthodox communities, people choose what is meaningful to them and avoid choices that lack meaning or seem foreign. Till this day, I cannot say whether my wishes for my father were governed by *hala-*

khah or my sense that this is what my father would have wanted had he thought about these particular matters. Eventually, though, my mother gave in to my wishes on these matters, probably because she understood my overall argument that Jewish tradition really mattered to my father even though he was not conventionally religious.

Although it is traditional for men to be buried in their own *tallit* (prayer shawl), it was very important to me to keep my father's *tallit*, and so he was buried in one that he did not own. Since my decision departed from what some regard as an established Jewish practice, this too can be considered an exercise in remix. The personal meaning of this choice continues to be significant for me and others in my family. When our youngest daughter was married eight years after my father's death, she and her husband were wrapped in his *tallit* for the final blessing of the bride and groom.

> When Reuben returned to the pit and saw that Joseph was not in the pit, he rent his clothes.
>
> —Genesis 37:29

In the worldview of the Torah, tearing one's clothing is a sign of grief. After Joseph's brothers had sold him into slavery, his brother Reuben returned to the pit in which he had been held, and upon seeing it empty, he believed that Joseph was dead and so he "rent his clothes." Later, when the brothers presented their father Jacob with Joseph's colored coat that they had dipped in an animal's blood, Jacob similarly "rent his clothes" and mourned his son for many days.[9]

According to *halakhah*, one is required to mourn only for one's parents, siblings, children, and spouse.[10] An aspect of this mourning process involves the *k'riah* ceremony, which entails the recitation of a blessing and the ripping of an article of clothing by the mourners as a sign of grief. The ceremony usually is performed at the beginning of the funeral. Today, it is pretty much a universal practice, although less traditional Jews often elect to rip a small black ribbon rather than an actual item of clothing.

I suspect the popularity of this ritual is due to the symbolism that physically ripping a piece of material entails. This action signifies the physical destruction of a relationship that can no longer be actualized.[11] The mourner is required to make the tear herself. Both of the times I was a mourner, I found that making a tear in one of my scarves provided a cathartic release. The requirement of wearing the torn item during the entire *shiva* period also provided me with a sense of comfort that I still do not fully understand. In the case of deceased parents, the *k'riah* tradition entails some special rules. First, the clothing is torn on the left side over the heart. For me, this symbolized that my heart was broken and would never be quite the same. Also, although in general an item used for the *k'riah* can be completely mended after a period of thirty days, the clothing torn for a parent should never be permanently repaired. I believe the symbolism, poignancy, and meaning attached to *k'riah* undoubtedly contributes to its enduring popularity among Jews of all levels of observance.

Another hallmark of a Jewish funeral is that family members and others in attendance shovel dirt onto the casket. This allows the mourners and others to act out a personal farewell to the deceased. Particularly when performed for a parent or other close relative, this final goodbye can be extremely powerful and emotional. Rabbi Maurice Lamm explains in his seminal work on Jewish mourning that there also is a beneficial quality inherent in this practice because it spurs the beginning of healing by dispelling the illusion that one's relative is still alive.[12] Personally, I am not sure if I found this practice psychologically beneficial for this reason, but, as with the tearing of my scarves, there was a cathartic element to this experience. It was helpful to have a physical action accompanying the depth of emotion at this time.

The shoveling of dirt onto the casket is not the only demonstration of physicality during a Jewish funeral. After the burial service has been concluded, all the people in attendance form two parallel lines through which the mourners pass as they retreat from the site of the grave. As the mourners exit between these lines, the following customary greeting of condolence is recited by the attendees: "May you be comforted among the mourners of Zion and Jerusalem" (traditionally this is said in Hebrew). The performance of this ritual changes the focus of the funeral from honoring the dead to comforting the mourners, and it provides a palpable bridge to the *shiva*, the following stage of mourning. Both times I moved through these lines, the inherent symbolism of this practice allowed me to physically transition not only from the funeral to the *shiva*, but also from the status of having two parents, then just my mother, and ultimately neither parent.

THE *SHIVA*

[Joseph] observed a mourning period of seven days for his father.
—Genesis 50:10

Although I was very close to my maternal grandmother and still remember the sharp pain of her loss that lasted for months, my recollections of the *shiva* for her are rather vague. My mother's sister hosted it at her home on Long Island because she lived close to my grandfather and that was easiest for him. I recall we slept over at my aunt's home and that my family sat *shiva* for three days rather than a full week.

The phrase "sitting *shiva*" refers to this official stage of mourning following the burial in which the mourners remain at home and visitors come to offer their condolences. According to Jewish tradition, the mourners do not sit on regular chairs but instead reflect their depressed state by literally sitting closer to the ground.[13] Today that can mean removing a pillow from the couch or even sitting on a stool so the mourner's position is noticeably lower than everyone else's.

Looking back, I am not surprised my family sat *shiva* only for three days. My family was far from Orthodox and my mother and aunt felt that my grandfather could not handle more than this number of days. The three-day *shiva* is a popular remix of the traditional seven-day ritual, although there are certain times when a particular Jewish holiday will truncate even a traditional seven-day *shiva*.[14] Still, according to Lamm, there is a basis in Jewish tradition for distinguishing the first three days of *shiva* from the remainder of the week. For example, mourners have a greater degree of latitude after three days with respect to leaving their homes for certain specified purposes, including indigent mourners' need to work. Lamm also writes that the first three days are characterized by intense grief, during which time the traditional mourner does not even respond to greetings. Throughout the remainder of the week, however, the mourner is up for more engagement.[15] Despite this differentiation of the first three days, today it is not uncommon for non-Orthodox Jews to sit *shiva* for even less than three days.

During the *shiva* for my grandmother, I also recall that my family ordered tons of food to feed the visitors. At that time, I had no idea that this is not the traditional practice when it comes to food and *shivas*. I learned how more traditional communities operate when my mother-in-law passed away many years later. Before we left for the funeral, which was out of town, the executive director of our synagogue asked me who would be the "*shiva* coordinator." I was not familiar with this concept, and I fumbled around for an answer. But before long, a few friends called to volunteer. Clearly they were well versed in the more traditional practice that calls on friends and other family members to supply all of the meals for the mourners and the deceased's immediate family. Once we returned home, people furnished kosher food for us for every meal during the remainder of the *shiva*. Consistent with the traditional practice, we ordered no food for either our family or our visitors.

One benefit of a traditional *shiva* is that mourners are not alone in their first week of grief because the home is filled with people all through the day. Although in theory the food in a *shiva* home is not for the guests, in practice many traditional mourners are happy when there is a surplus of food available so that guests can nibble during their visits. It is also not uncommon for traditional mourners with small families to invite some guests to join them for a meal during a *shiva*. This grass-roots exercise of remix actually can serve as an important aspect of the healing process, which the *shiva* itself is designed to jump-start.

Due to the generosity of our community, my husband was able to concentrate on mourning and I could concentrate on helping him and our daughters through this time. Although I was not obligated to stay home or refrain from work during the *shiva* for my mother-in-law, the academic semester had already ended and it was easy for me to be around and available throughout the process. And our daughters saw firsthand what a difference it makes to have a supportive Jewish community that prioritizes taking care of those in need. This first experience with *shiva* made a hugely positive impression on them.

> Rabbi Hanin said: Wine was created only in order to comfort mourners in their distress.
>
> —Eruvin 65a, Babylonian Talmud

Unlike my mother-in-law's funeral, the burials for my parents were local. Both times, when we returned from the cemetery, my friends had prepared a pitcher of water at the entrance to our front door so we could wash our hands in accord with this ancient custom. They also prepared the meal of condolence, which is the first full meal the mourners eat after the burial. Often, mourners may not feel like eating so soon after burying a close relative. But by ensuring that a cooked meal is prepared and available, it is easier for mourners to manage eating just a little bit, and experiencing this small measure of normalcy, even if they are not so inclined. Usually this meal includes bread, considered the staff of life, hard-boiled eggs, and wine. Eggs are served because they represent the cycle of life and also are one of the few foods that become harder the longer they are cooked. They symbolize that human beings can, with time, also become stronger with time even in the face of adversity.

There was no doubt that I was going to do a seven-day *shiva*, even if I had to cancel all of my classes to do so. As it turned out, both of my parents passed away at times when I was not teaching. During the *shiva* for my father, I distinctly recall wondering what I would do for a whole week without working, going on my computer, or even watching television. I anticipated sitting around with endless long stretches of time on my hands. I couldn't have been more wrong. The entire week I had at most two hours to myself without any visitors. I did not specify the times that people could come, and so folks dropped in at all hours of the day, every day.

During a *shiva*, many observant mourners, including some who belong to Conservative synagogues, insist on reciting the *kaddish* prayer only in their own homes in order to follow the traditional practice. I adhered to this tradition for the evening services but I exercised an element of remix by leaving my home every morning to attend a *minyan* (prayer quorum) at my synagogue. I made this choice because I did not want to place an additional burden on my community by requiring people to come to my home so early in the day, and I was also concerned about whether having a *minyan* at my home would take people away from the synagogue *minyan* that is held at the same time. But this choice actually ended up having a very special meaning for me, especially in connection with the *shiva* for my mother, who died in the middle of May. That particular year, the weather in Chicago was unusually warm both on the day of her funeral and during the entire week of *shiva*. I have such fond memories of walking to and from my synagogue during that week, and thinking that the lovely weather I enjoyed each morning was somehow my mother's final gift to me!

Traditionally, the mirrors of a home are covered during a *shiva* because mourners are not supposed to be overly concerned with their external appearance. Similarly, women are supposed to refrain from using cosmetics during the *shiva* week. I found comfort in adhering to this tradition, but I made this choice because it felt right at the time, rather than because it was what I was supposed to be doing. On the other hand, I did not comply with the tradition's prohibition on showering. A mourner is not supposed to experience personal pleasures, and the sages of the Talmud determined that washing oneself for pleasure, as opposed to necessity, is off limits. So they allowed mourners to wash separate parts of their bodies but not the entirety at one time. Exceptions can be made for individuals who are ill or "inordinately delicate."[16] I drew a line at refusing to shower because I found this prohibition to be devoid of personal meaning and also instinctively troublesome. This was another way in which I exercised an element of remix in the context of an otherwise traditional *shiva*.

I found the *Shabbat* experience during the *shivas* for both of my parents extraordinarily meaningful, although in different ways. For me, a large part of the opportunity for meaning came from the observance of *Shabbat* itself, during which time several of the rules concerning *shiva* do not apply. For example, one does not wear the *k'riah* on *Shabbat* and there is no formal visiting of the mourner until after sundown on Saturday night. This enabled me to get a bit more rest than was the case the rest of the week. My father passed away in the dead of the winter and it was important to me to walk to synagogue on *Shabbat* rather than ride. So I decided to stay in a hotel that was much closer to our synagogue at that time to avoid a longer walk. My friends from synagogue prepared a lovely *Shabbat* dinner for us, including homemade challah, that we enjoyed at the hotel.

At the time of the *shiva* for my mother, all of our daughters had graduated from college and were living and working in the city. They, and their respective partners, decided to spend the entire weekend at our home. Since we did not have other visitors on *Shabbat*, we spent all of Friday night and Saturday after services just hanging out. As discussed earlier, a mourner generally is not supposed to leave the home, but I decided to join my family on a long walk to a nearby beach on Saturday afternoon. This beach walk was another way in which I relaxed the rules of mourning, another exercise of remix.

Our family time together during this *shiva* period was so meaningful that we collectively decided to rent a home for a weekend in a local resort the following summer so we could re-create this same sense of togetherness. The *shiva* experience not only created very sweet memories during this very difficult time but also reaffirmed that the combination of *Shabbat* and *shiva* can be an especially unique family experience that can impact the future. I know my mother would have strongly approved.

Still, I do understand that for some people, a week of *shiva* is a lot to handle. Not everyone is in a position to take a week off work and completely disconnect from all other aspects of life. Also, for those who are naturally introverted by nature, the thought of having multitudes of people in one's home, some of whom you barely know, can be extremely difficult. Jewish tradition dictates that visitors to a *shiva* home refrain from speaking excessively, and people are encouraged to keep all conversation related to the deceased. [17] In my experience as both a mourner and attendee, however, this is almost never the case except for *shivas* I've attended in ultra-Orthodox communities.

Although the week of *shiva* can be tiring and even stressful for mourners and their immediate families, I found great comfort in the forced disconnection from my day-to-day life. Still, both times I was ready to get back to a more normal routine. Right after the morning synagogue service on the seventh day of the *shiva* for my mother, I took the customary walk to mark the end of the *shiva* and then drove to my mother's former facility so I could visit with her nursing staff and her friends. These people were unable to come to our home for *shiva* due to either their working schedules or their inability to drive. As I reminisced about my mother with those who were closest to her in her final days, including those who were physically with her when she passed, the emotions washed over me in a way that I hadn't previously experienced or anticipated. I spent a full hour crying with them and, after that, felt strangely more at peace. It is almost as though my mother was saying to me, "Yes, of course I want you to be deeply sad . . . but not for too long, and it is now time to begin to mend!"

THE NEXT STAGES IN THE YEAR OF MOURNING

> And the Israelites bewailed Moses in the steppes of Moab for
> thirty days.
>
> —Deuteronomy 34:8 [18]

The official Jewish period of mourning for all relatives except parents is thirty days, including the *shiva* period. During this period, called the *sheloshim* (meaning "thirty" in Hebrew), Jewish tradition requires that mourners refrain from hair cutting, shaving, cutting nails, wearing new clothing, getting married, attending parties, and listening to music.

After the *sheloshim*, the mourner of a parent continues to say *kaddish* for eleven months, and, according to tradition, refrains from many of the same prohibited activities for a full year. [19] Growing up, my father frequently told me that he said *kaddish* for his mother three times a day, corresponding with the three daily services men are required to attend. In fact, he met my mother during the time he was saying *kaddish* and they married right after he finished his twelve-month mourning period. Although my father never explicitly asked me to say *kaddish* for him, I know my doing this was important to him.

The idea of a woman, even a daughter, saying *kaddish* is definitely a remix of the tradition, which puts the obligation of recitation on sons, rather than daughters, and even discourages women from saying the prayer. I still distinctly recall the reaction of an ultra-Orthodox woman whom I met shortly after I concluded the mourning period for my father as she expressed surprise—and frankly disapproval—upon learning that I had said *kaddish* for him daily for eleven months. Coming from her worldview, it was unfathomable that a female would, and should, do this. Coming from my worldview, it was unfathomable that I would not have said *kaddish* for him.

According to Lamm, a daughter may recite *kaddish* quietly to herself, along with other mourners, "especially if there is no son." He explains that the tradition makes a distinction between men and women in this regard so women do not feel compelled to carve out the time to attend daily services and say *kaddish*, given their familial responsibilities, even if a particular woman might be in a position to make the time to do so. In other words, absent a surviving son, no one has the primary obligation to recite *kaddish*. In the event there is no surviving son, or other suitable male relative, a male substitute such as a synagogue official can be hired to perform this service.[20]

The remix practice of women saying *kaddish*, nearly universal among liberal Jews, is also becoming more common in certain Modern Orthodox communities. In an essay about her essentially positive experience as an Orthodox woman reciting *kaddish* for her father, Jewish educator Adena Berkowitz noted that the women at her synagogue had even formed an informal daily "babysitting service to watch over the children during the service."[21] Still, use of remix to create an environment conducive to women saying *kaddish* is far from universal in Orthodox communities, as evidenced by writer Talia Bloch's account of her daily *kaddish* routine for her mother. Bloch discussed how she often felt women in her situation had to make themselves "small and silent" when all they wanted to do was just recite this simple prayer.[22] Personally, I had the same experience in some, but not all, of the Orthodox daily services I attended during the years I was a mourner. I hope that more Orthodox synagogues will embrace this aspect of remix and be more welcoming to women who want to say *kaddish*, because realistically, Orthodox daily services often are the only option available in many locations.

Candidly, I found it difficult during both eleven-month periods of mourning to carve out the time to get to services once a day, especially when I was traveling. But with very few exceptions, I managed. During the times I was home and in my regular routine, I don't think I ever missed a day. Occasionally, when traveling, there were a few times I simply did not have access to a synagogue. But I also had some wonderful—even unique—experiences, such as the time a *minyan* was convened especially for me in West Virginia where I was giving a lecture at the university. There was also a time at my university when the center for Jewish law I was co-directing sponsored a major conference. We had numerous Orthodox men in attendance and they formed a "pop-up" *minyan* so I could say *kaddish*.

Author Leon Wieseltier wrote in his book that he said *kaddish* for a variety of reasons, including duty to his father and to his religion, and that it would have been harder for him not to say *kaddish* because he would have felt regretful and guilty.[23] I can relate to all of these reasons. According to his account, at the time of his father's death, Wieseltier was no longer observing Jewish law, yet he still felt compelled to comply with this commandment. For him, the very act of saying *kaddish* was actually his way of exercising remix with respect to a tradition that he apparently still valued, but was no longer part of his life the way it once had been. Talia Bloch also wrote about the personal attributions she ascribed to saying *kaddish* in language that resonated strongly with my experience. For her, saying *kaddish* was a way to stay close to the time just after her mother's passing, and by extension, "a way to remain close to the time before she died."[24]

I adhered pretty closely to the other traditions of Jewish mourning with selective exercises of remix. I ignored the prohibitions on hair cutting after the *sheloshim*. In fact, even according to Jewish tradition, one is allowed to have a haircut and shave if someone tells you that your appearance requires it.[25] I learned this when an Orthodox friend essentially told me to tell him that he needed a haircut and beard trim sometime after his mother passed away. I just saw no need to go through this charade for a haircut.

With respect to music, I was fairly strict, especially in the first nine months of both yearlong mourning periords. Still, I exercised options of remix even within this framework. Attending weddings with music generally is prohibited during the twelve months one is mourning for a parent. During the *sheloshim* for my mother, my husband's best friend's daughter was married and the wedding was out of town. We had made our arrangements to attend prior to my mother's passing, and I decided to honor my commitment to attend the wedding with my husband. But I ate my meal in a separate room and only entered the wedding reception when the band was not playing. I also requested that the father of the bride, who is a rabbi, convene a *minyan* prior to the dinner so that I could say *kaddish*. Although these compromises would not necessarily have been sanctioned by the *halakhah*, I felt they struck the proper balance for me.

In order to attend other weddings that took place after the *sheloshim* during the years of mourning for my parents, I took advantage of a work-around sanctioned by the law that requires a mourner to perform some function of assistance, such as ushering, prior to the ceremony.[26] During both years of mourning, I also refrained from dancing as well as listening to music on the radio while in my car. During my years as a mourner, I never bothered to check whether radio, as opposed to live, music is permitted because refraining from listening to all music felt like an appropriate way to mark my status as a mourner (I learned while writing this chapter that recorded music also is off limits). After both periods of mourning, it was very meaningful and liberating for me to mark the distinction between being a mourner and returning to my normal life by returning to my favorite radio stations.

And then there was the matter of refraining from wearing new clothing. This prohibition was already familiar to me given that there is a three-week period in the Jewish calendar that precedes the saddest day of the Jewish year, the ninth of *Av*, during which one is not supposed to buy or wear new clothing. I have observed this practice since I was a teenager, and have always been attracted to it because I like the idea of having a mandatory time in which one does not have a green light to succumb to whatever purchasing impulses one has. I have always found it meaningful because it gives you the time to reflect and appreciate what you already own.

So based on this history, I decided to follow the tradition of not purchasing or wearing new clothing during the yearlong periods that I was in mourning for my parents. Of course three weeks is different from twelve months, and I will fully confess that this wasn't all that easy! On the morning of my mother's funeral, I had three new items hanging in my closet with the tags still on them. So I woke up early and wore each one for about twenty minutes before our rabbi came to meet with our family. Since the funeral had not yet taken place, the mourning traditions technically did not apply to me at that point. My rabbi was amused and chided me that, as a lawyer, I well understood the Jewish law's system of loopholes.

When I needed to purchase a necessity or two during these times (such as pajamas or something to that effect), I had one of my daughters wear it for a while so that the item was no longer technically "new" when I put it on.[27] This work-around is considered legitimate, but I elected to do this more because I felt it appropriate for my personal status, rather than because it was in accord with Jewish law. And on my birthday during the year of mourning for my mother, I agreed to accompany my oldest daughter to the city so she could have fun at the annual Nordstrom sale. And yes, I too purchased a few things that day that were not, strictly speaking, necessities. I was aware that these purchases probably went against the grain of Jewish tradition but I exercised a degree of remix by keeping them tucked away in my closet until my year of mourning had passed. I didn't want to reach the point where I felt resentful of the tradition, or that it was too onerous to be meaningful for me.

During each period of mourning, I was very ready to be done with the daily *kaddish* routine after eleven months, even though in general I found it to be a very therapeutic ritual.[28] Both times I also found the twelfth month of mourning difficult. The obligation to say *kaddish* was no longer there, but the remaining restrictions I had assumed remained in place. I felt like the end was in sight, and I wanted to be done, but I just wasn't there just yet. Toward the end of the yearlong period for my mother, I learned how to lead the congregation in the evening prayers, and I had the opportunity to serve as the prayer leader both on my last day of *kaddish* after eleven months as well as a month later on her first *yahrtzeit*. I felt very happy about having mastered this skill, knowing that my mother (and father) would have been so proud that I did this in her honor. My choice to lead services can be seen as yet another exercise of remix because, even at my traditional Conservative synagogue, most women do not lead prayers.

BACK TO (ALMOST) NORMAL

Earlier in this chapter I discussed my friend Kathy's approach to the unveiling of the tombstone for her husband. There are certain prayers that are prescribed for this ceremony, including the *kaddish* if a *minyan* is present. For the unveiling of both of my parents, we had a very small ceremony with just our immediate family. We kept the ceremony simple yet traditional. Kathy, on the other hand, created special booklets for her husband's unveiling that included some traditional content but also other readings and materials that were meaningful to her. This represents a very creative way one can follow Jewish tradition with a remixed twist.

The *yahrtzeit* of a close relative provides a yearly opportunity to formally honor and remember our loved ones. Throughout the Jewish year there are also four other holy days where special prayers known as *yizkor*, derived from the Hebrew word for "remember," are said for our close relatives who are no longer with us. Eli Feldblum has written about his experience saying *yizkor* despite not believing in the power of prayer. He finds personal meaning in saying *yizkor* and sees this prayer as an "internal, intimate, painful celebration of life" that allows people to imagine what the present would be like if their loved ones were still alive.[29] The *yizkor* prayers also contain a pledge for giving *tzedakah*, charity, in memory of a beloved deceased, which is a practice many people embrace, since they find meaning in this connection between honoring the memory of the dead and striving to perfect the world in the present. Many Jews also mark the *yahrtzeit* of a loved one by giving *tzedakah*.

The current practices in connection with both *yahrtzeit* and *yizkor* were influenced heavily by external cultural and historical factors—specifically, the persecution of the German Jews in the fourteenth century prior to the onset of the Black Death, as well as certain Christian practices in connection with mourning. For example, the term *yahrtzeit* comes from the same term used by German Christians to recall the souls of the departed on the anniversary of their deaths. Around this time, three of the four *yizkor* services were added to the Jewish calendar supplementing the original service on Yom Kippur. These additional services coincide with the major festivals of Passover, Shavuot, and Sukkot. According to Professor Ivan Marcus, the *yizkor* service combines elements from both the Christian All Souls' Day and the Christian All Saints' Day, during which times candles are lit and special masses recited. In the Jewish tradition, along with the special *yizkor* prayers, one is supposed to light a special memorial candle at home that burns for the entire day. This is also the practice for observing *yahrtzeit*.[30]

In my family, the candle-lighting ritual for *yahrtzeit* has fostered another element of remix. My cousin Carol is the only child of my mother's sister. She lights a *yahrtzeit* candle for both of her parents as well as my mother, with whom she was also close, but does so on the dates of death based on the Gregorian calendar. Although I observe the traditional practice of adhering to the date of death based on the Hebrew calendar, for Carol, the Hebrew date has no meaning. Instead, she chooses to light the traditional memorial candle, but on the date that has meaning for her.

As millennials mature and must grapple more directly with death, it will be interesting to see whether they choose to adhere to some of the Jewish practices surrounding mourning with a greater degree of frequency and intensity than other rituals. The success of the online platform Death Over Dinner, created in 2013 to facilitate conversations around the issues of dying and death, prompted the creation in 2016 of Death Over Dinner—Jewish Edition. Two Jewish organizations, Reboot and IKAR, collaborated with Death Over Dinner for this initiative, and it has proved very popular among Jewish millennials, demonstrating that they are eager to discuss death. The Jewish edition requires those desiring to host a dinner to select from among several designated reasons for their interest, which include learning about relevant Jewish traditions, rituals, and perspectives on death and finding comfort after a loss. In addition, younger audiences are gravitating toward books such as *Modern Loss*, authored by two Jewish women in their thirties, and the podcast *Kaddish*, started by Rabbi Ariana Katz. [31]

I would not be surprised if the Jewish rituals surrounding death and mourning continue to speak to liberal Jews, with remix being a large part of the equation. For one thing, the Jewish mourning rituals, particularly the yearlong process that applies to parents, send people a very different message from society's overall expectation that people need to "get over" their grief and just move on. The Jewish tradition's "ongoing opportunities to publicly remember the deceased" can provide a welcome sense of relief for those who simply are not in a position to terminate the grieving process so quickly. [32] Also, people seem to feel most vulnerable, and spiritually available, when grappling with the death of a loved one. The relevant Jewish practices have a logic and psychological appeal that responds to this vulnerability. These practices seem tailor-made to facilitate healing even as they allow the memories to survive and thrive.

Although my personal experience with Jewish mourning may be more on the traditional side of the spectrum, it should be evident that I still relied on the hallmarks of a remixed approach to Jewish tradition in my observances. I made choices in how and what I observed, and searched for personal meaning in those rituals that I embraced. This "pick and choose" approach is not unusual, even for Jews who care greatly about the tradition's preservation and respect its authenticity. But as the epilogue suggests, an attraction to authenticity when it comes to Jewish faith and practice is not uncommon among liberal Jews.

EPILOGUE

Faith, Fluidity, and Authenticity

All things are mortal but the Jew; all other forces pass, but he remains. What is the secret of his immortality?

—Mark Twain[1]

Tanya Schevitz, spokesperson of Reboot, a nonprofit dedicated to renewing and forging Jewish connections among young Jews, has observed that the millennial generation embraces a belief in "tools not rules."[2] Many non-Orthodox Jews, regardless of their age, function similarly when it comes to Judaism. Perhaps for this reason, much of the discourse about Jewish education for non-Orthodox Jews centers on how to provide Jews with content about Judaism they will find relevant. Still, the underlying message always seems to be that Jewish tradition has the capacity to make life better for those willing to give it a chance.

Many Jews (and also non-Jews involved with Jews) have the capacity to be drawn to this message, although it resonates more strongly with some people than others. But, in order for this attraction to occur, people need to be in a place in their lives where they have the inclination to explore and the mental, spiritual, and physical energy and time to devote to a spiritually oriented enterprise. For most people, this level of receptivity will vary over the course of their lives.

Also, for most non-Orthodox Jews, it is probably fair to say that although, in theory, they may value aspects of Jewish tradition, in practice they are not driven to devote significant energy to consistent observance. People tend to get caught up in their daily routines and generally relegate Judaism to liminal moments. Some of the chapters in this book attest to this pattern, as demonstrated by the continuing popularity even among nonobservant Jews of celebrating B'nai Mitzvah, breaking the glass at wedding ceremonies under a *chuppah*, and observing some of the practices related to the death of a loved one.

Of course, there are also some Jews who may not believe that Jewish tradition really has the capacity to make life better in general terms until they encounter a situation that changes their perspective. Illness, either one's own or that of a loved one, can create especially significant opportunities for embracing Jewish tradition. Anthropologist Gila Silverman performed an ethnographic study of prayer and healing consisting of fieldwork conducted in Tucson, Arizona, a city with one of the lowest levels of Jewish observance and affiliation in the United States. One of her publications focused on the *Mi Shebeirach*, the Jewish prayer for healing, and how the thirty-five non-Orthodox participants in her study felt about their experience in connection with this particular prayer.[3]

Silverman describes the subjects of her study in a way I believe is typical for the majority of non-Orthodox Jews. Specifically, "their Jewish identities ebb and flow across the life cycle: they take on, reject, reinvent, and/or combine Jewish practices with other practices in their search for personal meaning." She observes that "within this context, times of illness or loss become sites of negotiation, through which their relationships to Jewish traditions, practices, and communities shift and become transformed."[4]

Silverman's discussion suggests that the ability to say this prayer had a profoundly positive impact on some participants in her study. A small number of participants actually attributed physical improvements to the consistent recitation of this prayer, and some Jews also voiced a stronger interest in ritual observance based on their experience. But for most, their attachment to the *Mi Shebeirach* reflected a more generalized connection to Judaism grounded in history, community, peoplehood, strength, comfort, and emotional healing.

The *Mi Shebeirach* is a paradigmatic example of how Jewish tradition can be remixed. First of all, although the *Mi Shebeirach* traditionally is recited in a synagogue during the Torah reading, today it can be heard in many types of group settings, such as the cancer support group for Jewish women that Silverman attended as part of her research. Second, given modern versions that can be sung in English, it is an element of Jewish tradition that is capable of enormous personal attribution and is immediately usable by Jews with little or no knowledge of Hebrew or background in Judaism. Third, it can be interpreted to cover all emotional and spiritual dimensions of illness—for those who are ill, their caretakers, and their loved ones.

Silverman questioned her subjects about their hopes and expectations from their prayer experiences. She observed that the most common answer was that reciting the prayer "couldn't hurt and it might even help." In the words of a hospital chaplain whom she quotes, "There's a big difference between what we hold intellectually and how we respond to life and death emotionally."[5] I believe this remark reveals a fundamental truth about human nature and faith. Many people feel a general disconnect between the intellect and emotion when it comes to faith, but at certain moments of our lives, the intellectual barriers to faith recede. At these times, the emotional or spiritual pull takes over as comfort, history, tradition, and community assume more importance.

There are important questions whose answers defy logic: Why are so many Jews drawn to the *Mi Shebeirach*? Why do people gravitate toward tradition in their darkest times? Why do people continue to celebrate B'nai Mitzvah? Why do people choose to have a *ketubah* and a *chuppah* even in nontraditional weddings? Why do Jews feel like a much larger part of the population than our minuscule numbers suggest? Why do so many Jews say with a good dose of pride that they are "culturally Jewish?" And most significantly, as Mark Twain pondered, why have the Jewish people and Jewish tradition survived against all odds? Truly, the Jewish people can be likened to the burning bush in the Torah that was not consumed.[6]

I have faith in the beauty, wisdom, and power of Jewish tradition to speak to Jews from all different backgrounds. The Torah actually supports this perspective. An ancient rabbinic source tells us that even at the time of Revelation, God's voice came "to each Israelite with a force proportioned to his individual strength."[7] This source underscores the importance of human individuality even with respect to how the Torah was received by humans. Also, the sacred texts of the tradition reveal multiple meanings on their face. For example, the Bible incorporates numerous, and sometimes competing, views of God. The history of the Jewish people is complicated, as is the Jewish tradition itself. Judaism has never been a one-size-fits-all religion.[8]

Equally important, Jewish tradition had no choice but to be flexible and responsive to outside cultures given that the Jewish people have been living in foreign cultures in the Diaspora since before the destruction of the Second Temple in 70 CE. The importance of flexibility was recognized in the Talmud by Rabbi Simeon Ben Eleazar, who is quoted as advocating that one should "be pliable like a reed, not rigid like a cedar" (Ta'anit 20b). The underlying message here is that a tree that bends will survive the elements, but one that is rigid will not.

Throughout history, the Jews demonstrated their flexibility by constructing their particular identities according to an interesting process that allowed for adaptation, and even at times subversion, of elements from their surroundings. One interesting example involves the *brit milah*, known colloquially in Ashkenazi Jewish circles as the *bris*. Although the Torah states that God commanded Abraham to circumcise every male at the age of eight days, the rabbis in late antiquity prescribed the particular prayers and blessings for the *bris*. But many of the familiar customs were actually derived from the Christian baptism, a reality not all that surprising given that baptism replaced circumcision in early Christianity. This process of adaptation occurred in connection with so many aspects of Jewish tradition, resulting in the creation of a distinctive Jewish subculture in all the locales in which the Jews lived.[9] Given these dynamics, fluidity is actually hardwired into the Jewish tradition.

FLUIDITY, CHOICE, AND ATTRACTION TO AUTHENTICITY CHARACTERIZE JEWISH FAITH AND PRACTICE

Faith is not a subject that most Jews are comfortable discussing openly. Silverman also co-authored a separate paper with Kathryn Johnson and Adam Cohen focusing on belief in God, incorporating research from both her Tucson study as well as national surveys. This piece discusses how, given the tradition's multiple perspectives about God and the long history of Jewish suffering, faith is a more complex matter for Jews.

Also, Jewish identity involves matters of ethnicity, tradition, and ritual as much as personal beliefs about God and theology. [10]

Their work demonstrates that Jewish representations of God are too complex to reduce to a framework of whether one does, or does not, believe. It concludes that Jews "on average" do believe in God, although this belief spans a range of diverse perspectives and even shifts on the part of any one person. Based on their interviews and survey data, the authors conclude that "Jewish beliefs about the nature of God are often unclear and in flux."

> For many Jews, God is sometimes represented as a benevolent being amenable to relationship; but, just as often, God is represented as an energy or cosmic force, or as ineffable, inconceivable, unfathomable, beyond knowing, and past finding out. Given the complex nature of Jewish representations of God, *belief* may not be the correct verb, and measures of belief may not be able to capture the variety of ways in which this population conceives of, and relates with, God. [11]

Significantly, this work may suggest that among non-Orthodox Jews there might be greater faith than is generally evidenced by existing survey data. Still, this faith is characterized by degrees of fluidity and lack of definition.

Even those who self-denominate as Orthodox are not immune to degrees of fluidity when it comes to faith. Gil Perl, a Modern Orthodox educator, has written that his yeshiva students seem to live in a world of fluidity. They are bothered by "their inability to determine whether objective value systems do—or ought to—exist at all." The result is that even in his world "boundaries taken for granted only a generation ago— between private and public, leader and laity, normative and deviant, even male and female, are increasingly evaporating." [12]

It is also not necessarily the case that Perl's observations are confined to younger Modern Orthodox Jews. There is a documented group of Modern Orthodox Jews who identify as "socially Orthodox." According to an article in *Commentary* magazine, this group exercises choice in their selection of ritual observance "without fear of divine retribution." Socially Orthodox Jews are affiliated with Orthodox institutions such as synagogues and day schools and purport to follow an Orthodox lifestyle, but maintain an identity steeped "much more in Jewish culture, history, and nationality than in faith and commandments." [13]

Studies also show that belief in God is not necessarily universal among Orthodox Jews. According to a 2017 study of the Modern Orthodox community by Nishma Research, belief in the existence of God ranged from 75 percent to 99 percent.[14] Similarly, the 2013 Pew Report, the most comprehensive survey of the entire American Jewish community, showed that only 77 percent of Modern Orthodox Jews are "absolutely certain" of their belief "in God or a universal spirit."[15]

I was surprised not only by these statistics regarding faith among self-denominated Orthodox Jews, but also by the range of observance within the Modern Orthodox sector specifically. For example, the Nishma Study revealed a range from 82 percent to 100 percent in terms of observance of *Shabbat*, and a range from 53 percent to 92 percent affirming that "Orthodox observance is an extremely important part" of life. These findings led Mark Trencher, the president and founder of Nishma, to conclude that among Jews who identify as Modern Orthodox, the variations "in beliefs, practices and worldview . . . are striking," and the data suggests this group is significantly fragmented.[16]

It stands to reason that Jews who are more religiously identified will manifest higher degrees of faith and observance, a reality confirmed by the 2013 Pew Report with respect to all the denominations. But the data regarding the beliefs and practices of the Modern Orthodox community specifically demonstrates that fluidity, and individual choice, exist even among those Jews who identify as part of the Orthodox community. Given these realities, how can we not expect non-Orthodox Jews to display an even wider degree of fluidity in their practices?

There is also reason to believe that non-Orthodox Jews today exhibit a large degree of fluidity in their denominational loyalties. The study of the Tucson Jewish community discussed earlier showed that many of the people interviewed revealed multiple affiliations and a mixture of Jewish engagement patterns.[17] Speaking anecdotally, I think these findings are right on target. Many of my own non-Orthodox friends and acquaintances in the Chicago area and elsewhere have a similar mixed pattern of Jewish engagement, often extending into involvement with Orthodox outreach groups.[18] This showing of fluidity is a question that liberal Jews and their leaders need to ponder. Why are people who are not conventionally religious still attracted, even if only sometimes, to Chabad and other forms of Orthodox outreach? The strength of these Orthodox communities, and certainly their appeal to nonreligious Jews, would not have been predicted in the aftermath of the Holocaust. What is the perceived value of these groups to non-Orthodox Jews who likely have no intention of ever adhering to the letter of Jewish law?

One answer that is obvious to anyone who has ever participated in an event sponsored by Orthodox groups who do *kiruv* is that many people are drawn to the warm, charismatic, and encouraging personalities of those who do outreach. Consider Adam and Judy, who have built up a remarkable following in the more than twenty years they have been part of a suburban Midwestern community, hosting classes, prayer groups, trips to Israel, and other special programs. By any account, they are considered a remarkable *kiruv* success story. Yet their success does not include converting the majority of their followers to Orthodoxy. The truth is that their followers represent people very interested in their personal Jewish journeys but who do not necessarily feel a need to go "all in."

I believe that aside from Adam and Judy's magnetism, a large part of what draws people to participate in their events, and those sponsored by other Orthodox *kiruv* groups, is the perception that they represent a sense of authenticity. Paradoxically, more than a few non-Orthodox Jews who thrive on their fluidity of beliefs and practices still are drawn to groups that advocate the perceived Jewish "real deal."

But freedom of choice regarding observance is not a novel concept with respect to Jewish tradition. In fact, the element of choice dates back to Revelation at Mount Sinai. According to the Torah, when Moses told the people all of God's commandments, the people answered with one voice and said "we will do" (Exod. 24:3). It was their collective choice to obey.

The Book of Ruth furnishes one of the most renowned examples of the importance of this choice. Ruth, a Moabite woman, married one of Naomi's sons, who later died. Naomi then urged Ruth to return to her own people, but Ruth refused to do this and instead uttered the famous pledge of loyalty including the words, "For wherever you go, I will go . . . ; your people shall be my people, and your God my God" (Ruth 1:16). This Biblical narrative concludes with Ruth marrying Boaz, a relative of Naomi's deceased husband, and bearing a son named Obed, who was the grandfather of King David. The placement of this lineage at the end of the text is particularly significant because according to the tradition, the Messiah will be a descendant of King David, and of Ruth, the woman who chose to be Jewish. [19]

But despite this tradition of choice, up until the second half of the nineteenth century there was a recognizable consistency in Jewish practice even though local customs often varied. The impact of the Enlightenment and the emancipation of the Jews in Europe eventually changed this landscape by opening up for Jews increasing options for participation in the surrounding cultures. Before long, Jews were no longer culturally and economically isolated, a development that led to the growth of divergent factions among Jews who embraced distinct views on the importance and relevance of Jewish law. In the United States, these factions evolved into the three major movements that still exert a significant influence on the state of American Judaism.

In 2005, I attended a lay leaders' retreat at the Shalom Hartman Institute in Jerusalem, where I heard the late Rabbi David Hartman open his plenary address by saying that for most Jews today, Judaism is considered a choice, and that it is impossible to put this genie back in the bottle. I still recall being struck by his words, and they have impacted my thinking about Judaism ever since. Although the issues facing non-Orthodox Jews today with respect to transmission are not entirely without precedent, as a practical matter we do live in an era where cultural forces make it more difficult than before to secure a balance between fluidity and choice, on the one hand, and authenticity on the other. We cannot escape the reality that too much fluidity and choice can compromise the stable, authentic content upon which successful transmission depends.

THE ART OF JEWISH TRADITION

My husband often says that religion is an art and not a science. The arts are, of course, critical for the richness of life's tapestry. The idea of seeing Jewish tradition as a form of art has the potential for helping non-Orthodox Jews think through the difficulties they confront in transmitting Jewish tradition in our diverse world.

I have always viewed human artistic creativity as a spiritual type of enterprise, even before the time I began to write about this idea on a more formal basis. Any creative artistic work—be it literature, music, or visual art—is the product of the author's personal story as shaped by her own experience and her reaction to her surrounding environment. Early in my career as a law professor, I became an advocate for authors' rights, and much of my legal scholarship has focused on an author's right to receive attribution and to safeguard her work from unauthorized changes that compromise its message and meaning.

About fifteen years ago, my legal research led me to an important book written by the historian Daniel Boorstin, *The Creators*, in which he observes that the Torah's language that "God created man in His image" furnishes a path leading man to regard himself as a potential creator.[20] I had never thought about this insight before, despite having read the Biblical text many times. Around the time I encountered Boorstin's book, I had begun to reconnect with Jewish learning, which had occupied a large part of my adolescent and college years. It suddenly occurred to me that the Jewish tradition is very much like a work of art that has been composed jointly by its many human authors, and based (at least in my view) on its Divine origin. As such, the tradition can be understood as reflecting the personal and environmental circumstances of many of its authors, both the rabbis and laypeople. Therefore, both the laws promulgated by the rabbis and the practices of the people have a basis in the cultures that have surrounded the tradition's authors.

After this realization, it was not a particularly difficult stretch for me to see that so many of the issues I had written about involving artistic works were also relevant to the Jewish tradition. Specifically, how much can a work (or a tradition) undergo modification and still be considered representative of its original meaning and message? What does society lose when a given work (tradition) loses its essential character and becomes something completely different? Further, who gets to make these changes and pursuant to what type of authority? At base, these questions are all concerned with "authenticity."

These questions loom large in a postmodern age where it is expected that the audience will interpret texts and forge new meanings. They apply not only to artistic works, especially in our digital era, but also to Jewish tradition. Many argue that Jewish tradition, like art, should be subject to new interpretations, and invested with a sense of personal meaning, especially given the challenges of modernity.

There is a value to changes in any cultural tradition, particularly in more liberal pockets of the community. Still, changes that are not grounded in the fabric of the cultural tradition can compromise important values unique to the tradition. This concern with loss of value and dilution of the tradition's authenticity justifies a perspective that embraces a degree of selectivity with respect to implementing changes in the tradition. This concern is particularly relevant to the Jewish tradition, which represents a minority culture in the Diaspora. The issue of how much change and evolution it can tolerate and yet retain its authenticity is one that has occupied much of the discourse in certain circles of Jewish thought since the inception of the Enlightenment.

I agree with my husband that Judaism is not a science but rather a form of art—a cultural product composed of law, wisdom, and narrative—all of which have been shaped by social forces over time and diverse geographic space. But I am also concerned about the potential loss of Jewish tradition on a more global level. Judaism has offered hope, comfort, and a good life path for thousands of years. The current trends showing an increasing disinterest in Jewish practice are disturbing. If this pattern continues, Judaism may wind up as the exclusive property of the most religiously observant of our people. I am not alone in this fear. In 2018, Jane Eisner, the former editor of *The Forward*, wrote that if Jews continue to abandon "the norms of Jewish behavior . . . who will keep alive our rituals and traditions other than an Orthodox segment"?[21]

Jewish continuity matters, including the religious component of Judaism. This perspective seems to be shared by the majority of professionals involved with Judaism, including those on the most liberal side of the religious spectrum. When the staunchest advocates for interfaith hospitality, such as Edmund Case, the founder of Interfaith Family, articulate why their position makes sense, it is with the notion of safeguarding continuity. Case has observed that we need to be more confident that "Jewish traditions are so compelling that people will gravitate to them once exposed."[22] Similarly, when the Reform movement adopted the Patrilineal Resolution in 1983, so that the children of non-Jewish mothers would be considered legitimately Jewish as long as they were raised with a strong Jewish identity, the movement was concerned with continuity.

Today, the most religiously liberal rabbis advocate co-officiating with the clergy of other religions in order to "keep the next generation of Jews." Even the discourse in much of the Conservative movement about interfaith inclusivity is grounded in the idea of Jewish continuity and keeping the next generation. Those Conservative rabbis who have broken with the rabbinic standards of their movement and have elected to perform intermarriages rely on this same reason to justify their decisions.

In short, Jewish continuity is very much on the radar of liberal Jewish leaders, and their followers, even though they have different ideas from their Orthodox brethren about what measures should be invoked to achieve this continuity. I believe that the majority of Jews today, even those who are among the most assimilated, still would not agree with Gabriel Roth's call for complete assimilation discussed in the introduction. In their hearts and souls, many nonreligious Jews still find value in Jewish tradition. And an explicit remixed approach to Jewish tradition represents a particularly fruitful way to facilitate its transmission to future generations of non-Orthodox Jews.

ESTABLISHING PERSONAL AND FAMILY JEWISH NORMS

The concept of remix Judaism appears in the Talmud, although it is not labeled as such. According to a well-known narrative, Moses visits the academy of Rabbi Akiva, who lived about 1,400 years after him. But Moses fails to understand anything Rabbi Akiva is saying. It is all just so unfamiliar to him. Even so, Moses is comforted when Akiva cites the law as it was transmitted to Moses at Sinai as his original source. The point here is that Akiva and his colleagues were operating on the assumption that their work was indeed part of the tradition dating back to Moses, even as they applied a significant degree of remix.[23]

This narrative often is used by rabbis of the more liberal denominations in support of new interpretations of Jewish law that may even conflict with prior tradition. Realistically, though, because they lack sufficient knowledge of the tradition and its development to make judgments with respect to the authenticity side of the equation, the majority of Jews today cannot be equated either to the students of Rabbi Akiva or to modern rabbis. As a result, free choice usually will prevail at the expense of safeguarding transmission.

In the coming generations, our religious, cultural tradition is in danger of becoming a relic outside of Orthodox and other very traditional communities. The simple truth is that most Jews need to be more proactive when it comes to preservation of Jewish tradition—both religiously and culturally. To achieve transmission of Jewish tradition, personal and family Jewish norms need to be thoughtfully developed and implemented. Initially, this entails sufficient knowledge acquisition so that it is possible to select from the tradition personally meaningful practices that can be consistently performed. Realistically, these norms should be centered on *Shabbat* and holidays, as well as the dietary traditions. These pillars of Judaism are still perceived even by non-Orthodox Jews as the most foundational elements of the tradition.

Readers who have gotten to this point understand that I am not suggesting that transmission of Jewish tradition will only be effective if Jews strictly keep *Shabbat*, the holidays, and the dietary laws. But absent consistent observance of at least some of these fundamentals, transmission becomes a difficult proposition. In short, the key to fighting extinction of Jewish tradition in liberal communities is an emphasis by individuals and families (as well as institutions) on the proactive development of more Jewish norms of ritually centered engagement, even if that engagement looks different from the norms of more traditionally observant Jewish families.

Reform Rabbi Clifford Librach recognized this reality when he wrote that in Israel, "the near-universal embrace of the *Shabbat* dinner reminds all of the power of simple religious norms to give integrity to a culture."[24] And in 2018, the Reconstructionist movement rebranded itself through an organizational name change designed to convey the importance of *doing* Jewish rather than being Jewish. Rabbi Deborah Waxman announced the name change to Reconstructing Judaism, a decision fueled by an explicit need for those affiliated with this group to be more proactively engaged in ritual and other aspects of Judaism.[25]

Parents and grandparents also need to respond to our current reality by paying more attention to their own Jewish journeys as well as their children's. This requires not only verbal communication as to why Jewish tradition is important, but also action. Every action toward this end—no matter how small—matters.

Remix as the tool for transmission of Jewish tradition in non-Orthodox communities is based on the idea that new approaches to Jewish tradition must be steeped in historical authenticity and performed consistently. This is not the same thing as simply relaxing standards out of convenience. Remix involves education so that intentionality can be exercised on an individual basis. It involves thoughtful appropriation with an eye to what is being abandoned. It involves a continual rethinking of what has been abandoned, and what should be recaptured. It requires engagement.

REMIX AND CREATIVE COMMUNITIES

> It is a tree of life for those who grasp it, and all who uphold it are blessed. Its ways are pleasantness and all its paths are peace.
> —Proverbs 3:18, 3:17[26]

Jews who regularly attend most any synagogue will recognize this prayer as it is sung when the Torah, having been read, is returned to the ark. I particularly love this part of the service. The traditional melody that accompanies this prayer is a slow, rhythmic one that prompts my group of friends to link arms as we sway and sing along with the rest of the congregation.

Still, in future decades, the number of Jews who will be able to recognize the beauty and power of this prayer can easily shrink. All the available studies of the non-Orthodox American Jewish community point to the likelihood that synagogue affiliation is likely to decrease in the coming years, along with the number of people who regularly attend services.

The emerging similarity between Reform and Conservative Jews when it comes to synagogue attendance as well as other markers of observance also is significant. The 2013 Pew Report revealed that only 39 percent of Conservative Jews and 17 percent of Reform Jews attend synagogue at least monthly. These figures show that Jews of these two movements are much more similar to one another than to Orthodox Jews, 74 percent of whom report at least monthly attendance. Similarly, when it comes to markers of *Shabbat* observance and keeping a kosher home, Conservative Jews show greater degrees of observance than Reform, but still far lower levels than even Modern Orthodox Jews.[27] Not surprisingly, the National Jewish Population Studies from as early as 1990 and 2000 show that Conservative and Reform Jews share a great deal in terms of patterns of personal observance as well as outlook on issues such as interfaith marriage, same-sex marriage, ordination of gay rabbis, and whether Jewish membership should be determined by either one's mother or father.[28]

The findings of these studies are supported by strong anecdotal evidence that can easily be found in most non-Orthodox communities. Whether a formal merger of Reform and Conservative institutions will ever become a reality, there is much to suggest that American Jews are entering into a post-denominational phase, with the divisions grouped along the lines of "traditional versus liberal" rather than according to specific denominational affiliations.

In light of these realities, the clergy and professional staff of liberal groups need to focus less on membership numbers and more on creating a richer cultural, religious tradition among their members. This means educating their members about the pillars of Jewish tradition such as *Shabbat* and the dietary laws, affirmatively encouraging them to embrace more tradition, and helping their followers to develop a sense of intentionality and personal meaning with respect to those elements they choose to practice. Unfortunately, these types of initiatives are difficult for many pulpit rabbis to implement given that often their time is occupied more by administrative rather than spiritual matters. Their spiritual influence is at its strongest during their sermons and in connection with family life cycle events. But in the majority of non-Orthodox synagogues, most members do not attend services with any degree of regularity. Under these circumstances, it is difficult for most congregants other than "the regulars" to receive the encouragement needed to develop patterns of ritual consistency that are vital to the creation of thicker cultural, religious traditions.

But despite the challenges facing most non-Orthodox rabbis and professionals in creating stronger religious norms among their followers, certain synagogues, pop-up synagogues, and organizations are successfully employing a remix philosophy to attract more participants—especially around the High Holidays. According to recent articles, communal observance by millennials is on the rise when traditional stodgy venues give way to unconventional venues such as popular restaurants, bars, and even bowling alleys.[29]

And it is not just the locations that are being remixed. In many instances, creative rabbis and professionals are discarding the format and content of the prescribed service, replacing it with programming that focuses more on education and discussion of the holiday themes. These departures are likely to be appealing to younger Jews as well as other non-Orthodox Jews who do not believe they are commanded to recite the traditional prayers in order to fulfill religious obligations.

To illustrate how remix is operating in the context of these communal settings, consider Rabbi Lori Shapiro's introduction of "goat yoga" as a means of reenacting the traditional Yom Kippur *avodah* service in her Venice Beach location. The *avodah* service entails commemorating the ritual of the High Priest in the ancient Temple. A central feature of this traditional service is the prostration by clergy and even willing congregants during the renowned *Aleinu* prayer. Shapiro elected to have her congregants do the traditional prostration with a goat on their backs given the important role of two goats in the High Priest's ritual.[30] According to Shapiro, this is about "making Judaism relevant again." As another example, the nondenominational Chicago congregation Mishkan rented out the Old Vic theater for its 2018 High Holiday program. Attendees were given glow sticks to create a concert-like vibe for *Neilah*, the final service for Yom Kippur, which is recited standing for at least an hour.[31]

Remix does not have to be confined to more liberal Jewish communities. There is plenty of room for a remixed approach to prayer and Jewish communal space within all of the denominations as they currently exist, and even in a world that extends beyond our current denominational structure. Modern Orthodox Rabbi Ari Hart runs a one-hour afternoon program on both the first day of Rosh Hashanah and Yom Kippur for anyone who wants to connect with Jewish tradition. I mentioned this option to my youngest daughter last year and she and her husband attended. They brought back rave reviews. When I asked my daughter why she liked the service as much as she did, she explained that they not only recited certain prayers but the rabbi also explained their meanings and relevance. She also liked that he discussed the meaning of certain rituals such as striking one's chest during the recitation of the Yom Kippur confessional. Although the High Holidays may be a time when Jews are more spiritually available, the successes of these ventures can extend beyond the beginning of the Jewish New Year. The High Holiday programs, and those that build on these communal models for other holidays and programming, offer the hope that a remixed approach to Jewish tradition has the ability to inspire creativity among the spectrum of clergy and Jewish professionals.

I do not prescribe any one path for non-Orthodox Jews. One of the main values of a remixed approach to Jewish tradition is that it recognizes the value of individuality, just as was true of the narrative of the Revelation of the Torah at Mount Sinai. I hope that the value of this book lies not in its advocacy for any one particular path, but rather in its overall call to individual Jews to forge their own paths of keeping Jewish tradition alive. I anticipate that these remixed paths will entail an individualized balance of fluidity and authenticity. My goal for all who seek to attempt this process proactively is the development of a stronger connection to Jewish tradition, and a greater ability to transmit this tradition to the next generation.

The Torah tells us that God promised Abraham that he would be "the father of a multitude of nations" (Genesis 17:5). The Jewish patriarch is assured that his offspring will be like the stars of the sky, and the sands on the shore.[32] Some Jews believe we are still here because of God's promise. Other Jews may not be as sure of why we still exist but find enormous comfort and pride in the reality that we continue to survive and thrive. Anyone who knows even a little about Jewish history cannot help but realize that our existence as a people throughout time and space is miraculous and defies logic. The recognition of this reality, even if at subconscious levels, likely is part of what accounts for the continued strong Jewish pride that still exists among the majority of Jews.

But pride is not enough to ensure continuity. We need more action-oriented religious tradition. Some people may argue that partial efforts will never be enough for successful transmission. But consider this scenario, even if it is implausible. If every Jew celebrated a remixed *Shabbat* every week, and attempted to keep a remixed version of the dietary laws, would successful transmission of Jewish tradition among non-Orthodox Jews be more possible than it is right now? The answer, I suggest, is clearly affirmative.

Finally, implausible scenarios have their place in Jewish tradition when they represent aspirational visions. Not long ago, I confided to my friend Betsy, a rabbi, that I simply could not recite the final paragraph of *birkat ha'mazon*, the prayer after meals. I felt that its theme was completely unrealistic, especially the following line: "I was a youth and also have aged, and I have not seen a righteous man forsaken, or his children begging for bread."

Betsy's response completely changed my thinking. She pointed out that this paragraph is not meant to describe reality but, rather, that it is aspirational. She even illustrated the different feel one can experience by singing this particular line with a more spiritual tune rather than the upbeat, marching-type melody that is often heard. Her explanation, and the tune she sang to illustrate it, made a complete difference in how I subsequently perceived this part of the prayer, and I have not failed to recite it ever since. Our beautiful Jewish tradition has shown for thousands of years that there is value in the aspirational.

NOTES

INTRODUCTION

1. Gabriel Roth, "American Jews Are Secular, Intermarried, and Assimilated: Great News!," *Slate*, October 3, 2013, https://slate.com/human-interest/2013/10/american-jews-embrace-your-secular-intermarried-selves.html.

2. Roth, "American Jews."

3. Pew Research Center: Religion & Public Life, "Chapter 3: Jewish Identity," in *A Portrait of Jewish Americans: Findings from a Pew Research Center Survey of U.S. Jews*, October 1, 2013, https://www.pewforum.org/2013/10/01/chapter-3-jewish-identity(hereafter cited as Pew Report, Chapter 3).

4. Roberta Rosenthal Kwall, *The Myth of the Cultural Jew: Culture and Law in Jewish Tradition* (New York: Oxford University Press, 2015), 277–80.

5. In her ELI Talk, Jewish educator Stacey Aviva Flint observed that studies show that 11–20 percent of American Jews self-identify as Jews of color. "Many Faces—One Community: K'hal Amim" (lecture, ELI Talks from the AVI CHAI Foundation, August 2017), https://elitalks.org/stacey-aviva.

6. Kwall, *Myth of the Cultural Jew*, 265.

7. According to a report by the Pew Research Center, more than half of all Israelis emphasized the importance of passing down Jewish traditions to their children. To compare, 35 percent of non-Orthodox Jews in the United States report not eating pork and only 16 percent say that they always or usually light Sabbath candles (citing the 2014 U.S. Religious Landscape Study as the source of data for American Jews on these points). Pew Research Center: Religion & Public Life, *Israel's Religiously Divided Society*, March 8, 2016, 83, 51 (hereafter cited as Israel Pew Report). The report pdf is available at https://www.pewforum.org/2016/03/08/israels-religiously-divided-society.

8. For example, consider the fact that, unlike a growing number of American Jews, virtually no Israeli Jews say they have no religion, despite the fact that roughly half self-identify as secular. Pew Research Center, Israel Pew Report, 6.

9. Anshel Pfeffer notes that in Israel there are on average twenty marriages a year between Jews and Arabs. "What We Really Mean When We Talk of Assimilation's Threat to Jewish Identity," *Haaretz*, January 2, 2016, https://www.haaretz.com/israel-news/.premium-what-we-really-mean-when-we-talk-of-assimilation-1.5384720.

10. See Pew Research Center, Israel Pew Report, 62; Pew Research Center, Pew Report, Chapter 3.

11. Alex Sinclair, *Loving the Real Israel: An Educational Agenda for Liberal Zionism* (Teaneck, NJ: Ben Yehuda Press, 2013), 108–9.

12. Gal Beckerman, "Shabbat Meals: For the Love of Challah!," *Forward*, June 22, 2011, https://forward.com/food/138975/shabbat-meals-for-the-love-of-challah.

13. This concept has been used by copyright law scholars arguing for a greater ability to use works that are protected by copyright law so that new works can be contributed to society's store of culture. See Lawrence Lessig, *Remix: Making Art and Commerce Thrive in the Hybrid Economy* (New York: Penguin Press, 2008).

14. Erica Brown and Misha Galperin, *The Case for Jewish Peoplehood: Can We Be One?* (Woodstock, VT: Jewish Lights Publishing, 2009), 162.

15. Amanda Gordon, "At the Intersection of Faith and Secularity," *New York Jewish Week*, June 26, 2018, https://jewishweek.timesofisrael.com/at-the-intersection-of-faith-and-secularity.

16. See Susan Scafidi, *Who Owns Culture? Appropriation and Authenticity in American Law* (Piscataway, NJ: Rutgers University Press, 2005), 54.

17. Steven M. Cohen and Arnold M. Eisen, *The Jew Within* (Bloomington: Indiana University Press, 2000), 9.

18. "You shall kindle no fire throughout your settlements on the sabbath day." Exod. 35:3.

19. See b.Ros Has.9a.

20. See Judith Hauptman, *Rereading the Rabbis: A Woman's Voice* (Boulder, CO: Westview Press, 1998), 61.

21. Leslie Hill Hirschfeld, "A Loving Ritual Calms the Chaos," *JUF News*, January 28, 2019, https://www.juf.org/news/local.aspx?id=446859.

22. This is particularly true of the Babylonian Talmud, as opposed to the Jerusalem Talmud. See Steven H. Resnicoff, "Autonomy in Jewish Law—In Theory and in Practice." *Journal of Law and Religion* 24, no. 2 (2008): 507, 528–29, https://doi.org/10.1017/S0748081400001697.

23. B.Ketub.62b.

24. Kwall, *Cultural Jew*, 248.

1. A CELEBRATION OF *SHABBAT* AND HOLIDAY TRADITION

1. Hillel Halkin, "You Don't Have to Be Orthodox to Cherish the Sabbath," *Jewish World Review*, December 13, 2002, http://www. jewishworldreview.com/hillel/halkin121303.asp. Ahad Ha'am was the Hebrew and pen name of Asher Zvi Hirsch Ginsberg. His name means "One of the People."

2. Halkin, "Cherish the Sabbath."

3. "You shall kindle no fire throughout your settlements on the sabbath day." Exod. 35:3.

4. This list of prohibitions is contained in the Mishnah, Shabbat 7:2, the earliest codification of the Oral Torah. The rabbis derived these thirty-nine tasks from the main types of work that were necessary to construct the Tabernacle, the story of which is recounted in the Torah.

5. This special prohibition is called *muktze*.

6. Sadie Whitelocks, "A Sharpie Pen as Eyeliner and Hairspray to 'Fix' Foundation? The Long-Lasting Make-Up Tricks of Orthodox Jewish Women During the 24-Hour Sabbath," DailyMail.com, updated May 23, 2013, https:// www.dailymail.co.uk/femail/article-2328532/A-SHARPIE-pen-eyeliner-hairspray-fix-foundation-The-long-lasting-make-tricks-Orthodox-Jewish-women-24-hour-Sabbath.html. The word *isha* in the website is a transliterated version of the Hebrew word for "woman."

7. Daniella J. Greenbaum, "Whom Have You Brought to Shabbat," *Wall Street Journal*, June 16, 2017, https://www.wsj.com/articles/whom-have-you-brought-to-shabbat-1497570577.

8. Jonathan Sacks, *A Letter in the Scroll: Understanding Our Jewish Identity and Exploring the Legacy of the World's Oldest Religion* (New York: Free Press, 2000), 138.

9. Deut. 5:14.

10. David J. Wolpe, *Why Be Jewish?* (New York: Henry Holt, 1995), 75.

11. Daniel Judson and Kerry M. Olitzky, "Entering Shabbat: Broad Strokes of Shabbat Observance: Dan's perspective," in *The Rituals & Practices of a Jewish Life* (Woodstock, VT: Jewish Lights Publishing, 2002), 65.

12. Rabbi Jonathan Sacks, "Renewable Energy (Beshallach 5776)," Office of Rabbi Sacks: Covenant & Conversation, January 18, 2016, http://rabbisacks. org/renewable-energy-beshallach-5776.

13. Ariel Okin, "How to Host a Shabbat Dinner and Why You Should—Even if You Aren't Celebrating," *Vogue*, March 9, 2017, https://www.vogue.com/article/how-to-host-friday-shabbat-dinner.

14. Ari L. Goldman, *Being Jewish: The Spiritual and Cultural Practice of Judaism Today* (New York: Simon & Schuster, 2000), 198–99.

15. Sacks, "Renewable Energy."

16. *Tisha b'Av*, the ninth day of the Hebrew month of Av, is a fast day that commemorates the destruction of the two Temples in Jerusalem as well as other tragedies in the history of the Jewish people. This day is known as the Black Fast.

17. Abraham Joshua Heschel, *The Sabbath: Its Meaning for Modern Man* (Boston: Shambhala, 2003), 20.

18. Sacks, "Renewable Energy."

19. Daniel S. Nevins, "The Use of Electrical and Electronic Devices on Shabbat," The Rabbinical Assembly, Committee on Jewish Law and Standards, May 31, 2012, https://www.rabbinicalassembly.org/sites/default/files/public/halakhah/teshuvot/2011-2020/electrical-electronic-devices-shabbat.pdf.

20. David L. Lieber et al., eds., *Etz Hayim: Torah and Commentary* (Philadelphia: Jewish Publication Society, 2001), 473. See accompanying text discussing Exod. 23:12.

21. b.Beitzah 16a.

22. Mordecai M. Kaplan, *The Meaning of God in Modern Jewish Religion* (New York: Jewish Reconstruction Foundation, 1947), 59–63, 81–81, 90–91, 96–103.

23. Craig A. Kaplan and Janet Davidson, "Hatching a Theory of Incubation Effects," in *The Artificial Intelligence and Psychology Project* (Pittsburgh: Carnegie Mellon University, 1989), 3.

24. Henri Poincaré, "Mathematical Creation," in *The Creative Process*, ed. Brewster Ghiselin (Berkeley: University of California Press, 1952), 22, 27.

25. Graham Wallas, *The Art of Thought* (New York: Harcourt, Brace, 1926), 87.

26. This importance is illustrated by a search from the years 1997–2007 by two researchers in Google Scholar "for the term *incubation* along with either *creativity, insight,* or *problem*," resulting in the appearance of 5,510 articles. This search was limited to the subject areas of arts, humanities, and the social sciences. Ut Na Sio and Thomas C. Ormerod, "Does Incubation Enhance Problem Solving? A Meta-Analytic Review," *Psychological Bulletin* 135, no. 1 (2009): 94, 95, https://doi.org/10.1037/a0014212.

27. Ap Dijksterhuis and Loran F. Nordgren, "A Theory of Unconscious Thought," *Perspectives on Psychological Science* 1, no. 2 (June 2006): 95, 96, https://doi.org/10.1111/j.1745-6916.2006.00007.x.

28. Ap Dijksterhuis and Teun Meurs, "Where Creativity Resides: The Generative Power of Unconscious Thought," *Consciousness and Cognition* 15, no. 1 (2004): 135, 145, https://doi.org/10.1016/j.concog.2005.04.007.

29. Dijksterhuis and Nordgren, "Theory of Unconscious Thought," 102 (quoting Dijksterhuis and Meurs, "Where Creativity Resides," 138), 104, 108.

30. Benjamin Baird et al., "Inspired by Distraction: Mind Wandering Facilitates Creative Incubation," *Psychological Science* 23, no. 10 (October 2012): 1117, https://doi.org/10.1177/0956797612446024.

31. The well-known *Shabbat* song *Mah Yedidus* specifically says thinking about weekday matters is permissible. See Rabbi Nosson Scherman, *The Family Zemiros* (New York: ArtScroll Mesorah Publications, 1981), 47. See also Rabbi Eli Mansour, "Talking or Thinking about One's Business on Shabbat," DailyHalacha.com, accessed February 1, 2019, http://www.dailyhalacha.com/m/halacha.aspx?id=1010.

32. Haiyang Yang, Amitava Chattopadhyay, Kuangjie Zhang, and Darren W. Dahl, "Unconscious Creativity: When Can Unconscious Thought Outperform Conscious Thought?" *Journal of Consumer Psychology* 22, no. 4 (October 2012): 573, 579, https://doi.org/10.1016/j.jcps.2012.04.002.

33. Chen-Bo Zhong, Ap Dijksterhuis, and Adam D. Galinsky, "The Merits of Unconscious Thought in Creativity," *Psychological Science* 19, no. 9 (September 2008): 912, 917, https://doi.org/10.1111/j.1467-9280.2008.02176.x.

34. Zoë Miller, "This Shabbat, Try a Digital Detox," *Tablet Magazine*, March 2, 2017, https://www.tabletmag.com/scroll/226457/this-shabbat-try-a-digital-detox.

35. The rabbis instituted the additional *Yom Tov* days for outside Israel in the early centuries of the Common Era. Tacking on an additional day ensured that at least one of the days of celebration in the Diaspora would represent the actual day of the holiday. Today in Israel, days of *Yom Tov* other than Rosh Hashanah are celebrated according to the times prescribed in the Torah, and do not include these additional days. For a more detailed account of this history, see Rabbi Daniel Kohn, "Why Some Holidays Last Longer Outside Israel," My Jewish Learning, accessed January 31, 2019, http://www.myjewishlearning.com/article/extra-festival-days-in-the-diaspora.

36. Former Chief Rabbi Lord Jonathan Sacks, "The Pursuit of Joy," Orthodox Union, accessed January 31, 2019, https://www.ou.org/torah/parsha/rabbi-sacks-on-parsha/the-pursuit-of-joy.

37. "To Life! (*L'Chaim*)," in *Fiddler on the Roof*, lyrics by Sheldon Harnick, music by Jerry Bock, New York: RCA Victor, 1964.

38. Isa. 58:13.

39. See Chabad-Lubavitch Media Center, "The Separation of 'Challah,'" Chabad.org, Jewish Practice, http://www.chabad.org/library/article_cdo/aid/633188/jewish/The-Separation-of-Challah.htm.

40. See Num. 15:17–21.

41. Sophia Marie Unterman, "Gumbo Shabbat in New Orleans—Treyf but True?," *Forward*, February 22, 2017, https://forward.com/food/363792/gumbo-shabbat-in-new-orleans.

42. Unterman, "Gumbo Shabbat in New Orleans."

43. "For the Lord your God will bless all your crops and all your undertakings, and you shall have nothing but joy." Deut. 16:15.

44. Of course, joy and pleasure are not the mainstays of all Jewish holidays, as there are times in life where a more somber, reflective mood is necessary. The reality of so much historical persecution has resulted in the designation of several days that are designed to commemorate death and destruction. As discussed earlier, the most significant one is *Tisha b'Av*, the ninth day of the Hebrew month of Av.

45. Pew Research Center: Religion & Public Life, "Chapter 4: Religious Beliefs & Practices, Polling & Analysis," in *A Portrait of Jewish Americans: Findings from a Pew Research Center Survey of U.S. Jews*, October 1, 2013, http://www.pewforum.org/2013/10/01/chapter-4-religious-beliefs-and-practices.

46. See Reboot, "Sabbath Manifesto: Slowing Down Lives Since 2010," accessed February 1, 2019, http://www.sabbathmanifesto.org.

47. Alina Dizik, "Why I Started Lighting Shabbat Candles," *Tablet Magazine*, November 14, 2014, https://www.tabletmag.com/jewish-life-and-religion/186849/lighting-shabbat-candles.

48. Amy Guth, e-mail message to author, February 1, 2016.

49. Cindy Sher, "How's His Faith?," *JUF News*, March 29, 2016, https://www.juf.org/news/local.aspx?id=438615.

50. Edgar M. Bronfman, *Why Be Jewish? A Testament* (New York: Twelve, 2016), 80.

51. Kerry M. Olitzky, "Millennial Engagement in the Jewish Community," eJewish Philanthropy, Readers Forum, October 25, 2016, https://ejewishphilanthropy.com/millennial-engagement-in-the-jewish-community.

52. Sandy Cardin, "Shabbat and the Sacredness of Healing," eJewish Philanthropy, Readers Forum, November 17, 2016, https://ejewishphilanthropy.com/shabbat-and-the-sacredness-of-healing.

2. FOOD

1. Anita Hirsch, *Our Food: The Kosher Kitchen Updated* (New York: Doubleday, 1992), 9.

2. Hirsch, *Our Food*, 9.

3. Barbara Kirshenblatt-Gimblett, "Kitchen Judaism," in *Getting Comfortable in New York: The American Jewish Home, 1880–1950*, ed. Susan L. Braunstein and Jenna Weissman Joselit (Bloomington: Indiana University Press, 1991), 7.

4. See Leah Koenig, "What Is 'Jewish Food'?," *Tablet Magazine*, April 27, 2018, http://www.tabletmag.com/jewish-life-and-religion/260575/what-is-jewish-food.

5. Gabriel T. Rubin, "Baseball Rules Are Complicated Enough, Now Add Passover," *Wall Street Journal*, April 5, 2018, https://www.wsj.com/articles/baseball-rules-are-complicated-enough-now-add-passover-1522941723.

6. Hallie Lieberman, "Atlanta Emerges as the Jewish Foodie Capital of the South," *Tablet Magazine*, November 6, 2017, http://www.tabletmag.com/jewish-life-and-religion/248122/atlanta-jewish-foodie-capital-of-the-south.

7. Cathryn J. Prince, "For Many NY Jews, Delis Are the 'Secular Version of the Synagogue,'" *Times of Israel*, May 15, 2016, https://www.timesofisrael.com/for-many-ny-jews-delis-are-the-secular-version-of-the-synagogue.

8. Lieberman, "Atlanta Emerges."

9. Anna Goren, "Kosher Meets Hipster," *The Atlantic*, September 24, 2014, https://www.theatlantic.com/national/archive/2014/09/the-new-kosher/380707.

10. Michael Ledeen, "After 500 Years, an Italian Jewish Rebirth," *Wall Street Journal*, July 14, 2017.

11. See Alice Hancock, "Jewish Food: The Most Comforting Trend of 2017," *Spectator Life*, July 17, 2017, https://life.spectator.co.uk/2017/07/jewish-food-the-most-comforting-trend-of-2017; Elizabeth Kratz, "Vienna's Growing Kosher Scene a Case Study of Thriving Jewish Life in Europe," eJewish Philanthropy, January 30, 2018, https://ejewishphilanthropy.com/viennas-growing-kosher-scene-a-case-study-of-thriving-jewish-life-in-europe.

12. Rachel Shukert, "My Mother's Cakes, Memory, and the Meaning of Me," *Tablet Magazine*, September 11, 2015, https://www.tabletmag.com/scroll/193553/my-mothers-cakes-memory-and-the-meaning-of-me.

13. Shukert, "My Mother's Cakes."

14. Derek Attig, "How Froot Loops Helped Me Create a Culinary Connection to the Jewish World," *Tablet Magazine*, February 16, 2017, http://www.tabletmag.com/jewish-life-and-religion/160418/froot-loops-jewish-food.

15. Attig, "How Froot Loops Helped."

16. Josefin Dolsten, "The Jewish Food Society Wants to Preserve Your Grandma's Recipes—Before They're Lost Forever," *Jewish Telegraphic Agency*, August 25, 2017, https://www.jta.org/2017/08/25/life-religion/the-jewish-food-society-wants-to-preserve-your-grandmas-recipes-before-theyre-lost-forever.

17. Yvette Alt Miller, "It's the End of an Era for America's First All-Kosher Supermarket," *Jewish Telegraphic Agency*, April 10, 2018, https://www.jta.org/2018/04/10/united-states/its-the-end-of-an-era-for-americas-first-all-kosher-supermarket. Hungarian was sold to Orian Azulay in April 2018, and the new owner has pledged to keep the business as a mainstay of the Chicagoland kosher community.

18. Liz Alpern, telephone conversation with author, November 21, 2017.

19. Ari Y. Kelman et al., "The Social Self: Toward the Study of Jewish Lives in the Twenty-First Century," *Contemporary Jewry* 37, no. 1 (April 2017): 53, 67, https://doi.org/10.1007/s12397-016-9182-5.

20. Adam Rosen, "Finding Faith in Sukkot," *Tablet Magazine*, October 3, 2017, http://www.tabletmag.com/jewish-life-and-religion/246140/finding-faith-in-sukkot.

21. Rosen, "Finding Faith in Sukkot."

22. Rosen, "Finding Faith in Sukkot."

23. Attig, "How Froot Loops Helped."

24. Lieberman, "Atlanta Emerges."

25. Barbara Fenig, "Jewish Food Renaissance Is Here to Stay, According to Hazon Food Conference," *Forward*, August 25, 2017, https://forward.com/food/381002/jewish-food-renaissance-is-here-to-stay-according-to-hazon-food-conference.

26. Jenna Weissman Joselit, "Breaking the Fast," *Tablet Magazine*, September 28, 2017, http://www.tabletmag.com/jewish-life-and-religion/244748/breaking-the-fast.

27. Micheline Maynard, "It's Official: Philadelphia's Zahav Is the James Beard Awards' Favorite Everything," *Forbes*, May 7, 2019, https://www.forbes.com/sites/michelinemaynard/2019/05/07/its-official-philadelphias-zahav-is-the-james-beard-awards-favorite-everything.

28. Michael Solomonov and Steven Cook, *Zahav: A World of Israeli Cooking* (Boston: Rux Martin, Houghton Mifflin Harcourt, 2015), 198.

29. Solomonov and Cook, *Zahav*, 22.

30. Liz Alpern, telephone conversations with author, November 21, 2017, and January 28, 2019.

31. Lieberman, "Atlanta Emerges."

32. Lucy Cohen Blatter, "This New Kosher Deli May Be Miami's Hippest Restaurant," *Jewish Telegraphic Agency*, January 26, 2017, https://www.jta.org/

2017/01/26/life-religion/this-new-kosher-deli-may-be-miamis-hippest-restaurant.

33. See Lev. 11:2–31; Deut. 14:3–21.

34. Edward L. Greenstein, "Dietary Laws," in *Etz Hayim: Torah and Commentary*, ed. David L. Lieber et al. (Philadelphia: Jewish Publication Society, 2001), 1460–61. The prohibition of consuming blood appears in the Torah as early as Genesis 9:4, in the story of Noah.

35. Historian Roger Horowitz details the story of animal science professor Temple Grandin and *shechitah*, demonstrating how she "deserves much credit for averting wide challenges to *schechita* in the United States" after the infamous scandals involving Agriprocessors in Postville, Iowa. Her view, and that of others, is that when done properly, kosher slaughtering entails little or no pain. Roger Horowitz, *Kosher USA* (New York: Columbia University Press, 2016), 225, 241–42.

36. See Exod. 23:19, 34:26; Deut. 14:21.

37. See b.Hul. 111b; b.Zevachim.96b.

38. David C. Kraemer, *Jewish Eating and Identity through the Ages* (New York: Routledge, 2007), 100.

39. Haym Soloveitchik, "Rupture and Reconstruction: The Transformation of Contemporary Orthodoxy," *Tradition* 28, no. 4 (1994): 2, 37 n.18.

40. Haym Soloveitchik, "Religious Law and Change: The Medieval Ashkenazic Example," *AJS Review* 12, no. 2 (Autumn 1987): 205, 206–20, http://www.jstor.org/stable/1486380.

41. See b.Hul. 104b–105a.

42. See Kraemer, *Jewish Eating and Identity*, 88–89 (citing Moses Maimonides, *Mishneh Torah: Ma'achalot Assurot* 9:28).

43. Sue Fishkoff, *Kosher Nation* (New York: Schocken Books, 2010), 47. These agencies are "the Manhattan-based Orthodox Union, the Star-K in Baltimore, the OK Kosher Certification in Brooklyn, and the Kof-K Kosher Supervision in Teaneck, New Jersey." According to Fishkoff, "in 1923, Heinz Vegetarian Beans became the first food item to carry national kosher certification." Fishkoff, *Kosher Nation*, 8, 48.

44. See Samuel C. Heilman, *Sliding to the Right: The Contest for the Future of American Jewish Orthodoxy* (Berkeley: University of California Press, 2006).

45. Fishkoff, *Kosher Nation*, 175. Fishkoff writes that checking vegetables for bug infestation is the most time-consuming part of the job of a rabbinic food supervisor. Fishkoff, *Kosher Nation*, 167.

46. See Kraemer, *Jewish Eating and Identity*, 158. Kraemer notes that the eminent halakhic authority of the twentieth century, Rabbi Moshe Feinstein, was lenient on this matter. According to Fishkoff, the level of observance of a particular household can be indicated by whether or not it contains light boxes

to check vegetables and separate ovens and refrigerators for meat and dairy. Fishkoff, *Kosher Nation*, 267.

47. See Fishkoff, *Kosher Nation*, 233.

48. Fishkoff calls bacon "almost a separate category." Fishkoff, *Kosher Nation*, 229. On the connection between Jews and Chinese Food, see Roberta Rosenthal Kwall, *The Myth of the Cultural Jew: Culture and Law in Jewish Tradition* (New York: Oxford University Press, 2015), 286 n. 150.

49. Kirshenblatt-Gimblett, "Kitchen Judaism," 78, 80.

50. See Fishkoff, *Kosher Nation*, 233.

51. Horowitz, *Kosher USA*, 123, 125. According to Fishkoff, only 14 percent of the 11.2 million American consumers of kosher food are kosher Jews. Fishkoff, *Kosher Nation*, 6. Kosher products that contain dairy are marked with a "D." In contrast, products that do not contain any dairy are marked "Pareve" so they can be eaten with either meat or dairy meals. Foods that are specially made for Passover are user-friendly for those who need to avoid gluten.

52. See Fishkoff, *Kosher Nation*, 243.

53. Eric H. Yoffie, foreword in *The Sacred Table: Creating a Jewish Food Ethic*, ed. Mary L. Zamore (New York: CCAR Press, 2011), 18–20.

54. David A. M. Wilensky, "Pulled Pork Kugel and Other Transgressive Traditions from the Ultimate Treif Banquet," Jewish Telegraphic Agency, January 11, 2018, https://www.jta.org/2018/01/11/life-religion/pulled-pork-kugel-and-other-transgressive-traditions-from-the-ultimate-treif-banquet. The event was organized by Alix Wall, the founder of an organization called Illuminoshi, composed of local Jews working in the food service industry. See David A. M. Wilensky, "Tradition and Transgression at 'Trefa Banquet 2.0,'" Jewish News of Northern California, Jew in the Pew, January 8, 2018, https://www.jweekly.com/2018/01/08/tradition-transgression-trefa-banquet-2-0.

55. Mark Sameth, "'I'll Have What She's Having': Jewish Ethical Vegetarianism," in Zamore, *Sacred Table*, 225, 227.

56. Rabbi Abraham M. Heller, "Kashruth: Advancing the Cause of Jewish National Survival," in *The Jewish Examiner Prize Kosher Recipe Book*, ed. Balabusta (New York: Judea, 1937), 184.

57. Greenstein, "Dietary Laws," 1460, 1464.

58. See Mark Sameth, "The Broad Spectrum of Kashrut," in *The Rituals & Practices of a Jewish Life: A Handbook for Personal Spiritual Renewal*, ed. Kerry M. Olitzky and Daniel Judson (Woodstock, VT: Jewish Lights Publishing, 2002), 41, 44, 51, 52. Subsequently, Sameth articulated the rationale for a Jewish vegetarian diet. Sameth, "'I'll Have What She's Having,'" 225, 227.

59. Liel Leibovitz, "What I Gained by Losing Weight," *Tablet Magazine*, September 20, 2017, http://www.tabletmag.com/jewish-life-and-religion/245558/what-i-gained-by-losing-weight.

60. Jenni Person, quoted in Zamore, *Sacred Table*, xxxvii.

61. Ellen Umansky, "Three Sets of Dishes," Jewish Book Council, Prosen-People, February 20, 2017, https://www.jewishbookcouncil.org/_blog/The_ProsenPeople/post/three-sets-of-dishes.

62. Umansky, "Three Sets of Dishes."

63. See Peter Knobel, "What I Eat Is Who I Am: Kashrut and Identity," in Zamore, *Sacred Table*, 439, 442.

64. Sameth, "Broad Spectrum of Kashrut," 41, 45.

65. Liel Leibovitz, e-mail message to author, May 7, 2018.

66. Eugene B. Borowitz, "Real Life/Real Food: A Holy Moment at McDonald's," in Zamore, *Sacred Table*, 117–18.

67. See Bennett F. Miller, "The Joy and Privilege of Blessings Before and After a Meal," in Zamore, *Sacred Table*, 418, 421–23.

68. Aish HaTorah, "Purchasing Power: Daily Lift #1240," Aish.com, Spirituality, http://www.aish.com/sp/dl/46123397.html.

69. See Knobel, "What I Eat Is Who I Am," 439, 443.

70. Karen R. Perolman, "Meat Minimalism: Were We Meant to Be Ethical Omnivores?," in Zamore, *Sacred Table*, 261, 263–64. For a more complete discussion of *Yom Tov*, see chapter 1 of this book, on *Shabbat* and Holidays.

71. Borowitz, "Real Life/Real Food," 483–84. In her essay Zamore wrote that on a recent visit, her in-laws traveled more than three hours to a synagogue in Oslo, the only source of kosher meat in the country, and brought back kosher food for Zamore's family.

72. Mary L. Zamore, "Your Personal Kashrut: *Sh'leimut* and *Sh'lom Bayit*," in *Sacred Table*, 463, 466.

73. Horowitz, *Kosher USA*, 256–57, 263.

3. MARRIAGE AND FAMILY

1. Pew Research Center: Religion & Public Life, "Overview," in *A Portrait of Jewish Americans: Findings from a Pew Research Center Survey of U.S. Jews*, October 1, 2013, http://www.pewforum.org/2013/10/01/jewish-american-beliefs-attitudes-culture-survey(hereafter cited as Pew Report). See also Pew Research Center: Religion & Public Life, "Chapter 1: Population Estimates," in Pew Report. The Pew Report concluded that the NET Jewish population is 5.3 million Jewish adults, representing 2.2 percent of the United States population of adults.

2. See Rachel Biale, *Women and Jewish Law: The Essential Texts, Their History & Their Relevance for Today* (New York: Schocken Books, 1984), 50–51. In 1977, Israel enacted a law that made polygamy punishable with five

years in prison and a monetary fine. See David Sedley, "In Defiance of Israeli Law, Polygamy Sanctioned by Top Rabbis," *Times of Israel*, December 27, 2016, http://www.timesofisrael.com/in-defiance-of-israeli-law-polygamy-sanctioned-by-top-rabbis.

3. b.Qidd.2a-b.

4. See Gen. 24:57–58.

5. Judith Hauptman, *Rereading the Rabbis: A Woman's Voice* (Boulder, CO: Westview Press, 1998), 71, 73–74. See also Biale, *Women and Jewish Law*, 61. Despite the clear requirement that a woman must consent to marriage, the reality is that during the medieval period, the parents of the couple often exercised control over marriages rather than the couple.

6. Maurice Lamm, "The Purposes of Marriage," in *The Jewish Way in Love & Marriage* (New York: Jonathan David Publishers, 1991), 122–42.

7. Gilbert S. Rosenthal, "Marriage and Family," in *Etz Hayim: Torah and Commentary*, ed. David L. Lieber et al. (Philadelphia: Jewish Publication Society, 2001), 1353.

8. See Hauptman, *Rereading the Rabbis*, 60–61, 63, 67.

9. See Biale, *Women and Jewish Law*, 82–83.

10. Peter S. Knobel, "Love and Marriage: Reform Judaism and Kiddushin," in *Marriage and Its Obstacles in Jewish Law*, ed. Walter Jacob and Moshe Zemer (New York: Berghahn Books, 1999).

11. This provision is known as the "Lieberman Clause," named after its originator, Rabbi Saul Lieberman. See also Lorelei Laird, "Women in Chains: Lawyers Look for Secular Solutions to the Jewish Divorce Problem," *ABA Journal* 100, no. 8 (2014): 17, 20. It is not uncommon for Orthodox couples to have a prenuptial agreement binding the spouses to arbitrate marital disputes and providing that the husband agrees to pay the wife a certain daily amount until he grants her a get. These agreements have been enforced in some secular courts.

12. Exod. 21:7–11. A husband's duty to satisfy his wife sexually is based on a passage in the Torah that speaks of the basic rights of food, clothing, and conjugal rights that are owed to a female slave. The rabbis in the Talmud use these Biblically delineated rights for a slave as the basis for the rights of a free woman.

13. This translation appears in Biale, *Women and Jewish Law*, 130.

14. Compare b.Pesah.72b (Raba's statement indicating requirements represent a minimum) and b.Ber.22a ("Let not students of the law be with their wives too frequently like roosters").

15. For a discussion on this point, see Biale, *Women and Jewish Law*, 132–34.

16. Norma Baumel Joseph, "Rabbi Moses Feinstein," in Jewish Women: A Comprehensive Historical Encyclopedia, Jewish Women's Archive, March 1, 2009, https://jwa.org/encyclopedia/article/feinstein-rabbi-moses.

17. Biale, *Women and Jewish Law*, 144–45.

18. See Moses Maimonides, *Mishneh Torah: Issurei Bi'ah* 21:9.

19. b.Erub.100b.

20. Traditionally, after menopause a woman goes to the *mikveh* after her last period. Some women elect to do this even if they did not observe this practice consistently during their fertile years. There is inherent wisdom, and even a potentially universal appeal, in this practice. On February 7, 2017, an episode of the family sitcom *The Middle* aired called "Ovary and Out." This long-running show revolves around a Midwestern middle-class, Christian family with a middle-aged husband and wife and three quirky children. During this episode, the mother learns that she is now in menopause and she humorously laments this development with a monologue that concludes with the idea that she feels her ovaries should be celebrated with "a send-off for a job well done!" It is likely that the writers of this show had no clue about a woman's final post-fertility visit to the *mikveh* but it is fascinating that the very send-off her character seeks has existed within Jewish tradition for centuries.

21. Marjorie Ingall, "Transgender Jews Find a Place in the Mikveh," *Tablet Magazine*, November 17, 2017, https://www.tabletmag.com/jewish-life-and-religion/249597/transgender-jews-in-the-mikveh.

22. Allison Hoffman, "The New American Mikveh," *Tablet Magazine*, August 13, 2012, http://www.tabletmag.com/jewish-life-and-religion/109120/the-new-american-mikveh.

23. See Douglas E. Abrams et al., *Contemporary Family Law*, 4th ed. (St. Paul, MN: West Academic Publishing, 2015), 4; Eric Cohen and Aylana Meisel, "Jewish Conservatism: A Manifesto," *Commentary*, May 2017, 15, 21.

24. See also Biale, *Women and Jewish Law*, 202.

25. b.Yebam.64a.

26. See Sylvia Barack Fishman and Steven M. Cohen, *Family, Engagement, and Jewish Continuity among American Jews* (Jerusalem: Jewish People Policy Institute, 2017), 18, table 4, http://jppi.org.il/new/wp-content/uploads/2017/06/Raising-Jewish-Children-Research-and-Indicators-for-Intervention.pdf.

27. Pew Research Center: Religion & Public Life, "Chapter 2: Intermarriage and Other Demographics," in Pew Report (hereafter cited as Pew Report, Chapter 2). According to Pew, the intermarriage rates rose to 35 percent by 1974, 42 percent by 1984, 46 percent by 1994, and 55 percent by 1999. The report shows that the percentage of intermarriage has remained at 58 percent since the beginning of the twenty-first century. See also Laurie Goodstein, "Poll Shows Major Shift in Identity of U.S. Jews," *New York Times*, October 1,

2013, http://www.nytimes.com/2013/10/01/us/poll-shows-major-shift-in-identity-of-us-jews.html, discussing the Pew Report.

28. Fishman and Cohen, *Jewish Continuity*, 16, table 2; 18, table 4.

29. Abrams et al., *Contemporary Family Law*, 4.

30. See m.Qidd.3:12; Shaye J. D. Cohen, *The Beginnings of Jewishness* (Berkeley: University of California Press, 1999), 306.

31. For a more detailed discussion of these complexities, see Roberta Rosenthal Kwall, *The Myth of the Cultural Jew: Culture and Law in Jewish Tradition* (New York: Oxford University Press, 2015), 135–43.

32. Drawing on data from the Pew Report, Theodore Sasson and his colleagues find millennials of intermarried parents nearly twice as likely to be raised Jewish by religion compared to older counterparts, and for all ages data shows those with Jewish mothers nearly twice as likely to be raised exclusively Jewish. Theodore Sasson et al., "Millennial Children of Intermarriage: Religious Upbringing, Identification, and Behavior Among Children of Jewish and Non-Jewish Parents," *Contemporary Jewry* 37, no. 1 (2017): 99, 101, 111, https://doi.org/10.1007/s12397-017-9202-0 .

33. Theodore Sasson et al., *Millennial Children of Intermarriage: Touchpoints and Trajectories of Jewish Engagement* (Waltham, MA: Brandeis University: Cohen Center for Modern Jewish Studies, 2015), https://www.brandeis.edu/cmjs/pdfs/intermarriage/MillennialChildrenIntermarriage1.pdf.

34. Leonard Saxe et al., *Under the Chuppah: Rabbinic Officiation and Intermarriage* (Waltham, MA: Brandeis University: Cohen Center for Modern Jewish Studies, 2015), https://www.brandeis.edu/cmjs/pdfs/jewish%20futures/RabbinicOfficiation102616.pdf.

35. Sasson et al., *Millennial Children of Intermarriage*; Saxe et al., *Under the Chuppah*.

36. See Pew Research Center, "Overview," "Jewish Child Rearing" table. Among married Jews with only one Jewish parent, 83 percent are also intermarried, as compared to 37 percent of Jews whose parents are in-married. Pew Research Center, Pew Report, Chapter 2.

37. Fishman and Cohen, *Jewish Continuity*, 27, table 9.

38. For a flavor of the spectrum of positions on this issue, see George E. Johnson, ed., "What Will the Jewish World Look Like in 2050?," *Moment*, February 13, 2017, 44–55, https://www.momentmag.com/will-jewish-world-look-like-2050.

39. Mark Oppenheimer, Stephanie Butnick, and Liel Leibovitz, "Have Yourself an Unorthodox Little Christmas: Ep. 71," *Unorthodox*, podcast audio, December 22, 2016, https://www.tabletmag.com/jewish-life-and-religion/220570/unorthodox-episode-71-jewish-christmas-chinese-food-movies-trees-hanukkah.

40. See Sylvia Barack Fishman, *Double or Nothing? Jewish Families and Mixed Marriage* (Hanover, NH: Brandeis University, 2004), 52–54; Adina Bankier-Karp, "Catalyst of Continuity: A Study of Critical Experiences Influencing Self-Identification and Connectedness of Jewish Young Adults in Melbourne" (research, NRJE Emerging Scholars Mentoring Seminar, Brandeis University, June 6, 2017). Fishman has found that intermarried Jews and spouses often are surprised at how strongly they feel about religious identification *after* their children are born. Adina Bankier-Karp reached a similar conclusion based on her pilot study of critical experiences influencing the sustainment and transformation of the identification and connectedness of Jewish young adults in Melbourne, Australia. I am grateful to Adina Bankier-Karp for sharing her data on these points.

41. Jane Larkin, "Intermarried Couples Can Still Build Jewishly Engaged Families," *Tablet Magazine*, March 18, 2014, https://www.tabletmag.com/jewish-life-and-religion/163144/intermarried-jewishly-engaged.

42. David Lerner, "New Conservative/Masorti Ceremony for Interfaith Couples," *Times of Israel* (blog), March 26, 2015, https://blogs.timesofisrael.com/new-conservativemasorti-ceremony-for-interfaith-couples.

43. Felicia Sol, J. Rolando Matalon, and Marcelo Bronstein, "Why We Decided to Perform Intermarriages," *Forward*, June 21, 2017, http://forward.com/opinion/375221/bnai-jeshurun-rabbis-explain-perform-intermarriage.

44. Jane Eisner, "Why This Renegade Rabbi Says He Can Marry Jews—And the Jew-ish," *Forward*, June 9, 2017, http://forward.com/opinion/373982/conservative-jewish-intermarriage-renegade-rabbi.

45. Avram Mlotek, "Time to Rethink Our Resistance to Intermarriage," *Times of Israel*, June 13, 2017, http://jewishweek.timesofisrael.com/time-to-rethink-our-resistance-to-intermarriage.

46. See Yeshivat Chovevei Torah Rabbinical School, "Statement Regarding Intermarriage," yctorah.org, Newsroom, accessed February 20, 2019, http://www.yctorah.org/2017/06/statement-regarding-intermarriage.

47. Susan Katz Miller, "What Do Interfaith Families Want from Rabbis?," *Forward*, June 20, 2017, https://forward.com/opinion/375111/what-do-jewish-interfaith-families-want-from-rabbis. Katz Miller is the author of *Being Both: Embracing Two Religions in One Interfaith Family*, for which she surveyed more than three hundred interfaith family members across the United States (Boston: Beacon Press, 2013).

48. Edmund Case, "How Audacious Will Our Hospitality to Interfaith Families Be?," eJewish Philanthropy, June 12, 2017, https://ejewishphilanthropy.com/how-audacious-will-our-hospitality-to-interfaith-families-be.

49. See Pew Research Center: Religion & Public Life, "Chapter 3: Jewish Identity," in Pew Report. Of the NET Jewish population, 62 percent say being

Jewish is a matter of ancestry or culture; 15 percent say religion; and 23 percent say both religion and ancestry or culture. Even so, Pew also shows that 72 percent of this population do believe in God or a universal spirit. Pew Research Center: Religion & Public Life, "Chapter 4: Religious Beliefs & Practices, Polling & Analysis," in Pew Report.

50. For example, see Larkin, ""Intermarried Couples Can Still Build Jewishly Engaged Families." Jane Larkin, who writes about parenting for intermarried couples, received this advice when she and her husband took a class on interfaith relationships taught by both a priest and a rabbi.

51. Winnie Sandler Grinspoon, "PJ Library Family Study: How 25,000 Families Experience Jewish Life in the U.S. and Canada," eJewish Philanthropy, June 27, 2017, https://ejewishphilanthropy.com/pj-library-family-study-how-25000-families-experience-jewish-life-in-the-u-s-and-canada.

52. See Ariella Saperstein, "Strength in (Smaller) Numbers," eJewish Philanthropy, October 5, 2016, https://ejewishphilanthropy.com/strength-in-smaller-numbers; Ben Sales, "Outside the Synagogue, Intermarried Are Forming Community with Each Other," Jewish Telegraphic Agency, February 10, 2017, https://www.jta.org/2017/02/10/united-states/outside-the-synagogue-intermarried-are-forming-community-with-each-other; Rabbi Brian Field, "The Torah of Inclusion Offers Us a 'Yes' to Interfaith Couples," eJewish Philanthropy, May 23, 2017, https://ejewishphilanthropy.com/the-torah-of-inclusion-offers-us-a-yes-to-interfaith-couples. For an excellent analysis of innovation in prayer communities generally, see Jack Wertheimer, *The New American Judaism: How Jews Practice Their Religion Today* (Princeton, NJ: Princeton University Press, 2018), chap. 8, 183–210; chap. 10, 233–53.

53. Pearl Mattenson, Michael Wise, and Avi Rubel, "Honeymoon Israel: Building Ties That Bind," eJewish Philanthropy, December 20, 2016.

54. See Katz Miller, ""What Do Interfaith Families Want from Rabbis?"; Case, "How Audacious Will Our Hospitality to Interfaith Families Be?"

55. Fishman and Cohen, *Jewish Continuity*, 10. This study also has implications for the topic of "grandparenting," which is discussed further in chapter 5.

56. Clare Ansberry, "The Teenage Spiritual Crisis," *Wall Street Journal*, June 14, 2017, A15.

57. Fishman and Cohen, *Jewish Continuity*, 22.

58. See Eli T. Cohn, "Engaging Millennial Couples through Non-Traditional Weddings," eJewish Philanthropy, June 21, 2016.

59. See Janine Stein, "Against My Best Advice, I Married a Non-Jewish Man," *Forward*, June 15, 2017, https://forward.com/scribe/374849/against-my-best-advice-i-married-a-non-jewish-man.

60. Bankier-Karp, "Catalyst of Continuity." For a discussion of Bankier-Karp's research, see n. 40, supra.

4. CHILDREN'S JEWISH EDUCATION AND
THE B'NAI MITZVAH EXPERIENCE

1. "There probably has been no other time when Jewish themed books, texts, sources, and ideas have been as available and accessible as in contemporary America." Barry Chazan, Robert Chazan, and Benjamin M. Jacobs, *Cultures and Contexts of Jewish Education* (Cham, Switzerland: Palgrave Macmillan, 2017), 69. See also, David Bryfman, "When You're Happy and You Know It—The True Purpose of Jewish Education," eJewish Philanthropy, November 28, 2016, https://ejewishphilanthropy.com/when-youre-happy-and-you-know-it-the-true-purpose-of-jewish-education; Pew Research Center: Religion & Public Life, "Chapter 3: Jewish Identity," in *A Portrait of Jewish Americans: Findings from a Pew Research Center Survey of U.S. Jews*, October 1, 2013, http://www.pewforum.org/2013/10/01/jewish-american-beliefs-attitudes-culture-survey(hereafter cited as Pew Report, Chapter 3).

2. According to a 2009 study, only 18 percent of all American Jewish children attend Jewish day school, and of this group, 80 percent are Orthodox. Chazan, Chazan, and Jacobs, *Contexts of Jewish Education*, 101, 111n39. Dr. Scott Aaron also notes that "American Jews are disaffiliating from Jewish congregational life at unprecedented rates, though congregations have historically educated the majority of American Jewish students and continue to do so." "Can Today's Congregational Schools Teach Tomorrow's Happiness?," eJewish Philanthropy, March 28, 2017, https://ejewishphilanthropy.com/can-todays-congregational-school-teach-tomorrows-happiness.

3. See Janet Krasner Aronson et al., *2017 Greater Washington Jewish Community Demographic Study* (Waltham, MA: Brandeis University: Steinhardt Social Research Institute, 2017), https://www.brandeis.edu/ssri/pdfs/communitystudies/DCJewishCommunityStudy.pdf; Matthew Boxer et al., *2017 Greater Pittsburgh Jewish Community Study* (Waltham, MA: Brandeis University: Steinhardt Social Research Institute, 2017), https://jfedpgh.org/file/scorecard/PittsburghJewishCommStudy021918.2.pdf; Jonathan Woocher, "Reinventing Jewish Education for the 21st Century," *Journal of Jewish Education* 78, no. 3 (2012): 191, https://doi.org/10.1080/15244113.2012.700636.

4. For example, consider BimBam, which provided a wide array of educational content through online animated short films for both children and adults. In 2019, BimBam closed but found a new online home at ReformJudaism.org. See "Beloved Jewish Educational Video Studio BimBam to Close & Finds New Home for Award-Winning Content Online at ReformJudaism.org" (URJ Press Release), Union for Reform Judaism, April 2, 2019, https://urj.org/blog/2019/04/02/beloved-jewish-educational-video-studio-bimbam-close-finds-new-home-award-winning. See also Chazan and his colleagues, who note that

"anyone seeking knowledge about Judaism . . . can do so with only a few clicks or taps from just about anywhere in the globe." *Contexts of Jewish Education*, 133. These authors also discuss the "democratization of traditional text study" stemming from increasingly popular programs of study for adults geared to learners with all levels of prior knowledge. Chazan, Chazan, and Jacobs, *Contexts of Jewish Education*, 133, 130.

5. Woocher, "Reinventing Jewish Education," 198.

6. Paul Steinberg, "Why? The Continuing Struggle for the Soul of Hebrew School," eJewish Philanthropy, March 2, 2018, http://ejewishphilanthropy. com/why-the-continuing-struggle-for-the-soul-of-hebrew-school.

7. Steinberg, "Why? The Continuing Struggle for the Soul of Hebrew School."

8. Woocher, "Reinventing Jewish Education," 182.

9. Roberta Rosenthal Kwall, *The Myth of the Cultural Jew: Culture and Law in Jewish Tradition* (New York: Oxford University Press, 2015), 277; Erica Brown and Misha Galperin, *The Case for Jewish Peoplehood: Can We Be One?* (Woodstock, VT: Jewish Lights Publishing, 2009), 71, 110.

10. Woocher, "Reinventing Jewish Education," 211.

11. The Federation was able to get this program off the ground by obtaining the necessary funding to design and implement a comprehensive program to support these religious schools. Elaine Kellerman and Lisa Klein, "Revitalizing Jewish Education Through Experts, Technology, and Life-Long Learning," Jeducation World, December 12, 2016, http://jeducationworld.com/2016/12/ revitalizing-jewish-education-through-experts-technology-and-life-long-learning.

12. Laura Novak Winer, Isa Aron, and Jerilyn Perman, *New Approaches to Supplementary Education in the Reform Movement* (New York: Union for Reform Judaism, 2017), https://urj.org/sites/default/files/URJNewApproaches SupplementaryEducationReport.pdf.

13. See Bryfman, "Purpose of Jewish Education"; Rebecca Rosenthal and Mirit Sands, "Transforming Synagogue Education through Project Based Learning," eJewish Philanthropy, April 4, 2017, https://ejewishphilanthropy. com/transforming-synagogue-education-through-project-based-learning.

14. Maayan Jaffee, "Project-Based Learning Offers 'Deeper and Better' Way to Teach Judaism," eJewish Philanthropy, October 6, 2015, https:// ejewishphilanthropy.com/project-based-learning-offers-deeper-and-better-way-to-teach-judaism.

15. See Mark S. Young, "Inspiring Things Are Happening . . . in Hebrew School?!," eJewish Philanthropy, March 14, 2017, https://ejewishphilanthropy. com/inspiring-things-are-happening-in-hebrew-school; Jaffee, "Project-Based Learning."

16. Lesley Litman, "What Really Matters in Synagogue Education: A Comparative Case Study of a Conventional School and an Alternative Program," *Journal of Jewish Education* 83, no. 4 (2017): 249–79, https://doi.org/10.1080/15244113.2017.1378564.

17. Julie Wiener, "Jewish After-School Stressing Flexibility," *New York Jewish Week*, October 3, 2012, http://jewishweek.timesofisrael.com/jewish-after-school-stressing-flexibility.

18. Laura Novak Winer, "New Partners in Jewish Education: Independent Afterschool Jewish Education Programs and Their Relationships with Congregational Supplementary Schools," *Journal of Jewish Education* 83, no. 3 (2017): 173, 176, https://doi.org/10.1080/15244113.2017.1344822.

19. Winer, "New Partners in Jewish Education," 177.

20. Winer, "New Partners in Jewish Education," 191.

21. Laura Novak Winer, telephone conversation with author, June 11, 2018; see also Winer, *New Approaches*.

22. Mordecai Kaplan, "The Function of the Jewish Religious School," *Jewish Teacher* 1, no. 1 (1916): 12; see also, 5–12, http://memory.loc.gov/service/gdc/scd0001/2010/20101216002je/20101216002je.pdf.

23. See Janice Elster, "No More Business as Usual: The Need for Drastic Changes in Supplementary Jewish Education," eJewish Philanthropy, August 8, 2017, https://ejewishphilanthropy.com/no-more-business-as-usual-the-need-for-drastic-changes-in-supplementary-jewish-education.

24. Bryfman, "Purpose of Jewish Education."

25. Bryfman, "Purpose of Jewish Education."

26. Woocher, "Reinventing Jewish Education," 200–201.

27. See, for example, Miriam Heller Stern, "A Historic Crusade for Learning: The Future of Hebrew School," eJewish Philanthropy, March 21, 2017, https://ejewishphilanthropy.com/a-historic-crusade-for-learning-the-future-of-hebrew-school.

28. Woocher, "Reinventing Jewish Education," 192.

29. Pirkei Avot, 5:21. Pirkei Avot is a compilation of rabbinic wisdom dating back to the early centuries of the Common Era; it states that thirteen is the age for observing the commandments (presumably referring to boys). This text appears in the Mishnah, one of the earliest codifications of Jewish law dating back to the first centuries of the Common Era.

30. For a discussion of age in connection with obligations and puberty, see b.Niddah 46a. Those Orthodox synagogues that do permit girls to celebrate a Bat Mitzvah do so when the young woman turns twelve rather than thirteen.

31. Ivan G. Marcus notes that this ceremony "reached a recognizable shape no earlier than the sixteenth century, and even then, only in central Europe."

The Jewish Life Cycle: Rites of Passage from Biblical to Modern Times (Seattle: University of Washington, 2004), 40.

32. Jonathan D. Sarna, *American Judaism: A History* (New Haven, CT: Yale University Press, 2004), 173, 287.

33. See Kwall, *Cultural Jew*, 193–224, for a fuller exploration of this issue.

34. Mark Oppenheimer, "Three Rules for a Better Bar or Bat Mitzvah," *Tablet Magazine*, March 3, 2017, https://www.tabletmag.com/jewish-life-and-religion/224030/rules-for-a-better-bar-mitzvah.

35. Jewish educator Katherine Schwartz confirmed the importance of reading Torah for the fifteen students in her dissertation study of post–B'nai Mitzvah students in the Denver area. Katherine Schwartz, telephone conversation with author, July 9, 2018.

36. Patricia Keer Munro, *Coming of Age in Jewish America: Bar and Bat Mitzvah Reinterpreted* (New Brunswick, NJ: Rutgers University, 2016), 122–23.

37. See Danielle Braff, "The DIY Bar Mitzvah," *Crain's Chicago Business*, April 3, 2015, http://www.chicagobusiness.com/article/20150403/ISSUE03/150409900/the-diy-bar-mitzvah; Miriam Kreinin Souccar, "Rent a Rabbi, Borrow a Torah for DIY Bar Mitzvah," *Crain's New York Business*, February 23, 2015, http://www.crainsnewyork.com/article/20150224/SMALLBIZ/150229957/rent-a-rabbi-borrow-a-torah-for-diy-bar-mitzvah.

38. Braff, "DIY Bar Mitzvah."

39. See Pew Research Center, Pew Report, Chapter 3. Sadly, Pew's 2013 Religion & Public Life Project reveals that only 28 percent of the NET Jewish population reported that being part of a Jewish community is essential for Jewish identity. Even among Orthodox respondents, this figure is a surprisingly low percentage of 69 percent. These findings suggest that the importance of community seems underappreciated across the Jewish spectrum.

40. Sylvia Barack Fishman and Steven M. Cohen, *Family, Engagement, and Jewish Continuity among American Jews* (Jerusalem: Jewish People Policy Institute, 2017), http://jppi.org.il/new/wp-content/uploads/2017/06/Raising-Jewish-Children-Research-and-Indicators-for-Intervention.pdf.

41. Munro, *Coming of Age*, 159.

5. THE GRANDPARENT FACTOR

1. Rabbi Berel Wein, "Your Grandchildren: Parshas Vayechi," Torah.org, January 12, 2006, https://torah.org/torah-portion/rabbiwein-5766-vayechi.

2. See "Babylonian Talmud: Tractate Baba Mezi'a: Baba Mezi'a 85a," n. 26, Come and Hear, http://www.come-and-hear.com/babamezia/babamezia_85.html.

3. See Gerald C. Skolnik, "Between Grandparents and Grandchildren," in *The Observant Life*, ed. Martin S. Cohen and Michael Katz (New York: Rabbinical Assembly, 2012).

4. Skolnik, "Between Grandparents and Grandchildren," 711.

5. Jack Wertheimer, "American Jewry's Great Untapped Resource: Grandparents," *Mosaic Magazine*, January 28, 2016, 3, https://mosaicmagazine.com/observation/religion-holidays/2016/01/american-jewrys-great-untapped-resource-grandparents.

6. Jewish Grandparents Network, *Case Statement* (report, Atlanta, GA, July 2018), JGN Case Statement July 2018.pdf.

7. David Raphael, telephone conversation with author, December 3, 2018.

8. Wertheimer, "Great Untapped Resource: Grandparents," 3.

9. The happiness people derive from being a grandparent may be somewhat related to an overall increase in happiness at this time of life. Contrary to what is often said about aging, research demonstrates that people over the age of fifty actually are happier than when they were younger. Scholars believe that a "U-shaped life-satisfaction curve" is common to both sexes around the world, regardless of marital status, education, or employment. See Emily Bobrow, "'The Happiness Curve' Review: Midlife Slump and Late-Life Upswing," review of *The Happiness Curve*, by Jonathan Rauch, *Wall Street Journal*, June 1, 2018, https://www.wsj.com/articles/the-happiness-curve-review-midlife-slump-and-late-life-upswing-1527809014.

10. Clare Ansberry, "Grandfather's Dilemma: Am I a PopPop or a Skipper," *Wall Street Journal*, May 24, 2016, https://www.wsj.com/articles/grandfathers-dilemma-am-i-a-poppop-or-a-skipper-1464119401; Rukhl Schaechter, "The Battle Over What to Call Your Grandma," *Forward*, February 8, 2017, https://forward.com/opinion/362209/the-battle-over-what-to-call-your-grandma.

11. Naomi Grossman, "Growing Older—With an Emphasis on 'Growing,'" *Tablet Magazine*, June 11, 2018, https://www.tabletmag.com/jewish-life-and-religion/263173/growing-older-with-an-emphasis-on-growing.

12. Wertheimer, "Great Untapped Resource: Grandparents," 5.

13. Wertheimer's study contained similar findings about grandparents wanting to rectify their past sins of omission. Wertheimer, "Great Untapped Resource: Grandparents," 6.

14. Wertheimer, "Great Untapped Resource: Grandparents," 5.

15. Wertheimer, "Great Untapped Resource: Grandparents," 5.

16. There is evidence showing that maternal grandparents are more likely to be close with their grandchildren than paternal grandparents, and this close-

ness impacts the ability to transmit Judaism. See the Cohen Center for Modern Jewish Studies discussion of the "Millennial Children of Intermarriage" study based on 27,000 respondents and in-depth interviews with twenty-seven children of intermarriage in four cities. "Grandparents and Jewish Identity," eJewish Philanthropy, November 16, 2015, https://ejewishphilanthropy.com/grandparents-and-jewish-identity. Wertheimer's findings also support the perception that daughters, rather than sons, make the primary decisions concerning how grandchildren will be raised. "Great Untapped Resource: Grandparents," 5.

17. Wertheimer, "Great Untapped Resource: Grandparents," 6.

18. These baskets are known as *mishloach manot* and their origin is from the biblical Book of Esther.

19. Jack Wertheimer observes that "growing numbers of families ignore when the rest of the Jewish people are celebrating the holiday and instead hold their Seder to suit the convenience of their guests." *The New American Judaism: How Jews Practice Their Religion Today* (Princeton, NJ: Princeton University Press, 2018), 44. This trend also was documented in the Jewish Grandparents Network's "Our Time Together," in *Case Statement*, 3.

20. Jewish Grandparents Network, "Our Stories," in *Case Statement*, 4.

21. Jewish Grandparents Network, "Goals," in *Case Statement*, 5.

6. TIKKUN OLAM

1. According to the International Council of Christians and Jews, this quotation was taken from an "an advertisement in the *New York Times* on September 29, 2000, the eve of Rosh Hashanah (the first day of the Jewish year 5761), as part of a series sponsored by the American Jewish Committee and featuring statements by prominent figures in American public life." Elie Wiesel, "What Being Jewish Means to Me," Jewish-Christian Relations, Observations & Experiences (454), http://www.jcrelations.net/What+Being+Jewish+Means+to+Me.1305.0.html?L=3.

2. Susan Rothstein, "Reclaiming My Jewish Self," *Tablet Magazine*, July 16, 2018, https://www.tabletmag.com/jewish-life-and-religion/262681/reclaiming-my-jewish-self-uganda.

3. Rothstein, "Reclaiming My Jewish Self."

4. Martin S. Cohen, preface in *Tikkun Olam: Judaism, Humanism & Transcendence*, ed. David Birnbaum and Martin S. Cohen (New York: New Paradigm Matrix, 2015), 3 (hereafter cited as *Humanism & Transcendence*).

5. Sam Sokol, "In Jerusalem, Ruth Bader Ginsburg Celebrates Her Commitment to Tikkun Olam," Jewish Telegraphic Agency, July 5, 2018, https://

www.jta.org/2018/07/05/united-states/in-jerusalem-ruth-bader-ginsburg-celebrates-her-commitment-to-tikkun-olam; Vernon Kurtz, *"Tikkun Olam*: Particular or Universal?," in Birnbaum and Cohen, *Humanism & Transcendence*, 383.

6. Kurtz, "Particular or Universal?," 383; Elliot N. Dorff, "What Is *Tikkun Olam* and Why Does It Matter? An Overview from Antiquity to Modern Times," in Birnbaum and Cohen, *Humanism & Transcendence*, 11.

7. See Birnbaum and Cohen, *Humanism & Transcendence*, supra n. 4, for thoughtful essays showcasing a range of viewpoints, including a critique from a liberal perspective by Admiel Kosman, *"Tikkun Olam:* An Over-Used Term and Its Missing 'Inner Point,'" 275.

8. Jonathan Neumann, *To Heal the World? How the Jewish Left Corrupts Judaism and Endangers Israel* (New York: All Points Books, 2018).

A representative range of responses appears online in the *Jewish Journal* in July 2018. See Gil Troy, "Why Tikkun Olam Can't Fix American Judaism," July 18; Jonathan Klein, "In Praise of Tikkun Olam," July 18; Elliot Dorff, "Tradition, Tikkun Olam Are Not an Either/Or," July 27.

Shaul Magid and Michael Weingrad also offer thoughtful, but oppositional, reviews. See Magid, "Social Justice and the Future of Judaism," *Tablet Magazine*, June 13, 2018, https://www.tabletmag.com/jewish-arts-and-culture/264145/social-justice-and-the-future-of-judaism; Weingrad, "How American Jews Came to Believe That Tikkun Olam Was at the Core of Their Tradition," *Mosaic Magazine*, August 1, 2018, https://mosaicmagazine.com/observation/religion-holidays/2018/08/how-american-jews-came-to-believe-that-tikkun-olam-was-at-the-core-of-their-tradition/.

9. When asked whether each of the nine identified elements is "essential to what being Jewish means," 73 percent responded "remembering the Holocaust"; 69 percent, "leading an ethical and moral life"; and 56 percent, "working for justice/equality." In contrast, only 19 percent responded "observing Jewish law." Pew Research Center: Religion & Public Life, "Chapter 3: Jewish Identity," in *A Portrait of Jewish Americans: Findings from a Pew Research Center Survey of U.S. Jews*, October 1, 2013, http://www.pewforum.org/2013/10/01/jewish-american-beliefs-attitudes-culture-survey.

10. Andrés Spokoiny, "Tikkun Olam: A Defense and a Critique," eJewish Philanthropy, October 17, 2018, https://ejewishphilanthropy.com/tikkun-olam-a-defense-and-a-critique.

11. See Exod. 21:2–6; 22:20–22, 25–26; 23:2–3, 9–11.

12. Lev. 19:9–10, 23:22; Deut. 24:19–21.

13. Deut. 26:12–13.

14. Jill Jacobs, *There Shall Be No Needy: Pursuing Social Justice through Jewish Law & Tradition* (Woodstock, VT: Jewish Lights Publishing, 2009), 12, 18; See Deut. 15:1–2, 7–10.

15. See m.Git. 4:3; Jacobs, *Pursuing Social Justice*, 33–34; Kurtz, "Particular or Universal?," 383–85.

16. See Kurtz, "Particular or Universal?," 383–85; Dorff, "What Is *Tikkun Olam*," 11–13; Alyssa Gray, in *My People's Prayer Book: Traditional Prayers, Modern Commentaries*, vol. 6, *Tachanun and Concluding Prayers*, ed. Lawrence A. Hoffman (Woodstock, VT: Jewish Lights Publishing, 2002), 142; Jacobs, *Pursuing Social Justice*, 27.

17. The mystical application of *tikkun olam* is complicated. For a fuller treatment, see Kurtz, "Particular or Universal?," 383, 389–90; Dorff, "What Is *Tikkun Olam*," 11, 14; Jacobs, *Pursuing Social Justice*, 34–37, and other readings cited in these sources.

18. Jacobs, *Pursuing Social Justice*, 37.

19. Jonathan D. Sarna, *American Judaism: A History* (New Haven, CT: Yale University Press, 2004), 310–11.

20. *Shulchan Arukh*, *Yoreh De'ah* 251:12

21. b.Shab. 31a.

22. See Gen. 3:21; Deut. 34:6; Dorff, "What Is *Tikkun Olam*," 11, 22.

23. Jacobs, *Pursuing Social Justice*, 2–4.

24. Because many of the speakers were interested in formalizing their remarks into a published essay, I crafted a written symposium that included essays of those who participated in the symposium as well as other interested academics. For my introduction to the published written symposium, see "Introduction—People of the Book: Judaism's Influence on American Legal Scholarship," *Rutgers Journal of Law & Religion* 16, no. 2 (Spring 2015), https://lawandreligion.com/volume-16.

25. Susan A. Bandes, "Civil Liberties and the 'Imaginative Sustenance' of Jewish Culture," *Rutgers Journal of Law & Religion* 16, no. 2 (Spring 2015): 238–46.

26. Kurtz, "Particular or Universal?," 392, 394.

27. Jill Jacobs, "Reintegrating Judaism," eJewish Philanthropy, May 10, 2018, https://ejewishphilanthropy.com/reintegrating-judaism.

28. Dorff, "What Is *Tikkun Olam*," 11, 34.

29. Jules Harlow, ed., *Siddur Sim Shalom* (New York: Rabbinical Assembly, 1989), 9.

30. See Isa. 49:6; 51:4; Elliot N. Dorff, *For the Love of God and People* (Philadelphia: Jewish Publication Society, 2007), 109; Rabbinical Council of America, Council of European Rabbis, and Chief Rabbinate of Israel, *Between*

Jerusalem & Rome: Reflections on 50 Years of Nostra Aetate, August 31, 2017, https://rabbis.org/pdfs/Rome_and_Jerusalem.pdf, 13.

For further discussion of the joint statement by the RCA, CER, and Chief Rabbinate of Israel, see Joshua Yuter's "Sacred Slogans Series," arguing that "light of nations" is the more accurate translation of Isaiah. "Ohr Lagoyim / Light unto the Nations," September 15, 2018, https://joshyuter.com/2018/09/15/special-features/sacred-slogans/ohr-lagoyim-light-unto-the-nations.

31. Abby Levine, "Social Justice and Jews—An Open Letter to Jonathan Weisman," eJewish Philanthropy, May 10, 2018, https://ejewishphilanthropy.com/social-justice-and-jews-an-open-letter-to-jonathan-weisman.

32. Samson Raphael Hirsch, "Fifteenth Letter," in *The Nineteen Letters* (New York: Feldeim, 1970), 104.

33. Alex Sinclair, *Loving the Real Israel: An Educational Agenda for Liberal Zionism* (Teaneck, NJ: Ben Yehuda Press, 2013), 131.

34. Elliot N. Dorff, *The Way into Tikkun Olam: Repairing the World* (Woodstock, VT: Jewish Lights Publishing, 2005), 33. See chapters 4–7 for Dorff's suggestions.

35. Rabbi Laura Geller, "On Getting Up from Shloshim," *Jewish Journal*, August 24, 2018, https://jewishjournal.com/columnist/237714/on-getting-up-from-shloshim.

7. REMIX AND THE POWER OF
JEWISH MOURNING

1. Eric M. Meyers, "Jewish Culture in Greco-Roman Palestine," in *Cultures of the Jews: A New History*, ed. David Biale (New York: Schocken, 2002), 171, quoted in Roberta Rosenthal Kwall, *The Myth of the Cultural Jew: Culture and Law in Jewish Tradition* (New York: Oxford University Press, 2015), 48.

2. Gila Silverman notes that "explanations about these practices, and the meanings [found] . . . in them, are much more about the individual and the ways in which these mourning rituals supported, or undermined" the grieving process. "'We Sat Shiva for Three Days': Jewish Mourning Among Liberal American Jews" (paper, Annual Meeting of the American Academy of Religion, Boston, MA, November, 2017). See also Leon Wieseltier, *Kaddish* (New York: Alfred A. Knopf, 1998).

3. My impression of this lack of empirical evidence was confirmed through responses to an inquiry about this matter I posted on the Association for the Social Scientific Study of Jewry LISTSERV on June 28, 2018. As explained by Gila Silverman, "Much more research is needed to fully understand" how

people's "relationship to these mourning rituals relates to their complex relationship to Judaism, and how that relationship impacts" grieving. "Jewish Mourning," 7.

4. Pew Research Center: Religion & Public Life, *A Portrait of Jewish Americans: Findings from a Pew Research Center Survey of U.S. Jews*, Pew Research Center: Polling and Analysis, October 1, 2013, http://www.pewforum.org/2013/10/01/jewish-american-beliefs-attitudes-culture-survey.

5. Maurice Lamm, *The Jewish Way in Death and Mourning* (New York: Jonathan David Publishers, 1969), xi.

6. For an extensive overview about Jewish tradition concerning death and mourning, see Lamm, *Jewish Way*; Carl N. Astor, "The Jewish Life Cycle," in *The Observant Life*, ed. Martin S. Cohen and Michael Katz (New York: Rabbinical Assembly, 2012).

7. Lamm, *Jewish Way*, 7; Astor, "Jewish Life Cycle," 287.

8. Lamm, *Jewish Way*, 5.

9. Gen. 37:29–34. The Torah contains many other examples of this Biblical custom. See Astor, "Jewish Life Cycle," 285.

10. Lamm, *Jewish Way*, 22.

11. Lamm, *Jewish Way*, 39.

12. Lamm, *Jewish Way*, 65.

13. Lamm, *Jewish Way*, 11.

14. Both the *shiva* and the *sheloshim* can occasionally be cut short by certain Jewish holidays. These rules are fairly detailed but well summarized by Lamm in *The Jewish Way in Death and Mourning*, 95–97.

15. Lamm, *Jewish Way*, 78, 111, 112–13. Lamm notes that mourners who are indigent must observe the first three days of *shiva* but are allowed to work afterward as "privately and inconspicuously" as possible. *Jewish Way*, 117.

16. Lamm, *Jewish Way*, 125.

17. Astor, "Jewish Life Cycle," 298.

18. The Torah also notes the same period of mourning for Moses's brother, Aaron. See Num. 20:29.

19. Lamm, *Jewish Way*, 145–46.

20. Lamm, *Jewish Way*, 167–68.

21. Adena Berkowitz, "An Enigma Wrapped in a Mystery," in *Kaddish*, ed. David Birnbaum and Martin S. Cohen (New York: New Paradigm Matrix Publishing, 2016), 276, 267–80.

22. Talia Bloch, "A Time to Mourn without a Place to Pray," *Tablet Magazine*, November 9, 2018, https://www.tabletmag.com/jewish-life-and-religion/213166/mourning-without-a-place-to-pray.

23. Wieseltier, *Kaddish*, 25–26.

24. Bloch, "Time to Mourn."

25. Lamm, *Jewish Way*, 127–28. Lamm observes that Jewish law incorporates this "social reproach" work-around.

26. Lamm, *Jewish Way*, 182.

27. Lamm, *Jewish Way*, 132–33.

28. Astor explains the eleven-month practice as follows: "The point of stopping the recitation of Kaddish a month early has to do with the popular understanding of Kaddish as a kind of intercessory prayer for the deceased. Since it was deemed vaguely insulting to the memory of one's parents to assume that they would require every last prayer possible to be recited on their behalf, the custom was to recite Kaddish for only eleven of the twelve months." "Jewish Life Cycle," 301.

29. Eli Feldblum, "I Don't Believe in Prayer—Yet I Say 'Yizkor' Every Year," *Forward*, September 17, 2018, https://forward.com/life/faith/410092/i-dont-believe-in-prayer-yet-i-say-yizkor-every-year.

30. Ivan G. Marcus, *The Jewish Life Cycle: Rites of Passage from Biblical to Modern Times* (Seattle: University of Washington Press, 2004), 232–33. See also Kwall, *Myth of the Cultural Jew*, 77.

31. See Michael Hebb and Sharon Brous, "How Death Came to Dinner," Death Over Dinner—Jewish Edition, https://deathoverdinner-jewishedition.org/#about; "Plan a Dinner: Your Intentions," Death Over Dinner—Jewish Edition, 2, https://deathoverdinner-jewishedition.org/#intent; Flora Tsapovsky, "Let's Talk about Death," *Tablet Magazine*, August 21, 2018, https://www.tabletmag.com/jewish-life-and-religion/268648/lets-talk-about-death. For further discussion of Reboot, see chapter 1 on *Shabbat* and holiday tradition.

32. Silverman, "Jewish Mourning," 7.

EPILOGUE

1. Mark Twain, "Concerning the Jews," *Harper's Magazine*, March 1898, https://sourcebooks.fordham.edu/mod/1898twain-jews.asp.

2. Flora Tsapovsky, "Let's Talk about Death," *Tablet Magazine*, August 21, 2018, https://www.tabletmag.com/jewish-life-and-religion/268648/lets-talk-about-death.

3. Gila Silverman, "'I'll Say a *Mi Sheberach* for You': Prayer, Healing and Identity Among Liberal American Jews," *Contemporary Jewry* 36, no. 2 (March 2016): 175, https://doi.org/10.1007/s12397-016-9156-7.

4. Silverman, "Prayer, Healing and Identity," 180.

5. Silverman, "Prayer, Healing and Identity," 176.

6. Exod. 3:2.

7. "To the old, according to their strength, and to the young, according to theirs; to the children, to the babes, and to the women, according to their strength and even to Moses according to his strength." Exod. Rab. 5:9.

8. Roberta Rosenthal Kwall, *The Myth of the Cultural Jew: Culture and Law in Jewish Tradition* (New York: Oxford University Press, 2015), 286.

9. David Biale, *Cultures of the Jews: A New History* (New York: Schocken, 2002), xxi.

10. Gila S. Silverman, Kathryn A. Johnson, and Adam B. Cohen, "To Believe or Not to Believe, That Is Not the Question: The Complexity of Jewish Beliefs about God," *Psychology of Religion and Spirituality* 8, no. 2 (May 1, 2016): 119–20, https://doi.org/10.1037/rel0000065.

11. Silverman, Johnson, and Cohen, "Complexity of Jewish Beliefs," 129.

12. Gil Perl, "Postmodern Orthodoxy: Giving Voice to a New Generation," *Lehrhaus*, November 6, 2017, https://www.thelehrhaus.com/commentary/postmodern-orthodoxy-giving-voice-to-a-new-generation.

13. See Jay P. Lefkowitz, "The Rise of Social Orthodoxy: A Personal Account," *Commentary*, April, 2014, 37, 42.

14. Nishma Research, "Profile of American Modern Orthodox Jews," Jewish Virtual Library, September 28, 2017, https://www.jewishvirtuallibrary.org/profile-of-american-modern-orthodox-jews.

15. Pew Research Center: Religion & Public Life, "Chapter 4: Religious Beliefs & Practices, Polling & Analysis," in *A Portrait of Jewish Americans: Findings from a Pew Research Center Survey of U.S. Jews*, October 1, 2013, http://www.pewforum.org/2013/10/01/chapter-4-religious-beliefs-and-practices (hereafter cited as Pew Report, Chapter 4). For ultra-Orthodox Jews, the survey showed 96 percent absolute certain belief.

16. Mark Trencher, e-mail message to author, August 30, 2018.

17. Silverman, "Prayer, Healing and Identity," 169, 176; Silverman, Johnson, and Cohen, "Complexity of Jewish Beliefs," 119, 12.

18. See also Jack Wertheimer, *The New American Judaism: How Jews Practice Their Religion Today* (Princeton, NJ: Princeton University Press, 2018), 211–32

19. See Amy Kalmanofsky, *Dangerous Sisters of the Hebrew Bible* (Minneapolis: Fortress Press, 2014), 157–74.

20. Daniel J. Boorstin, *The Creators: A History of Heroes of the Imagination* (New York: Vintage, 1993), 41.

21. Jane Eisner, "So Called 'Jews of No Religion' Are the Impetus for a Jewish Revolution," *The Forward*, September 3, 2018, https://forward.com/opinion/407183/so-called-jews-of-no-religion-are-the-impetus-for-a-jewish-revolution.

22. Edmund Case, "How Audacious Will Our Hospitality to Interfaith Families Be?" eJewish Philanthropy, June 12, 2017, https://ejewishphilanthropy.com/how-audacious-will-our-hospitality-to-interfaith-families-be.

23. See b.Menah. 29b.

24. Clifford Librach, "Paying the Price for Abandoning Jewish Peoplehood," *Tablet Magazine*, June 18, 2018, https://www.tabletmag.com/scroll/264582/paying-the-price-for-abandoning-jewish-peoplehood.

25. Deborah Waxman, "Why the Reconstructionist Movement Is Rebranding," *Times of Israel* (blog), February 2, 2018, https://blogs.timesofisrael.com/why-the-reconstructionist-movement-is-rebranding.

26. This translation is taken from the Conservative Movement's prayer book: Jules Harlow, ed., *Siddur Sim Shalom* (New York: Rabbinical Assembly, 1989).

27. Pew Research Center, Pew Report, Chapter 4.

28. See Elliot N. Dorff, *The Unfolding Tradition: Jewish Law after Sinai* (New York: Aviv Press, 2005), 454–56.

29. See Shayndi Raice, "Goat Yoga, Mosh Pits, Glow Sticks: Younger Jews Reinvent Yom Kippur," *Wall Street Journal*, September 6, 2018, A1, 12, https://www.wsj.com/articles/goat-yoga-mosh-pits-glow-sticks-younger-jews-reinvent-yom-kippur-1536160155; Shira Hanau, "Kol Nidrei in a Red-Sauce Joint?," *New York Jewish Week*, September 20, 2018, https://jewishweek.timesofisrael.com/kol-nidrei-in-a-red-sauce-joint.

30. According to this ritual, one goat was sacrificed and the other was sent out into the wilderness, bearing the people's sins.

31. Raice, "Younger Jews Reinvent Yom Kippur."

32. See Gen. 15:5, 22:17.

BIBLIOGRAPHY

Biale, David. *Cultures of the Jews: A New History*. New York: Schocken Books, 2002.

Biale, Rachel. *Women and Jewish Law: The Essential Texts, Their History & Their Relevance for Today*. New York: Schocken Books, 1984.

Birnbaum, David, and Martin S. Cohen, eds. *Tikkun Olam: Judaism, Humanism & Transcendence*. New York: New Paradigm Matrix, 2015.

Bronfman, Edgar M. *Why Be Jewish? A Testament*. New York: Twelve, 2016.

Brown, Erica, and Misha Galperin. *The Case for Jewish Peoplehood: Can We Be One?* Woodstock, VT: Jewish Lights Publishing, 2009.

Chazan, Barry, Robert Chazan, and Benjamin M. Jacobs. *Cultures and Contexts of Jewish Education*. Cham, Switzerland: Palgrave Macmillan, 2017.

Cohen, Martin S., and Michael Katz, eds. *The Observant Life: The Wisdom of Conservative Judaism for Contemporary Jews*. New York: Rabbinical Assembly, 2012.

Dorff, Elliot N. *The Unfolding Tradition: Jewish Law after Sinai*. New York: Aviv Press, 2005.

Fishkoff, Sue. *Kosher Nation*. New York: Schocken Books, 2010.

Fishman, Sylvia Barack. *Double or Nothing? Jewish Families and Mixed Marriage*. Hanover, NH: Brandeis University Press, 2004.

Goldman, Ari L. *Being Jewish: The Spiritual and Cultural Practice of Judaism Today*. New York: Simon & Schuster, 2000.

Hauptman, Judith. *Rereading the Rabbis: A Woman's Voice*. Boulder, CO: Westview Press, 1998.

Heilman, Samuel C. *Sliding to the Right: The Contest for the Future of American Jewish Orthodoxy*. Berkeley: University of California Press, 2006.

Heschel, Abraham Joshua. *The Sabbath: Its Meaning for Modern Man*. Boston: Shambhala, 2003.

Horowitz, Roger. *Kosher USA: How Coke became Kosher and Other Tales of Modern Food*. New York: Columbia University Press, 2016.

Jacobs, Jill. *There Shall Be No Needy: Pursuing Social Justice through Jewish Law & Tradition*. Woodstock, VT: Jewish Lights Publishing, 2009.

Kaplan, Mordecai M. *The Meaning of God in Modern Jewish Religion*. New York: Jewish Reconstruction Foundation, 1947.

Kraemer, David C. *Jewish Eating and Identity through the Ages*. New York: Routledge, 2007.

Kwall, Roberta Rosenthal. *The Myth of the Cultural Jew: Culture and Law in Jewish Tradition*. New York: Oxford University Press, 2015.

Lamm, Maurice. *The Jewish Way in Death and Mourning*. New York: Jonathan David Publishers, 1969.

Marcus, Ivan G. *The Jewish Life Cycle: Rites of Passage from Biblical to Modern Times*. Seattle: University of Washington Press, 2004.

Munro, Patricia Keer. *Coming of Age in Jewish America: Bar and Bat Mitzvah Reinterpreted*. New Brunswick, NJ: Rutgers University Press, 2016.

Oliztky, Kerry M., and Daniel Judson, eds. *The Rituals & Practices of a Jewish Life: A Handbook for Personal Spiritual Renewal*. Woodstock, VT: Jewish Lights Publishing, 2002.

Sacks, Jonathan. *A Letter in the Scroll: Understanding Our Jewish Identity and Exploring the Legacy of the World's Oldest Religion*. New York: Free Press, 2000.

Sarna, Jonathan D. *American Judaism: A History*. New Haven, CT: Yale University Press, 2004.

Wertheimer, Jack. *The New American Judaism: How Jews Practice Their Religion Today*. Princeton, NJ: Princeton University Press, 2018.

Wolpe, David J. *Why Be Jewish?* New York: Henry Holt, 1995.

Zamore, Mary L., ed. *The Sacred Table: Creating a Jewish Food Ethic*. New York: CCAR Press, 2011.

INDEX